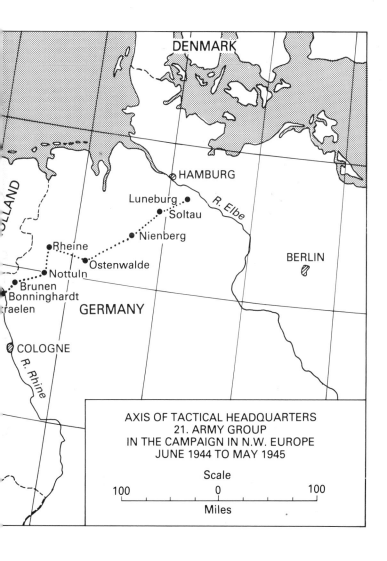

AXIS OF TACTICAL HEADQUARTERS
21. ARMY GROUP
IN THE CAMPAIGN IN N.W. EUROPE
JUNE 1944 TO MAY 1945

Scale

100   0   100

Miles

Aftermath of War

EVERYONE MUST GO HOME

Löibl Pass

Aftermath of War

EVERYONE MUST GO HOME

Carol Mather

'I cannot forecast to you the action of Russia, it is a riddle wrapped in a mystery inside an enigma'.

W. S. Churchill
1 October 1939

BRASSEY'S (UK)

LONDON · WASHINGTON · NEW YORK

First English edition 1992

UK editorial offices: Brassey's, 50 Fetter Lane, London EC4A 1AA
orders: Brassey's, Purnell Distribution Centre, Paulton, Bristol BS18 5LQ

USA editorial offices: Brassey's, 8000 Westpark Drive, First Floor,
McLean, Virginia 22102
orders: Macmillan Publishing Company, Front and Brown Streets,
Riverside, NJ 08075

Distributed in North America to booksellers and wholesalers by the
Macmillan Publishing Company, N.Y., N.Y.

Library of Congress Cataloging in Publication Data
Available

British Library Cataloguing in Publication Data
Available

ISBN 0-08-037708-4

Printed in Great Britain by B.P.C.C. Wheatons Ltd., Exeter

DEDICATION

To
The British Soldier

Contents

Preface   ix
Acknowledgements   xiv
List of Plates   xviii
List of Maps   xx
Glossary   xxi
Prologue   xxv

PART ONE – WAR-TORN EUROPE

Chapter I   Collapse and Chaos at the Heart of Europe   3

Chapter II   Post-Surrender in Germany   9

Chapter III   Everyone Must Go Home   15

Chapter IV   A Roving Commission in Post-War Europe   23

Chapter V   Austria – Letters from Vienna   33

PART TWO – THE SITUATION AT ALEXANDER'S HEADQUARTERS

Chapter VI   War on Three Fronts   43

Chapter VII   Final Phase and Surrender   49

Chapter VIII   War and Blood in the Mountains   53

PART THREE – THE VENEZIA GIULIA CRISIS

Chapter IX   Tito Moves In   65

Chapter X   Crossing the Alps   69

Chapter XI   Cleaning-up   73

Chapter XII   The Melting-Pot   78

Chapter XIII   Sorting out the Armies of Europe   83

PART FOUR – HOW WE ALMOST STUMBLED INTO WORLD WAR THREE

Chapter XIV   The Crisis Deepens   91

Chapter XV   History Repeats Itself 12–13 May   97

Chapter XVI	'The Klagenfurt Conspiracy'	104
Chapter XVII	Pre-requisite for War	109
Chapter XVIII	On the Brink	112
Chapter XIX	'I Must Clear the Decks'	118
Chapter XX	The Turning Point	125
Chapter XXI	The Climb-down	133

PART FIVE – WAR AVERTED – BUT A PRICE TO PAY

Chapter XXII	Balkan Backlash	141
Chapter XXIII	The Missing Signal	152
Chapter XXIV	Message from Stalin	157
Chapter XXV	Operation of War	161
Chapter XXVI	Alexander Visits 5 Corps	167

PART SIX – THE AFTERMATH

Chapter XXVII	Summer Solstice	175
Chapter XXVIII	Winter of Discontent	182
Chapter XXIX	Repatriation in Reverse	189
Chapter XXX	How it all Began	195

| *Epilogue* | | 201 |

Appendices:
A	Speech on Anglo-Soviet Relations. House of Commons 7 April 1987	215
B	Repatriation Statistics 21 Army Group (May–July 1945)	219
C	Truman's Telegram 12 May 1945	221
D	Signal by 5 Corps Defining Russian Nationals	224
E	Historical Note on the Cossacks	226
F	Anti-Tito Yugoslav Groups	239
G	Letter from P J Grigg (War Minister) to Anthony Eden (Foreign Secretary) 24 August 1944	242

| *Chapter Note* | 247 |
| *Index* | 265 |

Preface

On 8 May 1945 the German armed forces collapsed in unconditional surrender after five years of unprecedented aggression. From that moment on an immense repatriation movement began, right across Europe, in order to get everyone back to the countries where they belonged. Prisoners of war of all nationalities, slave workers and millions of other displaced persons comprising one of the biggest migration movements in recent human history.

Three factors influenced these proceedings.

First, the impossibility of feeding such vast numbers. The former European occupied territories were facing starvation, imminent epidemic and disease.

Second, only a full exchange of prisoners, Stalin made clear, would see the return of British and American prisoners of war in Soviet hands who were in German occupied territory over-run by the Russian advance. This exchange included deserters and other 'traitors', quislings, collaborators and the like whom both sides wished to see returned.

Third, there was a particularly ominous situation in Austria, to where many of the broken armies of Germany and her allies had fled, or been driven. Here the British, under Field Marshal Alexander, faced the outbreak of a major conflict with Tito's Yugoslav armies which had infiltrated into Venezia Giulia and invaded Austrian Carinthia. The attitude of Stalin, should hostilities have broken out, was an imponderable and menacing factor which presaged the advent of a third world war, only days after the second had ended.

In these circumstances, it was imperative for Alexander to 'clear the decks' in his impending area of operations, and his lines of communication and supply leading to it, unhappily cluttered with vast numbers of refugees.

The return of some of these German mercenaries to our allies (Russia and Yugoslavia) of only a few days before, has received plenty of attention from other authors who have described in vivid detail the loading of trains and lorries, and the eventual fate which overtook many of the repatriated people. It was a human tragedy. But I will maintain in these pages the inevitability and justification for many of the decisions made at that time, both in Austria and in Germany, at any rate in the immediate aftermath of war and in the light of knowledge at that time. I do not wish to belittle the efforts of previous writers to try and seek out the truth. But I question the relentless search for scapegoats, many of whom are no longer able to answer back.

To consider the Cossack and anti-Tito Yugoslav incidents in isolation is only to see half the picture. One needs a far deeper perspective to understand the motives for what may appear to many as callous acts. I hope therefore in this book to show how a temporary alliance, or 'marriage of convenience' between the Western and Eastern allies (America and Britain on one side, Russia and Yugoslavia on the other), led to intolerable strains once that war was over. And that this was an inevitable consequence, given the nature of that alliance. I was not in Austria to witness these events personally, but as I hope to show, I am in as good a position as any to interpret them. This story is perforce seen through British eyes. Very similar problems were being experienced in the American zones, but the political background was common to both. Uniquely, Britain had the special problem of Tito's incursion into Carinthia and its impact on peace or war.

My credentials for acting as 'interpreter' simply stated, are as follows. To begin with, I knew something of the nature of the Nazi terror which was sweeping Europe. I had witnessed, passing quite close by me, German mechanised columns on their way to the subjugation of Czechoslovakia. Foolhardidly, and against advice, I had entered Austria in the spring of 1939, in pursuit of my studies at Cambridge University. Alighting at Innsbruck station I found myself face to face with the war-machine of the Third Reich, which had occupied Austria the year before, now on its way to crush Czechoslovakia. The air was full of menace and I stood for a moment transfixed. Aware as I was of the dangers of this spectacle, I still did not quite realise that my fate was now sealed. Very soon we would all be dragged into the maelstrom.[1]

Next, as I shall show, I had a natural pre-occupation and awareness of developments in Russia through family connections and early friendships. My sympathies were with the White Russian exiles. Later, and this was before America had come into the war, our desperate situation brought home the need for a Soviet alliance, if we were to survive, let alone win the war.

Similarly, whilst writing this book, my feelings have been torn between a fellow-feeling and respect for the Chetniks or Yugoslav royalists (as we used to call them and with whom, I shared the discomforts and hunger of an Italian PoW camp at Bari in 1943), and the remorseless logic of the war.

Lastly, my 'worm's-eye view' of war, as a commando and SAS soldier, as a prisoner-of-war, escapee and fugitive, was tempered by a chance to see it from another vantage point, that of 'higher command'. By good fortune I was to be at Montgomery's side at three of the crucial battles of the Second World War, Alamein, the Normandy landings and the Ardennes offensive.

Two of the key personalities in my story are Montgomery and Alexander. On both was placed the onus of sorting out the mess in post-war Europe, the one in Germany, the other in Austria. At this early stage I should like to explain Montgomery's unique command system, and how it worked.

'Monty' (as he was affectionately known), leading British commander in the Second World War, had introduced a new element into the practice of command in war. His 'liaison officers' (LOs) were his eyes and ears on the battle front, giving him a sixth sense and feel for the progress of the battle. Of course he had his normal sources of communication, his frequent conversations with commanders, and his own visits to the front line. But there was nothing like the personal touch and the eye-witness account covering the whole day's fighting. The practice started during the battle of Alamein when his ADC, John Poston,[2] and his LO, myself, took it in turns to drive him about the battlefield, the other visiting commanders in different salients. It developed into a full team of LO's (including two Americans), when it came to the invasion of Europe. It may be wondered how comparatively junior officers could de-brief senior commanders and give verbal reports (nothing was in writing except the marks on one's map) to the Commander-in-Chief, perhaps on matters crucial to a campaign? It was all a matter of trust. If he trusted you, he trusted you absolutely, if he had any cause not to do so then you were 'out', straight away.

His habits were simple in the extreme. Regular as clockwork he would be woken at 6.00 am with a cup of tea; his day time activities included 'time to think' quietly in his caravan; at 6.00 pm he would receive his LO's who had arrived 'hot-foot' from the battlefront, marked up his map and who then gave him their impressions of the day's events. At 10.00 pm promptly, whatever the situation, he would retire to bed. I found that being so close to such a man was a refreshing and exhilarating experience; his system of command was a revelation in its simplicity; not for him the complex options of a planning staff. He laid down the plan, he issued the orders or broad 'directives', and it was up to his generals to get on with it and carry it out.

But, as a counter-illustration, let me describe his intervention at the time of the Ardennes offensive. It fell just before Christmas 1944. It was into the American sector that General Von Rundstedt made his famous counter-attack. There was snow on the ground. Communications between Bradley and his army commanders were completely severed. Montgomery was called in by Eisenhower to help, and was given command of the northern tier of American Armies. Colonel Tom Bigland and I were sent down to make contact with the Americans.[3] We found that 1(US) Army headquarters had fled, when the Panzers passed quite close to them, leaving their Christmas dinners on the table! The town of Spa was deserted. We returned post haste, he to Bradley's headquarters and I to Montgomery's. My Chief was extremely alarmed, for there was nothing now between Rundstedt and his main supply bases of Liege, Brussels and Antwerp. But Monty was in his element, he restored order out of chaos, riding roughshod over American feelings in the process. And this is where his Liaison Officers, British and American, proved their value, giving him an accurate picture of the battle situation, whereas before there had been virtually none.

By the end of six years of war, one was totally satiated with the experience; one had lived, eaten, slept and dreamed 'war' to the exclusion of everything else. After it was over I put a *cordon sanitaire* around the whole affair and forgot about it. Then the years passed and a subtle change took place, as succeeding generations grew up. The episode passed, almost unnoticed, out of the realm of 'experience' into the domain of 'history'.

The turning point for me must have come on the 40th anniversary of the 'D-Day' landings, in the summer of 1984, when I led a parliamentary delegation to Normandy. Now I played the 'Castiglione', extolling the art of war to those who had never experienced it. But there is a 'down side' to history as well as an 'upside', as I discovered when I visited the war museum at Bayeux, containing relics of the invasion. Could these pathetic scraps of uniform, covering stuffed dummies have been the flesh and blood that I knew? Could these broken weapons, water bottles and steel helmets really have belonged to my cheerful comrades and friends? Was it really like this? This sleeping beauty world, all covered in dust and cobwebs? Ashes to ashes and dust to dust! Maybe. But I came away from the museum like a disembodied spirit still connected to its former haunts. Murmuring to myself. Pathetic! Absolutely pathetic! And with growing anger – how could they hoodwink future generations with these miserable artefacts. Then I looked down the vista of whitened crosses of the war graves, row upon row, which gave me back my missing perspective. Acting as it were, as a causeway, between then and now. Reuniting flesh and blood, banishing time, so that past and present were one. And then the cloak of history fell again. Deadening. Unimaginative and obliterating.

But as I have been writing this and delving in the dusty files I do have a new perspective. What is my strongest impression? It is an impression of appalling suffering for mankind, hardly discernable to the individual engaged in his own personal war. Apart from the dead, there were the millions separated from homes and families as refugees, slave labourers or in remnants of Germany's broken armies. But the heartening thing I see is the spirit of man, in some amazing way, rising triumphant.

More and more war books came out and I became increasingly exasperated. Freed from the trammels of 'office' I at last had an opportunity to speak out in what proved to be my final speech in the House of Commons.[4]

Since I uttered those words, particularly with reference to the Gulf, that has indeed proved an explosive issue. Perhaps this latest war may help us to see these past events in greater clarity, and enable us to understand the needs and pressures of a nation emerging from 6 years of fighting. I did not foresee the renewed outbreak of trouble in the Balkans, but the causes are not far to seek and some may be discovered in the pages of this book.

CM

Moreton-in-Marsh
November 1991

Acknowledgements

As the main part of my research was carried out at the Public Records Office at Kew, I must first record my thanks to the officers and staff. I am also indebted to the staff of the Foreign Office Library and the Ministry of Defence Historical Section for making available PRO documents temporarily lodged there. All Crown Copyright material, including that in the Public Records Office is reproduced by permission of the Controller of Her Majesty's Stationery Office. I am grateful to this office, to the authors of the official War Histories, to the Cabinet Offices and to the Editor of the Official Report (Hansard), for their courtesy in expediting clearance.

I made full use of the research facilities offered by the Imperial War Museum, and my thanks are due to the Director, Dr Alan Borg, Christopher Dowling and the staff of the Museum, including their permission to use plates from the photographic collection.

I owe a particular debt of gratitude to Andrew Gibson-Watt for accompanying me on a visit to Carinthia and for giving me much sound advice (including reading of my script), from one who was present during the repatriation period in 1945. To Christopher Thursby-Pelham for joining me on a visit to northern Italy to gather material on the Partisan war, having advanced through this area with the Eighth Army, the depth of his experience was invaluable. My thanks also to our guide and interpreter on this visit, James Chamberlain of Udine University. This visit was made possible through the good office of Peter Lee, honorary librarian to the Special Forces Club and former member of SOE. Our contacts amongst former Partisans would not have been possible without the invaluable assistance of Dotoressa Paola del Din Carnielli ('Renata') of Udine, a former member of the Osoppo Partisan Group; of Dr Romano Marchetti of Tolmezzo, who also helped me with the map west of the Tagliamento River; of former Partisan leaders, A. Mosanghini, and Gian-carlo Chiussi; for the information supplied and translations made by Professor Laurenzina Deganutti and her sister. I must also record my thanks to Professor Gino Lizzero of Cividale and Giorgio Zardi of Udine both of whom came forward with help and information; for correspondence with Kim Isolani and Victor Gozzer. Professor Giancarlo Menis generously made available numerous extracts from his father, Pietro Menis's wartime diary. To Detalmo Pirzio-Biroli and his wife (Fey von Hassell) from Castello di Brazza, who painted a vivid picture of wartime years in Italy and Germany.

For all my contacts with the Special Forces I must thank my old friend and former parliamentary colleague Douglas Dodds-Parker; of those I must mention Ronald Taylor (who helped with the map east of the Tagliamento River); Pat Mosdell and David Godwin; Patrick Martin-Smith was a fund of knowledge on the Cossack con-tingents and their part in the Partisan war.

I must add a special acknowledgement to Francesco Berti for per-mission to quote extracts from that most exciting of wartime records *No.1 Special Force and the Italian Resistance*, published by Bologna University, and to its several authors including Count Gianandrea Gropplero di Troppenburg ('Freccia') and Dumas Poli ('Secondino'). For translations from the Italian I must record my thanks to Chris Pelham, Joe Gurney and my old friend the late A A 'Sandy' Robertson (a one-time fellow inmate of Campo di Concentramento PG 21 at Chieti).

For matters concerning Austria I am much obliged for correspon-dence with Dr Archie Thurn-Valsassina, the owner of Bleiburg Castle, and to Dr Walter Lechner who lent me books published in Austria on the Cossack repatriations. Also to my former comrade-in-arms, Colin Mitchell from whose letter I quote. All translations from the German were most generously done for me by Janus Paludan (for-merly of the Danish Foreign Service).

On the Yugoslav resistance movements I must thank my former wartime comrade Sir Fitzroy Maclean (who commanded the British Military Mission to Marshal Tito) who was good enough to read some of my manuscript; and to Mike Lees (former BLO with General Michailovic), and to Rear Admiral Morgan-Giles, who was in charge of naval supply operations to Tito across the Adriatic.

Eric Predite helped me on Latvia and the Baltic States. Lady (Masha) Williams, an old friend of the family, advised me on many matters concerning pre-revolutionary Russia, and events in Austria where she was Russian interpreter with the Allied Commission in Vienna.

Sir David Hunt was kind enough to read over and comment on the chapters concerning Field Marshal Alexander (whose chief intelligence officer he was in Italy). For background information on Montgomery and other leading personalities and events in those days there was no finer adviser than J R 'Johnny' Henderson (former ADC to Montgomery). For the campaign in NW Europe, he, Tom Bigland, Dick Harden and Paul Odgers, all former members of Montgomery's personal staff, have jogged my memory as to these events.

For verbatim accounts on the plight of allied PoWs held in Germany and Poland I am indebted to Tony Barber (the Rt Hon. Lord Barber of Wentbridge), and Peter Hanbury (whose war began and ended in 1940). Conversations with the late Jock (Sir John) Colville have clarified my mind on events during the Churchill years.

Although I carried out my research entirely independently and was not connected in any way with the *Cowgill Inquiry Report*, I have found that this most comprehensive analysis of the repatriations in Austria a most useful cross-reference, in particular the material from the United States National Archives and from the Institute of Military History, Belgrade, to which I did not have direct access. Subsequent conversations with Brigadier Anthony Cowgill have provided a most useful exchange.

I must record but cannot detail the numerous conversations I have had with brother officers, formerly serving with the 3rd Bn. Welsh Guards (including the Rev. Malcolm Richards), who were directly involved in the events in Austria. These exchanges have all taken place since these episodes achieved notoriety. Also with Sir Geoffrey Musson (former commander of 36 Infantry Brigade), with Tommy Wallis (late The Rifle Brigade); with Lord Desmond Chichester and Sir Rupert Clarke (former ADC's to Alexander in Italy) and to George Thorne his ADC at Dunkirk; with Lord Aldington (formerly Brigadier Toby Lowe, BGS 5 Corps), who kindly allowed me to see transcripts of the Court case.

I should acknowledge the help given by the following research establishments: the Berlin Documents Centre (under their US Director Dr B Marwell); the Bundesarchiv, Freiburg; the Hoover Institute of Stanford, California; the Leeds Russian Archive (Brotherton Library, University of Leeds); and the staff of the London Library, St James Square.

I am also grateful to the following. To David (Viscount) Montgomery of Alamein for permission to include the map from his father's book *Normandy to the Baltic*; to Toby (Sir Hereward) Wake for reminders of the army of occupation; to my brother Bill (Sir William) Mather for several stories of this period; to the Regimental Museum of the Royal Irish Fusiliers; to the British Red Cross; to Bob (Hon. Robert) Boscawen for allowing me to see the diaries of his mother, Lady Falmouth; to the All-Party Parliamentary War Crimes Group under the chairmanship of the Rt Hon. Merlyn Rees MP; to Alexander Bance who did some early reading for me; to my son Nicholas who made some thoughtful comments on reading the script.

I am much obliged to all the authors from whom I have quoted and their copyright holders. To any other benefactors I have left unmentioned I make my apologies in advance.

Fiona Rippon acted as long-stop and helped marshal numerous papers for me. Anita Rogers my secretary for the duration of this work, who typed the whole manuscript, devoted long hours in her spare time to this book, to her I am most grateful.

Peter Verney (son of the late Brigadier Gerald Verney, 1st Guards Brigade) advised me throughout on historical fact, and character sketches of Alexander. He kindly allowed me to quote from his father's private papers, including letters home from the front. His comments on reading my manuscript were both astringent and apt.

To Bryan Watkins (my Brassey's Editor) I owe a considerable debt of gratitude. He has given me much helpful guidance and shrewd advice during the editorial process, including work on the maps. I could not have wished for a better partner.

One debt which I cannot repay is to my wife Philippa. Finding oneself married to a writer must be a most traumatic experience. But her support and encouragement have kept me going, at the same time keeping my feet firmly on the ground. Apart from mastering an extremely temperamental photocopier, she had the tedious experience of reading every word I had written.

List of Plates

Frontispiece. Stragglers going through the Löibl Pass (From an original sketch by the Author)

1. The Author's grandmother and family in Russian peasant costume about 1880
2. 'The Chief' – General Sir Bernard Montgomery
3. Allied leaders tour French battlefields, June/July 1944
4. Montgomery with General Omar Bradley, Commander 1st (US) Army, Normandy
5. In the Ardennes. Montgomery's Liaison Officers
6. At Tac HQ, Zondhoven (Holland)
7. The Victory Dinner, Brussels 1945
8. The Surrender. Luneburg Heath 4 May 1945
9. Italian Partisans
10. Three Cossack soldiers with a German NCO
11. A Chetnik officer
12. Chetniks beg a lift
13. With the surrendered Hungarian Army in Austria – camp followers
14. Marshal Tito in his mountain hideout
15. General Mihailovic with a veteran Montenegrin leader
16. Brigadier Pat Scott and Lieutenant General Sir Charles Keightley
17. Crossing the Wörthersee. Field Marshal Alexander and Lieutenant General Keightley
18. Field Marshal Alexander and Brigadier Gerald Verney

List of Maps

1. The Road to Luneburg Heath (*Reproduced by kind
   permission of the Viscount Montgomery of Alamein CBE*)
   (*and front endpaper*)   2
2. The Final Phase in Italy 1945   42
3. Cossack Partisan Operations West of the River
   Tagliamento   56
4. Cossack Partisan Operations East of the River Tagliamento
   in Friuli   57
5. The Melting Pot: Carinthia 8–14 May 1945 (Sketch) (*and
   rear endpaper*)   140
6. The End of the War in Europe: Situation from the Baltic
   to the Adriatic. April 1945   194

Glossary

A & SH	Argyll and Sutherland Highlanders
ACABRIT	Assistant Commissioner Austria (British)
Adjt	Adjutant
AFHQ	Allied Force Headquarters
AGRA	Army Group Royal Artillery
AMG (AMGOT)	Allied Military Government (Occupied Territories)
BAOR	British Army of the Rhine
Bde	Brigade
BEF	British Expeditionary Force
BERCOMB	Berlin Command (British)
BGS	Brigadier General Staff
BLO	British Liaison Officer (SOE operations)
Bn	Battalion
Br	Bridge
BTA	British Troops Austria
CAB	Cabinet (Minutes)
CADC	Combined Administration Committee of the Joint Staff Mission in Washington
CAO	Chief Administrative Officer
CCS	Combined Chiefs of Staff (US/UK sitting in Washington)
Cdn	Canadian
CIGS	Chief of the Imperial General Staff
C-in-C	Commander-in-Chief
CO	Commanding Officer
Coln	Column
COS	Chiefs of Staff (British)
Coy Comd	Company Commander
DDMS	Deputy Director of Medical Services

DSO	Distinguished Service Order
DP	Displaced Person
DZ	Dropping Zone
EAM	Right Wing Greek resistance movement
ELAS	Communist Greek resistance movement
Flt	Flt (air force)
FM	Field Marshal
Fmn	Formation
FO	Foreign Office
G	General Staff (branches)
	See also:
	GSI Intelligence (British) G2 (US)
	A Personnel Administration
	(British) G1 (US)
	Q Quartermaster (British) G4 (US)
	Ops Operations (British) G3 (US)
Gds	Guards
GOC	General Officer Commanding
GUARD	Security grading for documents which were not to be shown to US
HMG	His Majesty's Government
Inf	Infantry
INNISKS	Inniskilling Fusiliers
Int	Intelligence
JCS	Joint Chiefs of Staff (US)
JSM	Joint Staff Mission (Washington)
JUGS	Used indiscriminately to describe Yugoslavs
KP	KP numbers are the serial numbers allocated to key papers in Brigadier Cowgill's works of reference
LF	Lancashire Fusiliers
LO	Liaison Officer
L of C	Lines of Communication
MA	Military Assistant
MACMIS	British Military Mission to Marshal Tito (Brig. Fitzroy Maclean)
Maquis	French (or Belgian) resistance movement
NKVD	Soviet security organisation (forerunner of the KGB)
NMA	Netherlands Military Administration
NCO	Non-commissioned Officer
OB	German General Headquarters (from *Oberbefehls-*

	haber – Commander-in-Chief)
Oberst	Colonel (German)
OC	Officer Commanding (a company or equivalent)
Ops	Operations
OKH	*Oberkommando des Heeres* (German High Command for all three Services – in Berlin)
OKW	*Oberkommando der Wehrmacht* (German Army Headquarters – equivalent to British War Office)
OR	Other Rank (British) (US Enlisted Man)
Org	Organisation
Osoppo	Element of the Partisans in Italy named after the small town of that name in commemoration of the part it played in the 1848 uprising of the Italians against the Austrians
OSS	Office of Strategic Services (US – forerunner of the Central Intelligence Agency and corresponding to British SOE)
Ost	East (German)
Ostmin	German Ministry for the Occupied Eastern Territories
PM	Prime Minister
POW	Prisoner of War (or PW/PsW)
PRO	Public Record Office
PWX	Ex-Prisoner of War
RB	Rifle Brigade
RE	Royal Engineers
Res.Min	Resident Minister
Rls	Railways
RWK	Royal West Kent Regiment
SA	*Sturmabteilungen* (German) Storm Troops (Brown Shirts)
SBO	Senior British Officer (POW Camps)
SD	*Sicherheitsdienst* (Security service of the German SS)
SEAC	South-East Asia Command
SEP	Surrendered Enemy Personnel
SHAEF	Supreme Headquarters Allied Expeditionary Force
SITREP	Situation Report
SOE	Special Operations Executive
Sp	Support
SS	*Schützstaffel* (Nazi organisation dedicated to Hitler

	and controlled by Himmler. *Waffen SS* was the field army element)
Stalag-Luft	German POW camp for air force personnel other than officers
Starets	Holy man (Russian)
Tac HQ	Tactical Headquarters
TCV	Troop Carrying Vehicle
Tits	Nickname for Titoists
TROOPERS	Signals address group for War Office
UN	United Nations
USNA	United States National Archives
Waffen SS	See SS
WG	Welsh Guards
WO	War Office (British)

Prologue

RUSSIAN BACKDROP

About the middle of the last century, it must have been in the year 1860, a lone traveller was making his way by sleigh on one of those interminable journeys in Russia. It was a night of frost and snow and it was quite clear that the driver had lost his way. After blundering about for some hours, a glimmering light was seen in the distance and before long, the tired horses drew up at a country house. Hospitality in such circumstances was given without question, whoever the travellers might be. But when the owner, Count Mura-vieff, discovered that the traveller was an Englishman, he was over-joyed, for despite the war in the Crimea, educated Russians were devoted to England.

The lone traveller was my grandfather, William Mather, who had been born in the year 1838, so he was only in his early 20's. Very soon he was making the acquaintance of the Count's wife and his two sisters-in-law the Princesses Shakovskoi (or more correctly in the feminine Shakovskaya). The whole family were passionately in favour of the emancipation of the serfs, an event that took place the following year and had the ear of no less a person than the Emperor Alexander. William Mather was therefore introduced at an early age to the social problems of Russia. But his chief reason for being in Russia, a country in which he was to spend half his working life, was to reconnoitre the prospect for his engineering 'works' which had been established during the last century.[1] He and other expatriates like him were members of the small English colony in St Petersburg, whose skills and enterprise helped to bring Russia out of the serf-economy into the modern industrial age of those days, so that by the outbreak of the First World War, Russia was in possession of at least some basic industry. His winter journeys were obligatory.

Most mills and rudimentary industry was located on the waterways, the great rivers of Russia, which even in later days no railway touched. It was much easier to travel by sleigh in winter time than in the morass of the spring thaw or the rough dust-bound tracks of summer.

Some years later, in February 1886, an important event took place in my family's history. William Mather was dining in Moscow at the home of a Russian lady, Madame Colley, when he received a telegram announcing the birth of a son:

'The event was naturally celebrated in hearty fashion,' the family history records, 'and the hostess then announced "The boy must have a Russian name, and I will be his godmother". He was named Loris after Loris Melikoff who was looked upon, at that time, as one of the greatest men in Russia'. And so my father came to bear a Russian name.

William Mather had written home to my grandmother: 'Loris Melikoff, Russia's commander in Armenia during the late war, is proclaimed dictator over the whole Empire. The Tsar has signed over to him all power within Russia over life death and property. He is reputed to be a good and strong man, honest, determined and clever. His mission of course is to root out nihilism'.[2]

On William Mather's last visit to Russia in 1912, at an audience at Tsarskoe Selo (Palace of the Tsar) he recounted to Nicholas II how his first arrival in Russia had coincided with the emancipation of the serfs and how he had visited Russia almost every winter since, which had added up to almost 22 years of his life.

The emancipation of the serfs did not have quite the effect that Tsar Alexander and liberal-minded noblemen had hoped for. The Russian people and their rulers could not really understand each other. The peasants believed that not only did freedom belong to them but that the land from which they had been cheated was theirs too. For their part, the landowners felt that, after emancipation, things would go on the same as before, albeit at greater cost. Agitators and *agents provocateurs* played on the sensibilities of the common people and revolution was never far beneath the surface. When the Revolution eventually came in 1917, the Russian people's hopes were to be disappointed, for a worse tyranny supplanted that which had gone.

These events have bound me ever since with a tenuous link to Mother Russia.

After the Revolution, my parents had many friends amongst the Russian exiles in London. It was a charmed but impoverished circle some of whose names I remember being: the Poustchines, Galitzines, Cantacuzines, Rodziankos (Paul, late of the Imperial Regiment of Chevaliers Gardes, taught me to ride), and many others, including the Sheremetievs, who I met later on in life. My mother who suffered from ill-health had several charming 'companions' drawn from this circle. Given these circumstances, 'the Revolution' was very near to us, for this shocking event had only taken place a dozen years before, and with emigrés our constant visitors, we children were only too well aware of it.

$$* \qquad * \qquad *$$

Soon after the outbreak of war, it must have been in the summer of 1940, I was stationed as a young officer at Sandown Park. I remember being taken by a brother officer to have tea with the Grand Duchess Xenia at 'the Wilderness', Hampton Court Palace. Xenia was the eldest of two sisters of the last Tsar of Russia, Nicholas II. It was a fortunate introduction for me, for although I cannot remember much of what we discussed, I still retain a vivid impression of her charm, beauty and vibrant personality. Then it was all forgotten, like so many other crowded events of those years.

Now this encounter assumes far greater meaning, for it gives me a living link with personalities at the centre of the Russian upheavals at the end of the First World War, which led on to the events I am about to describe.[3]

During the early days of 1940 a bizarre episode took place, in which I was to have a part. We almost found ourselves at war with Russia (then on Germany's side), through our attempt to come to the rescue of Finland, then under attack from the Soviets. Whilst I was an officer-cadet at the Royal Military Academy, Sandhurst, volunteers were called for (in January 1940), to join a special unit made up of ski-ers.[4] The destination was secret, but to those of us who joined there was no doubt in our minds that our destination was to be Finland. We were on the point of embarkation, having carried out essential training in France, when the armistice between Russia and Finland was declared. Our hopes were dashed but our lives were probably saved. We were saved also from a catastrophic action which would have altered the course of the entire war.

By 1941 the pendulum had swung the other way. Germany attacked Russia (codenamed Operation '*Barbarossa*'). Russia thereby came into the war on our side. As a member of the Tobruk garrison, then under siege, I shall never forget the spontaneous outburst of jubilation and relief that greeted the news on that day. It was 22 June 1941![5]

Three years later, having returned to England, after a spell in an Italian prisoner-of-war camp, I rejoined Montgomery in time for the Invasion.

A curious experience, whilst in the Normandy bridgehead in June 1944, alerted me to the nature of our alliance with the Soviets. In some farm buildings near Montgomery's battle headquarters I surprised a group of horsemen. They were wearing German uniform, but various characteristics told me that they were 'Cossacks' (whom one used to see at horse-shows and gymkhanas before the war performing their equestrian feats). We had no information that there might be Russians fighting on the German side. But soon we were to capture Russians in increasing numbers, much to the embarrassment of our Soviet allies, and ultimately to ourselves.

Having explored the background to my narrative, let me now take the reader by the hand and lead him gently into the reality of war-torn Europe, as we found it, in the early days of 1945.

PART ONE

WAR-TORN EUROPE

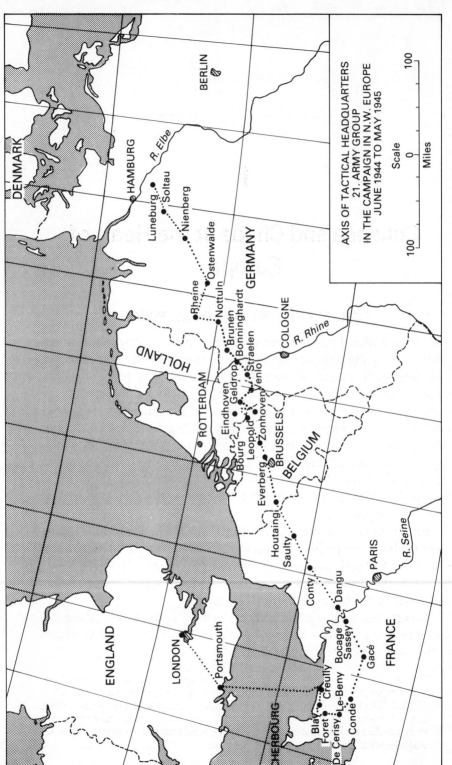

1. The Road to Luneburg Heath showing the author's own route across Europe in 1944-45 (*Reproduced by kind permission of the Viscount Montgomery of Alamein, CBE*)

I

Collapse and Chaos at the Heart of Europe

COLLAPSE OF THE OCCUPYING POWER

It is the 8 May 1945, the wheels of war have now stopped turning.[1] There is a deathly silence in Europe as millions of people clamber, like sleep-walkers, out of the fighting vehicles, their fox-holes, their cellars and their bunkers, scarcely able to grasp the fact that for them the war is over. The guns have stopped firing but the smoke and dust have scarcely cleared away from the battlefields. Millions of grey-clad figures, the crushed soldiers of the Third Reich, are standing in an attitude of surrender. The displaced people, the anonymous slave-army of the Reich, are emerging from their places of forced labour, bewildered and unbelieving, soon to wreck vengeance on their erst-while oppressors.

Other European armies, the allies of Hitler, lie broken and in tatters strewn about the plains and passes of Lower Austria: Hungarians, Cossacks, Caucasians, Azerbaijanis and Turcomen.[2] They are fleeing before Stalin's and Tito's armies, hoping for a softer option if they surrender to British and American soldiers.

The appreciation of a staff officer, writing at the time of the post-surrender period, gives an insight into the attitude of the Germans in the immediate aftermath of defeat.

'Initially the Germans were stunned by the disaster that had overtaken them. Superimposed on the universal confusion was a widespread fear of the RUSSIANS. The result of these factors was implicit obedience. This phase, which lasted for about 10 days, was followed by a period of limited recovery. Now their obedience was informed by the knowledge that the restoration of order was a result of allied orders and not their own.

3

Apart from their desire to be released, the prisoners were very apathetic. These was no criticism of commanders; their only crime was the losing of the war. Obedience and 'co-operation' were still the salient characteristics at all levels.

At this stage their motives do not emerge with clarity. They know that there is no future for the NAZI régime or for the German Armed Forces. Perhaps their first desire is to preserve what remains of GERMANY from deteriorating still further as a nation. No doubt the approach of winter is a potent factor in their appreciation.'[3]

There were very marked differences in the situations obtaining in the occupied countries of NW Europe. Holland had suffered more acutely than most during the Nazi occupation. So let us dwell for a time on the trials and tribulations of that country.

The Netherlands

In order to gain an understanding of conditions in the Netherlands, which greeted our arrival in the second half of September 1944, it is necessary to recapitulate the events which took place during the Occupation.

The *History of the Second World War* dealing with civil affairs, sets the background to the conditions of life in Holland as we found them:

'The circumstances of the Netherlands differed from those of France or even of Belgium. When the German forces overran the country in 1940 the whole of the Government, including its constitutional head, escaped to England. The queen and her Ministers set themselves up in London and continued to govern the Dutch colonies. Early in 1942, when Japan entered the war, the Netherlands East Indies were lost, after the Dutch Government had declared war upon the Japanese and ranged itself as an Ally alongside the British and Americans.'[4]

The essential difference was that the Dutch had decided to fight on. To the Germans they were a hostile nation, with an effective Resistance at home and free Dutch forces overseas, and the full rigours of Nazification were therefore imposed. The notorious Dr Arthur Seyss-Inqhart, himself a quisling, had been made *Reichskommissar* and reported direct to Hitler. Furthermore it was the Führer's intention that Holland should be annexed and incorporated into the Reich. This Nazification ran right through the provincial administration, and ensured that even petty officials were loyal to the Nazi Party and the aims of Hitler (of whom it may be said there was no great shortage). When the Royal Dutch Government began to formulate plans in London for the re-occupation of Holland and the provision of a caretaker government from their own resources, they were faced not only with a hostile local administration, but with the estrangement which had taken place between themselves, having spent a war in comparative safety, and the people of the Netherlands, who had suffered the full horrors of the Occupation. As they would be working with the Allies, the government in exile therefore deemed it not only tactful, but practical politics, to ensure that their leading representatives were in uniform. The Netherlands Military Administration (NMA) was therefore formed. Attached to General Eisenhower's Headquarters, they would enter Holland when the time was ripe and pave the way for the return of the Dutch Government in London. Operation 'Market Garden' (the Arnhem operation) by Montgomery's 21st Army Group supported by two American Airborne Divisions (82nd and 101st) opened the way into Holland.

For Monty's Liaison Officers, keeping in touch with the forward troops was a somewhat hazardous assignment. The axis of advance was upon one narrow cobbled road bounded on each side by canals. Minor roads and tracks supplemented this centre-line to some extent but even these roads were criss-crossed by waterways and it was not wise to stray far afield, as the enemy was trying desperately to sever our line of advance. Under the pressure of battle, we were only dimly aware of the condition of the few dejected inhabitants that we came across, but it was not until reaching Eindhoven, and setting up Tactical Headquarters (Tac HQ), that we realised that hunger had bitten deep into the population of Holland.

North of Eindhoven, approaching Nijmegen, our line of advance narrowed until we only controlled the strip of road itself, and it was here at Veghel, on 22 September, and at Uden on 24 September, that I encountered the German Panzers and they finally severed our L of C. Cut off from our main body, I spent the night in a primitive inn and failed to deliver my message to Montgomery that night, an unheard event, until communications were once more restored. It was a wet, muddy, slushy operation carried out in constant rain. Our painful earthbound movements were of course supplemented by a carpet of three airborne divisions dropped ahead across the Rivers Maas, Waal and the two branches of the Rhine, the last at Arnhem, our ultimate objective. Eisenhower had changed Montgomery's original plan, which was to be a combined Allied thrust towards the Ruhr on this same axis; and on towards Berlin. The scaling-down and delaying of this thrust led to all sorts of difficulties, especially at Arnhem, and has since been the subject of bitter dispute, but is not the subject of this book and has been fully covered else-where.[5]

The attitude of the Forces of the Interior (as the Dutch Resistance was known) was unfriendly and hostile towards the '*Engelandvaarder*' or the Netherlands Military Administration from the United Kingdom, who sought to impose their rule. The Resistance continued with their unlawful arrests of 'collaborationists', and by the end of June 1945, there were believed to be over sixty thousand in detention.[6]

All these events were profoundly unhelpful in alleviating the desperate need for food and medical supplies.

The most densely populated region of Holland, known as the B2 Area, containing Amsterdam, Rotterdam and the Hague, had not yet been reached. Here was the highest population and the industrial heartland of the country, the whole of it lying below sea level. It has been estimated that by 1944 the diet for the whole country had fallen to no more than 1,600 calories a day and in this densely populated area it was worse. (2,700 calories a day in Britain in 1945). Meantime, 21st Army Group had accumulated a food dump of some 30,000 tons, and General Eisenhower's Supreme Headquarters were sending 1,700 lorries from the United Kingdom. Reports received during the early months of 1945, from within occupied Holland told of the ration levels having dropped to 600 calories a day and lower in some cities. Yet the liberation of Holland could only be undertaken at the expense of the early defeat of Germany. It was a dreadful dilemma. Early in April 1945, news reached the Dutch Government in London that no food would be available for civilians after 28 April.

On 5 May 1945, the Germans capitulated in front of the advance of General Crerar's First Canadian Army, and the SHAEF Mission including the NMA moved in. Allied forces were greeted with wild enthusiasm. Let the head of the SHAEF Mission take up the story:

'On first appearances the condition of the people has proved unfortunately most deceptive. On the advent of Allied Troops, the soldiers were greeted with cheers and bunting, and made their progress through a smiling countryside. But it was deceptive because men and women who are slowly dying in their beds of starvation unfortunately cannot walk gaily about the streets waving flags. It is an empty country, inhabited by a hungry, and in the town, a semi-starved population. It is no exaggeration to state that, had liberation been delayed for another ten days or so, many thousands of people would surely have died of hunger.

The existing food supplies in the area are practically nil. A day's ration consists of a very small cup of nasty "ersatz" soup, a very small piece of an unappetising and sticky substance called bread, and a wafer of sugar beet. It is hardly surprising that a large proportion of the population, who were unable to buy on the black market, have lost on an average 45 pounds in weight.'[7]

More alarming was a random check of people on the streets. Out of 100 people 75 were suffering from under-nourishment or severe malnutrition. The infant mortality rate can be imagined. It was estimated that half the population were infected with lice and the report continues:

'There is an absolute lack of the necessities of life. There is no coal, consequently no light; no soap, and nobody has had any new clothes for five years. In many of the big towns there is no water pressure which means that the sanitary arrangements are "woefully deficient".'

A piece in the *Times* of 28 May 1945, quoted Sir Jack Drummond of the 'nutrition committee' as saying:

'Reports of a large number of deaths in the western Dutch towns from starvation are quite correct. We saw hundreds of people of both sexes and all ages as emaciated from starvation as any we had seen at Belsen concentration camp.'

A report by 21st Army Group, written shortly afterwards, points to the dangers of disease, the problems of flood control and basic transport:

'The conditions of life in Western HOLLAND were extremely grave. A large proportion of the population, apart from those actually dying of starvation, was found to be suffering from malnutrition and a prey therefore to sickness and diseases, such as enteric typhoid, dysenteric complaints, scabies, infestation, diphtheria and scarlet fever, the incidence of which was high. Large areas were under water and agricultural output and potential was seriously reduced. Road transport, horses, tractors and agricultural machinery had been very extensively removed by the Germans. Coal stocks were totally inadequate. The morale of the public was uncertain and that of the police forces low. One of the worst aspects was that the systematic stripping of HOLLAND by the Germans of its agricultural and industrial machinery, tools and transportation stock to an extent experienced by no other Western occupied country, had rendered a normally industrious and independent nation largely incapable of rehabilitation and reconstruction through a lack of the requisite physical means.'[8]

Holland had suffered far more devastation and deprivation than any other country in Western Europe at the time of the Occupation. And so we come to the end of this grim story:

'On 25 May, the exodus of the disarmed 25th German Army on its long trek to the concentration areas of the AURICH Peninsula commenced. These troops were passed across the IJJSSEL MEER by the causeway and by naval landing craft and taken over on arrival on the Eastern side by 2 Canadian Corps. Those who were in the automatic arrest category were previously taken into custody and on 11 May the notorious Reichskommissar SEYSS-INQHART with whom, only twelve days before, negotiations had had to be conducted for supplying food to the DUTCH, and who had made an unsuccessful attempt to escape by submarine, was handed over to SHAEF for trial.'[9]

The long line of Colonel General Blaskowitz's 25th Army as they trudged into captivity along the 20 mile long causeway across the Ijjssel Meer, silhouetted, Katgaresque, against the open sky and muddy waters, is a fitting exit for this most dishonourable army.

II

Post-Surrender in Germany

THE CLASH OF CULTURES

What were relations like with our Russian allies when we at last met them face to face? As the first troops made contact there was exultation, bear hugs, exchanges of cigarettes and a spirit of camaraderie. These Russians had been cracked up to be supermen, upstanding, patriotic, heroes to a man, and valiant fighters. But try living with them! That was a different story. Those who came back from Soviet occupied land told tales of a depopulated desert, of pillage, looting and raping. No German woman was safe from the Russian soldiery, and most of them fled towards the Allied lines. Their behaviour was the same in our territory. For those Russian slave-workers and ex-prisoners liberated by the Allies, rape and murder of their erstwhile enemies was the order of the day.[1]

'What are those notches on your rifle?' asked a British officer of a camp inmate in Schleswig-Holstein. 'For each of those notches' replied the Russian ex-prisoner cheerfully, 'I have killed a German, since the war is over.'

But there was a healthy respect for our Russian allies. After all, hadn't they pulled our chestnuts out of the fire? Where would we be without them? And was it not thanks to the feelings of friendship and respect at the Yalta Conference that enabled Germany to be finally defeated? If Yalta had ended in disagreement and estrangement between the Soviets and Western Allies, we should have been facing a hostile Russia across the dismembered body of Germany, and not an apparently friendly one. Or, we might indeed not have been celebrating victory over Germany at all, if we had forfeited Soviet good will. The Yalta Agreement, for all its imperfections, brought one inestimable boon to the fighting men and their families – an end

9

to the war in Europe. That is not to say that there was not rather more than a degree of realism about the future. With the collapse of Germany, we were face to face with one of the world's most powerful military machines with unlimited resources of manpower, which by skilful manoeuvring had gained a substantial toe-hold in Western Europe and had seized large parts of Poland and caused what remained of that country to occupy parts of Germany. But the unanswered question was always there, as I well remember hearing in officers' and sergeants' messes up and down the British zone, 'Why don't we go on?' Meaning why do we not, geared up as we are, deal with the other dictatorship in Europe – that of Stalin? An interesting thought. But alas, within months of the surrender, the Allied Command structure had been dismantled. Battle-experienced commanders had disappeared, and our fighting echelons were being decimated by demobilisation and Far East drafts. Whilst across the psychological non-man's-land sat the Soviet armies, sullen, watchful and intact.

> '*Churchill to Truman*   *12 May 45*
> An iron curtain is drawn down upon their front. We do not know what is going on behind. There seems little doubt that the whole of the regions east of the line Lübeck-Trieste-Corfu will soon be completely in their hands. To this must be added the further enormous area conquered by the American armies between Eisenach and the Elbe, which will, I suppose, in a few weeks be occupied, when the Americans retreat, by the Russian power.'

Churchill was worried by the huge belt of Russian-occupied territory which would now separate us from Poland, a country very much on his mind since Soviet intransigence at Yalta.

> 'Meanwhile the attention of our people will be occupied in inflicting severities upon Germany, which is ruined and prostrate and it would be open to the Russians in a very short time to advance if they chose to the waters of the North Sea and the Atlantic.'[2]

Up until the time of the Potsdam Conference in July 1945, it was assumed by the Western Allies that once the framework had been hammered out, Germany would be governed as a unified whole. All this changed when Stalin insisted that the traditional breadbasket of Germany, the huge agricultural tracts in East Germany, were no longer available for feeding the 3 million inhabitants of the Western Allied Sectors in Berlin, nor the huge population in the industrialised West of Germany. It was in this way that the two Germanies, East and West, were parted. Not, as is now supposed, as a safeguard against future German militarism. Other measures consolidated the economic imbalances. Russia stripped East Germany of most of her machinery and industrial infrastructure and shipped it off to the homeland to squeeze the last drop of reparations from her defeated foe. The Western Allies, on the other hand, were modestly stimulating coal production to refuel industry and provide the means in Western Germany for acquiring food.

The ambivalent attitude towards Russia was dictated, it must be said, by fear as much as anything else. Fear of a new conflict. Fear that our people, after almost six years of war, had had about enough. Fear that the Russians would not back the war against Japan. And, fear on the part of Britain and the United States that the Soviets would retain Western hostages, in the form of allied prisoners-of-war, overrun by their advance. And, fear of a new conflict was by no means irrational. For, since that moment, up to the year 1990 (in which I write these words), the Western Allies have been watching and waiting, at a constant state of readiness, on the line where the war ended. Waiting for a massive strike by Soviet armoured forces deep into the heart of Western Europe. A strike which, largely due to the nuclear deterrent, never came, but the threat of which lasted for almost 45 years, and which, with the collapse of the Warsaw Pact and the official ending of the Cold War at the Paris Summit in November 1990, has only just evaporated.

But there was a similar clash of cultures, and clash of personalities, between the British and Germans when they met for the surrender at Luneberg Heath. The German delegation, headed by Admiral von Friedeburg (as I know from eye-witness accounts), were extremely correct, their height accentuated by long grey and black greatcoats, even though it was the month of May. Montgomery was dressed as ever, very informally, in polo-neck sweater and corduroys.[3] Both he and Colonel Joe Ewart, his intelligence officer, of a decidedly unmilitary figure, were small of stature. Like all great moments in history, it must have had its ludicrous side as these two representatives of two vastly different cultures, or historical epochs one might say, advanced upon one another. Each must have looked to the other as strange as 'the man from Mars'. But Montgomery, never one to have the wool pulled over his eyes, reacted strongly to the delegation's suggestion that they do a deal 'by which they withdrew their forces as my forces advanced', in order to protect the civilian population. Montgomery reminded them sharply of the destruction of Coventry, 'the people who took the brunt of it' he reminded them 'were the women and children and the old men. Your women and children get no sympathy from me – you should have thought of all this six years ago.'[4]

And this describes the essential difference between the haughty, correct and rigid German military establishment, and their impish pursuer, whose caravans had indeed travelled from the Alamein line to this barren heathland in the heart of Hitler's Third Reich.

The war is over! But peace brings its own problems, for Montgomery is informed by the German High Command, that in Schleswig-Holstein, there are four hundred thousand Russian prisoners of war (POW), as well as an influx of two million civilians who had fled before the Russian advance. In ten days time there would be nothing for them to eat.[5]

RELEASE OF THE ALLIED PRISONERS

In the days following the Surrender, the release of allied POW seemed to be going according to plan. At least we were dealing with the Soviet fighting men and not at that stage with the NKVD. The evacuation of *Stalag Luft-I* at Barth near Rostock behind the Soviet lines, was a case in point, where some 9,000 (7,500 American and 1,500 British) troops, mostly airforce personnel were released within days of the cease fire. Even they, according to a British staff officer, Colonel Turner, 'were not even certain that they were not prisoners of the Russians'.[6]

This was a comparatively easy evacuation. But take the case of *Offlag VIIC*. The camp was located at Eichstat in Bavaria.

Lieutenant P F Hanbury, a Guards officer, who was captured at Boulogne at the time of Dunkirk, writes this account of liberation after 5 years in a POW camp:

'We were given orders to leave Eichstat Camp by the Germans one or two days before we actually departed early one morning in May. ... Armed with heavy packs, we set off from the camp along the valley. On the other side of the valley there was a railway line. I was in the earlier companies, and the tail was still in the camp, when two American planes flew over shooting-up a train or lorries (my memory fails me which) on the other side of the valley. They turned and then flew over our column, and some people thought they had dipped their wings, which American planes usually did when flying over the camp. I and a number of others thought they had not done this, so when the planes turned to come back over the column, we dived for ditches, and I went up a culvert under the road. The planes then flew to and fro machine-gunning the column until they ran out of bullets, I think, killing thirteen people and hitting fifty, including my step-daughter's father-in-law, who lost a foot. I reckoned they would radio for further planes, and that we should get out of the valley without delay. About twenty or thirty of us collected one of our German guards and ran as hard as we could with our heavy packs up the valley side into some woods.'[7]

At any moment it would have been possible to escape the German guards, but it was felt better at this stage of the war, with the Russians closing in on one side and the Americans and British on the other, to stick together. They were still in hostile country:

'We all went on to a huge camp, the name of which escapes me. It had about 29,000 people of all ranks and nationalities. We were put in a hut, and the American occupants were turned out to sleep in the open. I think this was part of German policy to create ill-feeling among the Allies. It did not work as far as we were concerned, as we suggested they come back and sleep on the floor between our bunks. The following day American tanks trundled past the camp firing at an SS division, which was holding the adjoining wood. Occasional bursts of fire went through our hut. No one was hurt, and I do not think that it was deliberate by the SS. That evening Patton came in in a Jeep to the cheers of everyone and said we would all be home shortly.'[8]

For these British prisoners the arrival of General Patton was most timely. By the numbers of Russians about, they could just as well had fallen into their hands, as indeed happened to the inmates of Lückenwalde, south of Berlin. This camp held 16,000 inmates including Russian POW in a state of semi-starvation. Flight Lieutenant Barber was a prisoner of war there. Later he described his experiences.[9]

'I myself was one of those aircrew who were held by the Russians after the end of the war in Europe. We realised at the time that we were being kept as hostages until the return of Russians who had been liberated by the British. If the Government had refused to return the Russians, I do not doubt that most of us would have accepted our unhappy lot as being a necessary consequence of the aftermath of war. In the event, a different decision was taken. The point I want to make is that it is all too easy for armchair critics who themselves have never had to take major decisions involving life and death, not to mention the wider international considerations; to moralise, generations later, about what should or should not have been done. I well remember at Dunkirk how we looked in vain for cover from the RAF. Many were killed on those beaches as a result of the decision not to risk our aircraft, yet that decision was undoubtedly the right one.
The winning of a war and the issues of peace were not quite as easy as the critics now pretend.'[10]

Tony Barber told me that after they had been overrun by the Russians they were free to wander out of the camp,

'We went outside to forage for food – to bring in horses and shoot them for food. But the SBO ordered us not to attempt to escape for fear of the Russians punishing those who remained. After a few days the Americans arrived to release us, and told us to climb into the trucks. As we did so, the Russians promptly fired a burst of machine-gun fire over our heads and that was that! We went back to our camp. Of course we realised we were being kept as hostages – for we were held in that camp for a further six weeks after the war was over.'[11]

It was not only British prisoners who were likely to be held as hostages by the Russians, as Mr Averell Harriman, then United States Ambassador in Moscow, records:

> 'Eisenhower and his staff were fearful that if they did not send back the Soviet prisoners, the Russians might seize upon one pretext or another to hold up the return of American prisoners from Eastern Europe.'[12]

As can be imagined, the return of prisoners, many of whom had been away from their wives and families for up to five years was a matter charged with emotion. In the eyes of the public it was a question of honour. A government which failed to honour this obligation, speedily and regardless of cost, would have been in deep trouble with public sentiment, already sorely tested by the privations of war, and now being asked to continue supporting a war in the Far East (where, incidentally, an even more emotional question of prisoners was involved). At what cost this was achieved we will see in a succeeding chapter.

As soon as the fighting was over, and in some cases before it had ceased, first priority for the British and Americans was to secure their own prisoners of war captured by the Germans.

Once the ex-prisoners were in British or American hands they were repatriated very rapidly, a huge airlift being organised for the purpose. As far as the British Zone of Germany was concerned a total of 157,000 British and Commonwealth ex-prisoners were dispatched to the United Kingdom from North-West Europe, 130,000 had arrived in the United Kingdom by 16 May, leaving a balance of 27,000, probably in Soviet hands to be repatriated later. It was this balance, together with ex-prisoners to be exchanged with the Soviets through Austria, which constituted the 'hostage' card which the Soviets had up their sleeve and would not play unless all their people, held by the British and Americans, whether willing or not, were first returned to them. Owing to these political factors, the repatriation of East-bound prisoners Russian, Polish and Yugoslav did not begin to take place until the end of May. Russian returnees were handed over at agreed exchange points and not until then was the return load of our Westbound people passed over. The Russians insisted on their 'pound of flesh' and it was on this basis that the exchanges took place.

III

Everyone Must Go Home

In the British Zone the military authorities faced a huge problem. A mass of humanity was on the move, initially estimated at 750,000, known as 'displaced persons' (DPs) if found outside their own country, but as 'refugees' if found inside their country of origin. This figure also included ex-prisoners of war (PWX). Every European nation was represented in this motley crowd, quite apart from the large number of Russians:

'Interminable "Covered waggon" convoys, on a scale never envisaged by a Cecil de Mille (sic) were encountered on a every military axis, and it was seldom possible, as had been hoped, to confine displaced persons to their camps until organised movement could be arranged. PWX became in most cases inextricably confused with DP. In addition to the considerable numbers of DP/PWX encountered East of the Elbe by 8 British and XVIII US Airborne Corps, a further problem was created by the retreat of the German armies in the North and the migration of the German population, in front of the advancing Russians, the total numbers involved estimated as being in the neighbourhood of one million.

Owing to the scale of this mass exodus and the effect it had on military operations, control became in effect the responsibility of military commanders, working through their staffs and the Military Government detachments deployed to formations. Effective organisation only became possible in the Barrier Zones established on the water obstacles of the rivers Elbe, Weser, Ems, Rhine and Ijissel, where movement became canalised by the scarcity of bridges. In the Barrier Zones DP/PWX were checked, sorted by nationalities and collected into Assembly centres run by Military Government staffs through appointed leaders provided by the DP themselves. Initial tendencies towards lawlessness and depredation on the surrounding countryside were brought under control and the feeding and clothing of DP by levies on the German population was organised. Measures of hygiene, including disinfestation, and sanitation were applied and medical attention provided for the sick.'[1]

Further mass movements swelled the numbers. 9 US Army had over-run part of the British Zone and the take-over by the British

21 Army Group approximately doubled the number of westbound DP/PWX, and quadrupled the number of eastbounds. Included in these were people fleeing from the Russian Zone and surrendered enemy personnel (SEP) from the occupying forces in Denmark:

> 'The evacuation of Eastbound DP/PWX presented even greater problems. After initial control, collection and sorting they had to be retained in national camps pending international agreements as to their disposal. One further complication encountered was the unwillingness of many Eastbound DP/PWX, particularly Poles and Baltic States nationals, to be repatriated; another was the incidence of stateless persons, whose nationality could not be determined, or who could not establish their right to the nationality claimed. Apart from those Russians handed over by local agreement in the Mecklenburg area occupied by XVIII US Corps, Eastbound movement from the British area did not commence until towards the end of May, when the Leipzig agreement provided for the exchange of Russians from the British and United States Zones for Westbound DP/PWX from the Russian Zone. As a supplementary measure as many Russians as possible were collected in the so called "Wismar cushion" in Mecklenburg, which fell within the Russian Zone and was eventually taken over by them.'[2]

The human débris of war in the British Zone of Germany alone therefore amounted to some two and a half million people, all of whom had to be looked after pending return to their homes. Quite apart from the pressure exerted by the Russians for the return of their people, 21 Army Group had little option but to repatriate all these people as speedily as possible, given the conditions in the zone and in particular the food problem. Montgomery's attitude was quite clear: the party is over – everyone must go home.

As the Army historian at 21 Army Group explains:

> 'The task created by the displaced persons problem was a gigantic one, involving as it did the processes of controlling and transporting the equivalent of the population of Wales and Monmouthshire in men, women and children; the setting up or adaptation of camps for them; disinfestation and organisation of hygiene and sanitation measures among the transitory population, many of whom through years of ill treatment, had been degraded almost to the level of animals; feeding, watering, and clothing; checking and documentation; the provision of medical attention and supplies, the control of disease, and in the case of those who were not to be speedily repatriated, the initiation of rehabilitation, education and entertainment. All this was necessary in the case of the relatively healthy majority. For the sick, including such political prisoners as the inmates of the horror camps who were being systematically starved to death, further special measures were required and provided.'[3]

F S V Donnison, explains in his later history of military government in Germany that the whole reason for setting up a civil affairs organisation at all was to keep refugees from impeding military operations, but of course the task as it turned out was of far greater magnitude:

> 'It was assumed that these persons would wish to return to their countries,

or that it would become necessary to send them back, whether they wished it or not, in order to relieve the countries in which they were found of the burden of feeding and caring for them.'[4]

Donnison agrees with the army historian on the grand total involved, 2,461,500 (Appendix B) but pitches the figures in a wider European context which gives the staggering figure of over eleven million refugees:

'In May 1944 it was believed, and events proved this figure very nearly right, that there were over eleven million refugees or displaced persons in France, Belgium, Luxembourg, Holland, Denmark, Norway and Germany. Some twenty different languages were spoken by these people. And this total took no account of any German refugees since it was intended that responsibility for looking after these persons should be pinned on to the people of Germany. As for the British share of this commitment, there were likely to be about two and a half million displaced persons within the British zone of Germany, as shown in the table below:

DISPLACED PERSONS WITHIN THE BRITISH ZONE OF GERMANY[5]

Westbound		*Eastbound*	
French	464,000	Russians	121,000
Belgians	219,000	Poles	580,000
Dutch	151,000	Czechs	422,500
Others	98,500	Italians	120,500
		Yugoslavs	114,000
		Others	171,000
Total	932,500	Total	1,529,000

Grand Total 2,461,500

It is interesting to note that it was Allied policy to place upon the Germans the fullest responsibility for 'control, care and repatriation' of enemy refugees (i.e. Germans) and displaced persons. Allied displaced persons who had suffered at the hands of the Nazis were to be looked after by the Occupying Forces.

THE FOOD SITUATION

No description of the situation facing the Western Allies in Germany is complete without mentioning the acute food situation. It had originally been intended that the defeated enemy should bear the responsibility for feeding the displaced people who had lived on such meagre rations whilst the German population, the *Herrenvolk*, waxed fat and had priority over all others. Following the surrender, German ration scales were therefore set lower than that for their former slave populations. Nor were the Germans to indulge themselves whilst the occupied countries went short at their expense. This was to be a measure of restitution. If suffering there was to be, the Germans must be the first to suffer. But the Morgenthau Plan, which set out the scale of reparations that the Germans must pay, which included the destruction of industrial power and cutting down the coal industry, ran counter to the Allies' intention. For without coal production, food manufacture and processing could not take place, nor could the Germans afford to import food which they were unable to produce. As we have seen, Western Germany had been cut off from its normal and natural breadbasket in the Eastern territories of the country, now occupied by the Russians. In no way, even in times of peace and plenty, could the British Zone feed the enormous population which now resided there. Dairying, which formed a large part of food production in the Zone, could not process foodstuffs without power, in those days entirely derived from coal. In 1945 there was almost no butter in the Zone and, as winter approached, the essential fats to keep people warm were absent.

The level of nutrition in Britain in the year 1945 was 2,700 calories a day, a meagre enough ration. For Germans it was set at 1,500 calories a day, and the following figures give a vivid picture of what could be expected:

GERMAN RATION SCALES – BRITISH ZONE 1945[6]

Ounces per day		Ounces per day	
Bread	12.7	'Nährmittel'*	2.5
Meat	0.7	Jam	0.3
Fats	0.5	Cheese	0.07
Sugar	0.6	Potatoes	10.5
Skimmed milk	0.2 pints		

*cereal products

The Germans had nothing to complain of, for the ration for Allied prisoners of war in German and Italian camps was probably in the order of 1,000 calories a day if they were lucky. In Italian POW camps this usually consisted of a greasy bowl of thin soup and a very small hard bread roll. The occasional Red Cross parcel made for a bit of variety but could not supply the bulk for which prisoners craved.

Anticipating that an entirely unplanned-for situation had arisen, that is the sudden collapse of Germany instead of a long drawn out advance, with the gradual over-running of displaced people, the 21 Army Group planners had provided for immediate relief supplies.

The first consignment of these, 135 tons, went to the surviving inmates of Belsen Camp, with 1,037 tons going for the relief of displaced persons. This consignment reached its destination by 7 June. The onus for supplying the rest was placed upon the people of Germany.[7]

THE USE OF FORCE

By the time I reached Germany at about the beginning of the month of July 1945, repatriation was in full swing. About half the total numbers had returned home. During the rest of that year and the beginning of the next, I never remember a major incident taking place in 8 Corps District or in the Hamburg area. As a Liaison Officer I should certainly have heard about it, it was my business to do so. Nor do I remember hearing from fellow LOs that major repatriation problems were being created.[8] The logistics of moving so many people were certainly a problem, and we monitored the whole operation on a regular basis. It was accepted that some Russians would be unwilling to travel, but no thoughts of exemplary punishment on arrival entered our heads. The question of traitors was a different matter. Treachery was a capital offence and was accepted as such on both sides. The penalty for treachery in war, that is putting the lives of one's fellow countrymen in jeopardy, was to be shot. Several Britons were executed, among whom was the errant son of former minister Leo Amery.[9] The Soviet interpretation of a traitor went much wider and included anyone who had given aid and comfort to the enemy in any form, including that of an impressed worker. For these people were considered to be contaminated by their experiences outside the Soviet Union and required de-contamination in the Gulags, or worse. But we have not actually reached the point where these matters reached a crisis. But a clearer definition of the repatriation rules was needed:

From: SHAEF to 21 Army Group   *14 June 1945*
'By direction of the State Department and of the Foreign Office, persons displaced by reason of the War uncovered by the Allied Expeditionary Forces after 11 February 1945 who claim Soviet citizenship or whose documents or other acceptable evidence indicated Soviet citizenship and who are identified and documented as such by authorised Soviet Repatriation Representatives are to be repatriated regardless of their personal wishes. Persons of any nationality residing, prior to the War, in Countries other than their own and who were not subsequently displaced because of the War are not to be repatriated against their will. Soviet citizens formerly residing outside the USSR and who were subsequently displaced by reason of the War and uncovered by the Allied Expeditionary Forces, if identified and documented as Soviet citizens by author-

ised Soviet Repatriation Representatives, are to be repatriated to the USSR whether or not they so desire.'[10]

How many Russians did we have to deal with in the British Zone of Germany? If one totals up the number of Russian forced workers and prisoners of war, because by this time it was quite impossible to separate them, the number approaches one million:

From:–Deputy Commissioner Military Government
To:–MA to Chief of Staff 21 Army Group

9 July 1945

'In the British Zone (including that part taken over from the US Army on British assumption of control) there were about 1,000,000 Russian PWX and DPs; PWX are not segregated from DPs. Of these over half a million have now been transferred to the Russian Zone. Transfers are now (8 July) commencing once more, after the temporary stoppage due to the readjustment of the interzone boundary completed on 3 July 45, and subject to Russian ability to accept, will continue at the rate of about 14,000 per day.

21 Army Group has striven to implement the spirit and terms of the YALTA Agreement, and it is believed that the local Russian authorities are generally satisfied with the efforts we have made to this end.

Requests made by the Senior Russian LO for repatriation have been met when possible and complaints promptly enquired into.

It is anticipated that all Russian DP/PWX will have been repatriated by about the end of August, though this depends on Russian acceptance rates. Russians are therefore unlikely to be a liability for accommodation during the winter.

Discipline among Russian DP/PWX has been and continues to be bad and has had adverse effects on the food situation in the British Zone.'[11]

But not all goes quite as smoothly as we might like to think. In August a conference is summoned because of serious difficulties arising over the repatriation of Russian DPs. It is held under the Chairmanship of Brigadier Kenchington, Chief of the PW and DP Division at the British Control Commission for Germany at Lubbecke. His paper for discussion sets out the problem as follows:

TOP SECRET

11 Aug 45

Subject: Repatriation of RUSSIAN DPs.
'Under the terms of the YALTA Agreement all DPs, who have been identified as Soviet Citizens to the satisfaction of the Military Authorities, are to be repatriated regardless of their personal wishes.
This ruling has led to two difficulties:
(a) The method of "identifying" Soviet nationality.
(b) The enforcement of compulsory repatriation.'

The paper goes on to explain that this is in accordance with a directive laid down by SHAEF. In the US Zone, when Soviet representatives claim a person is a RUSSIAN citizen, and it is disputed, then a board of officers is convened to adjudicate [no doubt including a Soviet representative]. This has not been working too smoothly but so long as the YALTA Agreement is operative, no other solution appears possible.

The paper continues:

> 'Serious situations are arising over the forcible repatriation of DPs who have been established to be Soviet Citizens.
>
> DPs have threatened mass suicide and in certain cases have committed suicide. When they refuse to return they can only be put into transport for repatriation by physical force. British Officers are loath to order their men to carry out this unpleasant task and even if they issue the orders there may be the possibility of their troops hesitating or refusing to comply with them.
>
> The British soldier will not bully civilians, especially children and old people, and even more so where the reason for doing so appears to him unjust and cruel.
>
> In one case the British Officer offered to withdraw his men so that the Russian LOs could force the DPs into transport, but the Russians declared that it was the duty of the British Military Authorities to carry out this task.
>
> As time goes on the above situation is bound to become aggravated, and if the existing regulations remain in force may well lead to mutinous conditions amongst the British troops concerned.'[12]

It is not clear from the above passage whether the author of this paper was generalising, and perhaps referring to the situation which has arisen in Austria, as no reports had come through at the time of serious incidents such as these.

MONTGOMERY BRIEFS THE WAR CABINET

Six months after the fighting had ceased, Montgomery attended the War Cabinet in London and gave a review of the situation in the British Zone, as recorded in the Minutes:

> *War Cabinet Meeting*   *3 January 1946*
> 'The Field Marshal Montgomery said ... that on the material side, they faced the risks of widespread starvation and disease. The existing food ration provided an average daily intake of 1,500 calories per head over the German population as a whole; and this represented the bare minimum required to prevent the spread of starvation and disease. This ration could be honoured if the Control Commission continued to receive the imports of wheat for which they had asked. If wheat imports into the British Zone ceased, the average calorie intake would drop to about 900 a day, which would be the equivalent of one-third of the present level of nutrition of the population in the United Kingdom. This would involve not only starvation, but disease. Arrangements for handling epidemics in Germany had now been completed. If, however, a serious epidemic occurred, these arrangements would not prevent the spread of disease to this country. Measures for reducing that risk were now under consideration.'[13]

The Soviet clamp-down on exports of wheat from West Germany's natural granary in the Russian occupied Zone had clearly begun to bite, and widespread famine was a serious possibility. Montgomery then explained:

> 'The human factor had not yet given rise to special difficulty. The 23 million Germans in the British Zone had hitherto been docile. But we must expect to have some trouble with them before long. In the first place, during the coming year they would begin to see the effects of reparations policy on German industry and would realise that they would derive little benefit from the recovery of the German economy. Secondly, our economic policy in Germany would give rise to widespread unemployment. Thirdly, there were dispersed within our Zone about 3 million former members of the German Armed Forces. Fourthly, we had removed from office a large number of competent Nazis, who now had no useful work to do and would have opportunities for stirring up trouble. This analysis led to two conclusions. First, we must not reduce too far the strength of the British occupational troops in Germany. Secondly, we should avoid undue haste in developing Trades Unions and political parties in Germany; the seeds of a healthy development had been sown, but it was desirable that they should be allowed to grow naturally and to produce the right type of leaders.
> Field Marshal Montgomery said that he did not find among the German people any sense of shame for the atrocities of the Nazi régime. The average German did not regard himself as having any responsibility for them, but considered them the work solely of the Nazis. It was essential to bring about a more complete change of heart among the German people. But it was difficult to make much impression on adults. It was the more important, therefore, to ensure that the education of the children was on the right lines'.[14]

Even in January 1946, the problem of displaced persons was still causing concern. But in the following passage, the C-in-C must be referring mainly to Baltic peoples (the Baltic Republics now re-occupied by Russia did not fall under the terms of the Crimea Conference at Yalta for mandatory repatriation as they were outside the boundaries of the USSR on 1 September 1939), and Polish DPs, who again came within the same category:

> 'Field Marshal Montgomery said that there might be further trouble over displaced persons. Their camps were comfortable, and too many of them were refusing either to return to their own country or to work. He was inclined to favour a policy by which every displaced person would be required to declare by the 1 April 1946, whether he was willing to return to his own country. Those who were not willing to return to their homes should then be required to go elsewhere, to the extent that other countries could be persuaded to receive them. Thereafter only those should be maintained in Germany who were willing to work.'[15]

As this chapter has shown, the problems which we faced were clearly on a vast scale. We were going to need all our ingenuity and understanding to solve them.

IV

A Roving Commission in Post-War Europe

THE SITUATION IN SCHLESWIG-HOLSTEIN

At Schloss Östenwalde, Montgomery's personal staff and his network of Liaison Officers had their base. The wartime command system still continued to function, and the LO's would be sent out on periodic sorties to the Corps area which had now become translated into Military Government Districts. The total destruction of Germany, her cities and her infrastructure had left enormous problems. In addition, as we have seen in Chapter III, vast numbers of refugees, displaced people and German prisoners, had to be dealt with and returned to their homes. There was not enough food to keep alive the 9 million people who were at that time herded into the British Zone. The information required was not of the battle front, but of the building up from scratch of the basic necessities of life, food and shelter, and the urgent evacuation of people to their homelands.

Getting people home was not just a matter of convenience, for there was a real danger that famine, epidemic and disease would establish its grip on Central Europe and cut a deadly swathe through those still left standing. This was not 'a policy' but rather an 'imperative' that everyone recognised and obeyed. This led, as soon as the Germans had laid down their arms, to the collection of as many Russians as possible into the 'Wismar Cushion' in Mecklenburg which was about to be taken over by the Soviets, so that those masses would not be a burden upon the people in the British Zone.

A series of my liaison reports to Montgomery, written at the time, have survived and give a vivid picture of conditions. They cover chiefly the province of Schleswig-Holstein, and the city of Hamburg. The

23

area was typical of the zone as a whole, but carried some of the biggest concentrations of displaced persons and surrendered enemy personnel, German prisoners of war, or mercenaries. Included in the area was the old Hanseatic port of Lübeck, the naval base at Kiel, and the Kiel Canal. At the centre of the province was a beautiful place called Plön, almost an island, so surrounded was it by lakes. Here it was that 8 Corps and Military Government District had its headquarters. And its commander and 'military governor' was Lieutenant General Sir Evelyn Barker. To the north lay the fishing port of Flensburg and the Danish frontier.

The following paragraphs give typical intelligence of the day, as reported by me to the C-in-C:

> *To C-in-C from CM*
> *8 Corps District 23–28 July 1945*
> 'The most remarkable events that are happening in the Corps area this week, are the disturbances caused by the Polish DPs. An average of two murders a day (of Germans) are being committed by the Poles. It is a good way of getting rid of the Germans but last week a British soldier was attacked and seriously wounded by rifle fire. The Poles are also committing rape, thefts and cattle raising. Their crimes are daily on the increase and the unarmed German Police, who it may be said are acting courageously against them, are virtually powerless. The Poles leave their DP Camps after dark, collect their arms hidden about the local countryside and then start their expeditions against the farmhouses.
>
> WARSAW Radio continues to encourage Polish DPs to return home, and Russian LOs have been known to enter camps saying that RUSSIA is ready to accept them, although the official Russian attitude remains the same: that the Poles cannot start until Russian repatriation is over. It is causing great unrest in the camps.
>
> The other matter of interest is the great fear that the people of SCHLESWIG-HOLSTEIN have of the Russians. They are convinced that the Russians are coming to take over their country. Rumours are rife and none of the Military Government officers are in a position to say that the frontier between BRITAIN and RUSSIA is fixed.
>
> Mistrust by the civilians of our non-committal attitude on the Russians was started by the situation in WISMAR. German civilians knew that the Russians were coming to take over. To stop a rush of refugees, we denied this. We then clapped a 24 hour curfew on the town and moved out whilst they were confined to their houses.'[1]

Not only the Russians had been confined to the 'Wismar Cushion', but German civilians were prevented from crossing into the British Zone by the curfew described. The Americans had over-run Mecklenburg and Wismar and were now pulling out to allow the Soviets to occupy this area, as agreed at Yalta.

My report on German prisoners was that:

> '370,000 have been demobilised since 18 June. Out of the 942,000 that now

remain in Schleswig-Holstein 129,000 are non-German. In the concentration areas there has been trouble between the Germans and their mercenaries – particularly the Hungarians [and they had to be separated]. Boys camps would also be formed for the large number of boys under 17.'

As regards Displaced Persons, the numbers given for the province (excluding Area's F and G, it being divided into seven areas) were 125,000 DPs, and 32,000 PWX. 10,000 convalescents from Belsen were reported as leaving for Sweden, and 16,000 Italians departing for North Italy. After the Italians, would go the Yugoslavs. Then the Russians, followed by the Poles. This would leave a good number of Baltic nationals, and a number of 'assorted Levantines'.

The remarks on Army morale are of interest. Divisions were being 'bled' to satisfy the dual needs of demobilisation and drafts to the Far East war and concern was being expressed as to the prospects of a career in the Army.

'there is still interest and concern as to prospects ... very soon they will have lost interest. Both officers and men still trying to make up their minds what they are going to do. Many are determined to get out of the Army as soon as possible on principle, although they have no idea what they are going to do in civilian life ... If only a note of encouragement could be introduced, and they could be given some aim on which to direct their energies; instead of, as they think, rotting for ever in Germany seeing their wives only once in six months.'

I cannot remember if any of these pleas fell on fruitful ground. The Labour Government's strategy had not yet emerged. But an ominous note is added, showing that political propaganda had begun seeping into the Forces.

'There was a wide-spread rumour at Election-time that a LABOUR Government would double the speed of Demobilisation.'[2]

And then a few notes on the crisis upon the civilian front:

'It is estimated that there is enough coal to stop people dying of cold during the winter, but not enough to heat houses and run factories. Food will shortly have to be reduced owing to continued exports to the RUHR and BERLIN. It is hoped to get most people in SCHLESWIG-HOLSTEIN undercover by 1 October.'

Major H Wake reported to the C-in-C, following a tour of the area, from 6–11 August 1945, echoing the same concern about the loss of officers and men.[3]

To the C-in-C from HW
'Many units are losing their most important officers and NCOs either to SEAC [South East Asia Command] or on release. Some brigade commanders are losing practically the whole of their staffs. The vacancies are being filled as and when

they occur, but when it is not known whether the unit or formation is to be kept or dissolved it is impossible to plan ahead.'

NEUENGAMME CAMP

In my reports, the German prisoner of war situation is commented on as follows. There were 274,000 PW in area F, 184,000 in area G, and 176,000 in the remainder of 8 Corps District, 9,700 SS in Neuengamme Camp, which is mentioned for the first time. There are still 34,000 German PW in Denmark, and 94,000 German PW to come from Norway, 16,500 having already landed. In addition 50,000 PW have been released for the BARLEYCORN operation, our emergency scheme to get the harvest in. It was reported that a Soviet LO shot a Russian PWX who refused to get on a British vehicle taking PWX to the Russian Zone at Flensburg on 8 August.

To the C-in-C from CM   *13–17 Aug 1945*
'The wave of crime from Polish DP camps was still a cause of concern. Senior commanders' views differed on the way to deal with this outbreak. One view was that proclamations issued in the name of the Corps Commander in DP camps threatening dire reprisals, were counter-productive. The only way to deal with the Poles was to try and help them out. Another view was that the Poles were a complete menace, in the LÜBECK area their behaviour was held to be a complete scandal. In the TRAVEMUNDE area in the last ten weeks they had looted enough meat to feed 144,000 adult civilians for a week.'

General Barker's views were equally strong. He had had quite enough of them. The trouble was that the Polish DP camp leaders were PWX and pro-London, and the DP's themselves pro-Lublin.[4]

'Amongst the British troops the manpower situation was becoming desperate. One Brigade Commander wondered how he was going to carry on. By November, 75 per cent of his company commanders would have been demobilised. The end of the war had not been heralded with great enthusiasm. Officers listened to the King's speech, and some even stood to attention when "God Save the King" was played, but when the cheers from London, Blackpool and Edinburgh came through on the BBC the wireless was turned off."

To the C-in-C from CM   *17 Aug*
'I visited NEUENGAMME camp where all the SS are concentrated. Previously this camp had been used by the GESTAPO and 40,000 political prisoners had lost their lives there. The victims' shoes were heaped up on a monstrous pile. The present SS PW are living under very squalid conditions. There are 9,700 SS being looked after by 500 Belgian MAQUIS. None of the Belgians have had any military experience except the Commandant.

When I arrived at ten o'clock in the morning, he was just getting out of bed. He could give me no useful information except how unagreeable the work was. I went round the prisoners' quarters. They were inhabiting a brick factory. Some had wooden bunks, others were sleeping in low dark tunnels where the bricks were baked on the ground – the air was stifling.

The officers of all ranks were sleeping jammed together on narrow duckboards on the concrete floor of a passage. Washing arrangements were very limited. Cooking facilities were very bad. The punishment was to stand to attention in rain or sun for not less than one day, on any movement one hand or both would be raised. The MAQUIS push them around a lot with bayonets. Last week one of the MAQUIS learnt from home that a relation of his was an inmate of BELSEN. He promptly shot seven Germans with his Sten.

It seems to me that "a certain standard" of harsh treatment should be introduced. It is being guarded by BELGIANS, but it is a BRITISH responsibility. I was revolted by the whole place. The Commandant is useless.' Thus ended my Report.

The events that followed were dramatic. The same evening that Monty received my report, he got on to the Corps Commander, (General Barker), and ordered the camp to be closed down forthwith.

My next visit came on 20–23 August. I report the latest on Neuengamme Camp.

'There is a great stir in 8 Corps over this camp. All non-arrest category (harmless) PW are now to be evacuated to area F starting 24 Aug. with daily loads of 500. Evacuation will take six days.'

Not surprisingly, General 'Bubbles' Barker was furious that one of his camps was closed down on the say-so of a junior captain, even though he came as an emissary from the Commander-in-Chief. I had evidently been declared 'persona non grata' in 8 Corps District. My next message to Monty soft-pedalled the reception I had received when next I saw the Corps Commander.

'General Barker was a little upset that I had not quoted to the C-in-C his comment on NEUENGAMME Camp. This was that the conditions were satisfactory. He is trying to get rid of the BELGIAN Commander of the Camp'.

I often wonder whether I was right to be the instrument for the closure and dispersal of the SS camp at Neuengamme. I had been a prisoner of war myself. Did this influence me? Was I really aware at that time of the depth of depravity of Himmler's SS? Was not General Barker's attitude of seeming indifference more acceptable under the circumstances? That they were only getting their just deserts? I must confess that in retrospect I think it was, and the C-in-C's concern over my report was a little overplayed.

Montgomery believed that the population of Germany, for which he was responsible, was part of his extended family, whether civil or military, and as such he was responsible for their welfare. It was thought in some quarters that he had 'gone soft' on his former enemies, but it was the simplistic attitude so typical of the soldier and the man.

Bubbles Barker's comment to me on Monty's last proclamation

was that it stressed too much our desire for the co-operation of the German people, and not enough what we wanted them to do and that many Germans would be surprised at its mildness. The German people he said would prefer Military Government to continue to govern – instead of helping.

CONDITIONS IN HAMBURG

An interview with the Burgomeister of Hamburg is equally revealing.

> 'The Burgomeister of HAMBURG has some very definite views on the general situation. He was asked to speak frankly. He said that unless a great deal more coal was brought into HAMBURG for the winter, disease would surely break out. Oct. 1st was the target for houses, but he is terribly short of labour and needs 10,000 more labourers. He suggested GERMAN Labour Bns from areas F and G but understands that the men can only be released individually.
>
> Secondly, the citizens will not work properly because they see no hope for the future. They have no ships and shipping was their industry. If they could be told that trade will start again at a certain date, he said, that would make a tremendous difference. 45,000 tons of wheat has arrived in HAMBURG so far and has greatly improved the situation.
>
> The city is entirely dependent on her economic life and if communications and economic exchanges are not resumed with the RUSSIAN Zone within one year, he says it will be certain death, not for HAMBURG alone but for the whole of GERMANY. The essentials he stressed as Coal, Resumption of Trade, and the Economic Unity of GERMANY within a few months. If there was a barrier between the RUSSIAN and BRITISH Zones for another two years, he said, the results would be quite disastrous. RUSSIAN Cells he mentioned and knew them to be active in his district. Communism he expects as a first result of a split GERMANY.'

The general impression of Hamburg when I visited it was of a huge pile of rubble. Street after street was reduced to just heaps of bricks and mortar. How Hamburg survived I do not know, for economic unity, which the mayor considered so essential, never became a reality. But Hamburg did survive and went on to prosper exceedingly. Hamburg, even in its hour of ruin, was more civilised and international than its rivals. Society was cosmopolitan. Clandestine parties used to take place, amongst the *demi-monde* of Military Government officers before the end of non-fraternisation; where British officers mingled with German girls. But it would have been quite improper and unseemly for an emissary of the Field Marshal to have taken part, in view of the strict non-fraternisation rules and knowing also his master's views on women!

THE POLISH PROBLEM

My next visit was on 20 August. Polish crime continued unabated:

To: The C-in-C from CM   *20–23 August 45*
'The average of two murders a day in SCHLESWIG-HOLSTEIN continues, increasing slightly in some districts. At LÜBECK for instance there were 6 murders in one night. A GERMAN Countess (ENGLISH by birth), was raped by POLES in the LAVENBERG area last week.

I had a very interesting talk with Lt. SAPIEHA in charge of 3,500 POLISH DPs in the ITZEHOE area. He himself is pro-LONDON and for political reasons cannot go back to RUSSIAN occupied POLAND. He takes great interest in his POLES and says that there is no wide gulf between the DPs and PWX. The DPs are not pro-LUBLIN – they are not pro-anything. They just want to go back to their country and see their families. If the POLISH crime is to be stopped they must be given work. If given extra food and better living conditions they will work at anything – farms, town repair or roads. The idleness makes the crime. He also added that the culprits are those young boys who were taken from their country between the ages of 14–24, none of whom are now over 30. As slave workers it was their patriotic duty to sabotage the GERMANS by any methods, and a dead GERMAN was counted a tremendous score. Now their ignorant minds are told that this quite suddenly is no longer a patriotic duty – the change-over must necessarily be gradual.[5]

From returned POLES he painted a lurid picture of RUSSIAN occupied POLAND. Pro-LONDON he was, but I still believed him. All POLES who return thus with an inside story of their country he tried to stop entering DP camps. It is fatal if they are allowed to talk, for then the DPs would never be prepared to return. Luckily 90% of them still wish to go back.'

LAISSEZ-PASSER TO EUROPE

As the months went by, the crisis atmosphere gradually subsided, and the excitement with it! It gave way to boredom amongst the troops and a cold and hungry winter for the German population, and only slightly less so for the remaining displaced people of which there were still a considerable number. The Germans were learning the bitter taste of defeat, as so many of their victims had done over the past five years. One word sums up Germany in 1945. Misery!

Fortunately I was sent on missions far afield for the next two or three months, a welcome break from the sombre routine to which we had become accustomed. To Denmark, accompanied by Toby Wake to establish contact with our Mission in Copenhagen. To Czechoslovakia, with the same travelling companion to take a message and a gift to the Czech Army Commander from Montgomery. Armed with a variety of '*Laissez-passer*' papers we drove in a 'Queen Mary' staff car through the ever-hospitable American Zone of Bavaria, albeit the scene of some hilarious misunderstandings, and on through Bohemia and into Prague. In Prague we found a very warm welcome.

At that time it was 'unoccupied' and the mediaeval city showed no war scars. But its inhabitants were deeply apprehensive about a Soviet take-over – unfortunate circumstances which overtook them only two years later, much to the discredit of the West.

In November, I started on the first of three assignments to Switzerland. I travelled this time by train, encountering the usual difficulties of railway travel in the wake of a military campaign. Long halts in desolate locations, only the gentle hiss of steam to assure one that the train was still alive. The intermittent tapping of wheels at unknown stations. Disembodied cries, followed by the brutal shock as buffers collide in a shunting operation. My 'mission extraordinary' is not part of this book. Suffice it to say that at about this time, Montgomery went down with pneumonia, which ended in a Swiss convalescence, followed by an official visit to Berne before he left.

Our visit to Switzerland had been like a fairy tale. We had not seen such things since the palmy days of 1939. Such food we had not tasted for five years. Every artifice that Swiss skill manufactured was there in plenty, from watches to wooden bears, from cheese to chocolate, tumbling over each other in the shop windows. But the outward signs of neutrality were too overpowering and began to cloy. This was not the real world, nor the sober truth.

THE IDES OF MARCH

On 10 March 1946 I paid my last recorded visit to 8 Corps District, after an absence of some 3 months, and this is what I wrote:

'In all towns that I visited I could not help being impressed by the miserable condition of the Germans. After an absence of several weeks in a civilized country this was brought home very forcibly. A change could also be detected in the Germans themselves. They appeared to be more dejected, ill clad and surly than before. My car was broken into twice and the windows smashed in the streets of HAMBURG. They seemed to be very badly off for clothing and those garments that they wore could hardly keep out the damp bitter winds. The picture in HAMBURG was one of utter dejection and misery. It is hard to get a balanced impression if one lives in that atmosphere the whole time; coming back to it after a period away one is very forcibly reminded of the truth.

Of course, the food situation has hardly begun to dawn on the average civilian.

Briefly the situation in Schleswig-Holstein and HAMBURG is this. Each person now lives on 1000 calories a day – semi-starvation level. The basic food is bread; and there is no other basic food – in the form of potatoes or anything else. This means that a person gets three "Hovis loaves" a month. And this he can draw at the beginning of each month, so, believing that the British will not let him down, he will probably consume the ration in the earlier stages of the month, so that the last week in March is the time that one may expect trouble. That is if he can overcome his apathy to take any action.

There is enough grain to last to the end of April, after this the food values must drop through 600 to 400 calories.

The Colonel controlling the Food Office in HAMBURG described the situation as desperate.

I attended the last day of the War Crimes Trials in HAMBURG. Three of the leading members of a chemical firm were on trial for supplying large quantities of gas for the extermination of 5,000,000 human beings at AUSCHWITZ concentration camp. Two were condemned to death. Trials were open to the public, but no members of the Press had bothered to turn up.

The crew of the GRAF SPEE were due to dock in HAMBURG on 10 March. Many of the crew were bringing "Argentine brides".'

So ends my last report to 'the Chief'. What an ironic note on which to end the war.

Two months later, I was invalided out of the Army. By September, I had wangled my way back in again, and was setting sail to joining my regiment in Palestine.

VALEDICTORY DISPATCH FROM GERMANY

Montgomery left Germany on 1 May 1946, to take up his post as Chief of the Imperial and General Staff (CIGS) in London. The day he left Germany he sent this valedictory dispatch to the British Chiefs of Staff Committee. It is an historic statement of the situation in Germany at that time but its irony will not be lost on present day readers.

'The general over-all picture is sombre if not black. For the present, the food crisis over-shadows all this but is not the only serious factor in the situation. We have a sick economy, coal is short, only the basic industries can be developed while the others lie idle. There are few consumer goods produced and nothing in the shops for people to buy.

We have reached agreement on the future level of the German economy – there will soon begin the removal and destruction of a large part of German industry. This will cause distress to the German people and may produce unemployment on a large scale in the British Zone. The present level of production is such that our exports do not pay for our imports. There is little to buy with marks, people are tending to use a system of barter to get food, marks are gradually becoming of no value. Under such a system industry cannot be got going since there is no incentive. This is the beginning of inflation, i.e. the phase where money begins to lose its value.'[6]

He then referred to the 'great mass of human material' we have in Germany. He asked for a concrete plan ... we must have more consumer goods ... we must decide what is to constitute Germany. The Eastern frontier was decided on at Potsdam. The Western frontier is not yet agreed. It is wrapped up with the whole problem of the

Saar and the Ruhr. We must tell the German people what Germany is to consist of, and the German people must have a reasonable standard of living:

> 'I do not feel confident that the Russians ever intend to treat Germany as an economic whole as we understand that phrase. I am certain that they will not do it unless we join with the other Allies in exerting strong pressure upon them. We must decide whether we are going to feed the Germans or let them starve, basically we must not let them starve. It does not look at present as if we can increase the ration beyond the present 1040 calories – this means that we are going to let them starve.'

In his conclusion he described the four pillars on which to build a secure German people:

> 'Such a Germany if it looked towards the East would be a menace to the security of the British Empire; on the other hand a contented Germany with a sound political framework could be a great asset to the security of the Empire and the peace of the world.'[7]

V

Austria

Since the happy winters of my youth, less than a decade before, tragic changes had taken place in Austria. Then, I must admit, my knowledge of Austria ran only surface deep. I was aware, of course, of the shattering events which had shaken the Republic. The murder of Chancellor Dolfuss in 1934. The Nazi *Putsch*. The rise of Prince Starhemberg's patriotic *Heimwehr*. The imposition of the Nazi Dr Arthur Seyss-Inquart as Interior Minister. Hitler's ultimatum and arrest of Chancellor Von Schuschnigg. And finally on 11 March 1938, the *Anschluss*. Even so things appeared to be happy and relaxed to a foreign visitor, outside the main cities. But I was not aware, as I made my last visit to Austria in the spring of 1939, that even then the streets of Vienna were reverberating to the cries of the Nazi wolf-pack.

'Sieg Heil! Sieg Heil! Sieg Heil!'
'Ein Volk, ein Reich, ein Führer!'

and more ominously, a cry that was to be heard throughout Europe:

Jud-aaa verr-rreckt!' (Judah perish)[1]

And so it was that the manhood of Austria was drawn into a bitter war, many to perish on the Eastern Front. And now, that was over, what was there left? A desolate and hunger-stricken land, once more occupied and humiliated.

The Western Allies knew little of what was going on inside Austria in the final stages of the war, and even less since the Russians had entered Vienna on 13 April 1945. It was some months before the

Russians allowed and welcomed their other allies into their own sectors of Vienna, which had been previously allotted. During the interval, news from inside the Soviet occupied parts of Austria (which included the province of Styria, supposedly a British responsibility), was hard to come by. The British were anxious to know the internal situation in Vienna for they had some responsibility for feeding part of the city.

The first hard piece of news that reached the Foreign Office was from three civilians (claiming to be representatives of the Renner Government[2] but who later denied they had any official mandate), who arrived at 5 Corps Headquarters at Klagenfurt on 23 May. They had left Vienna on the 14th, and this is what they reported:

> 'All vehicles have been requisitioned; food situation is catastrophic; there is no gas supply although water supply seems to be working in most districts. The Russians have removed currency from the Banks and machinery from factories and are showing no respect for persons or property. 80,000 cases of rape have been reported. These civilians add that the Renner Government has no authority as the Russians will not give it practical means of asserting itself.'[3]

On 31 May, another communication was received by the Foreign Office. This time from Sir George Franckenstein, a much respected former Austrian Envoy in London.[4] He had severed his ties with Austria when the Nazis marched in and had remained in London during the wartime years. He comes to the Foreign Office with urgent and disturbing news from an old friend of his in Vienna. But he is most anxious to conceal the identity of his correspondent, whose letter runs as follows:

> 'Vienna, May 14 1945.
> The last years were by no means easy for all of us. The last months, when we had the heavy air raids, were often rather awful. Vienna had suffered badly. the Opera-house, the Burgtheater, the Albertina and the Schwarzenberg palace are destroyed and so are a great number of residential houses. But all this was not to be compared with what we have and had to go through since Vienna was besieged by the Russians. Our flat, which was damaged by bombs on February 13th, was set on fire on May 1st by drunken Russians and completely burned out. There is no fire service and the Russians never think of bringing any fire under control. Do not worry, the pictures, silver and sculptures are stored in a safe place. All the rest is lost. I personally, just as all other people, was robbed of all belongings and possess only a few suits and hardly any underwear. I tried to oppose some drunken Russians (here a very frequent sight) who tried to rape women and received a bullet wound through my shoulder as well as a bad hit with a heavy pistol in my face.'

Franckenstein's correspondent continued:

'In general the situation can be summarised as follows: It seems impossible to re-establish any form of economic life at the moment. The Russians drive away all live-stock, slaughter all pigs and thus bring the country into a state of certain starvation. There is no shed in the Marchfeld where any cattle has been left. In the factories the machinery has been dismantled. Siemens, AEG, Saurer, Graf & Stift, Vereinigte Farbereien, Simmeringer Waggonfabrik, etc., to quote only the more important ones, are but empty shells. It is a systematic looting of a country which must lead to a catastrophe. Everybody over here was apparently waiting daily for the British and Americans to arrive, but apparently in vain. It looks as if we had been bargained away. ... (some personal sentences) ... If nothing is done, anarchy is bound to follow.[5]

I include this letter as it gives a strong flavour of the times and shows only too clearly the shock of the Soviet Army's arrival. Berlin in fact received far worse treatment. Not only was it pulverised by years of allied bombing, working up to the 1000-bomber raids, but what remained was shattered by the Russian forces as they battered their way into the centre of the city. But Vienna felt aggrieved that it was being treated like a committed combatant when it must have been known that it entered the alliance with Germany by force and with no enthusiasm.

Another report, dated 29 May, reached the Foreign Office from the exiled Archduke Robert of Austria, who had heard from sources in the Austrian provinces:

'The food shortage is acute in the western provinces of Austria and it is feared that due to the shortage of agricultural labour, the harvest will be extremely poor. Bread, potatoes and meat are completely unobtainable. This is not only due to the shortage of transport but mainly to the fact that the peasants have not been allowed to make any reserves which would carry them over the coming winter. If the Allies do not send some food soon it is believed that a real famine might break out in the near future. The situation is very serious indeed. If some of the Austrian prisoners of war held by the Allies could be released for agricultural work, the situation could be eased but this must be done before August, otherwise it will be too late.

Upper-Austria is a little bit better off but the provinces of Salzburg, Tyrol and Vorarlberg, in short the Alpine regions, are in a very bad way. Report from the Russian held part of Austria demonstrate that not only does a régime of terror reign, murder, rape and other attrocities being committed by the Red Army but also do they live on the country which already is starving. They have confiscated all the cattle and all the food reserves which they are shipping towards the East. Deportation and murder of their political opponent and would-be opponent is going on on a large scale. Many parish priest have already been assassinated for having tried to save women and girls from the fury of Red Army men. It is also reported that the Russians are already dismantling industry and sending the machinery to Russia.'
[The corruptions in this message are as received at the time.][6]

Meantime, in Carinthia, into which the British and American

Armies had already entered, Tito's Yugoslavs, who were also there, were claiming the most extravagant stories about the behaviour of the British occupation. That the ill-treated Carinthian population was asking for Tito's protection; that former SS men were being employed by the British Military Administration and carrying out terrorism and atrocities against the Yugoslavs; that they were stalking the streets wearing British badges on their Gestapo uniforms, the depressed population wondering when the terror would cease. Such disinformation was, of course, being seditiously propagated to back up Tito's bogus claim to the Austrian province of Carinthia, about which we will hear more in later pages.[7]

Meanwhile Mr W H R Mack, designated to be the British Deputy Commissioner in Vienna (now waiting at Alexander's headquarters in Italy – AFHQ Caserta) telegraphed the Foreign Office on 26 May:

> 'You will notice that the departure of the Yugoslavs from Klagenfurt has made the atmosphere more friendly towards us, while at Leinz, where the Yugoslavs have not been, the atmosphere is distinctly sulky, as one would expect in as strong a Nazi a province as Carinthia.
> I rather expect that we shall find that the goings-on of the Russians in Vienna will have made the Viennese distinctly friendly towards us. Such information as trickles through from Vienna is to the effect that the Russians have looted everything there and that the second wave of Russian troops behaved in every way very much worse than the first. This is, in my view, a further reason why it is undesirable for political representatives to go in until the Commission's charter has been settled.'[8]

The fact that the Russians would not agree to discuss the charter for the Allied (American, British and Soviet) occupation of Austria led to our realisation that until such time as this was done and the occupation regularised by Treaty, we would be in a false position in occupying our sectors in Vienna, responsible for feeding and administering millions of people but without any agreement to say where the food was to come from.

Mack's telegram confirms the fact that Soviet intransigence was now recognised as a fact of life and that the Russians were undergoing a very rapid change from a former 'friend' to a very tricky customer who had to be treated with kid gloves. The stark facts were that in both Germany and in Austria the Russians controlled the food-bearing provinces and we were saddled with the hungry sheep. In both Berlin and Vienna, the Western Allies were responsible for the greater proportion of the populations. The Russians, in the East, were now denying food exports to the West. This was a crisis of profound consequence.

The Author's grandmother and family in Russian peasant costume about 1880
(*Author's papers*)

'The Chief' – General Sir Bernard Montgomery at first press conference, Normandy, June 1944 (*IWM*)

Allied leaders tour French battlefields, June/July, 1944 (L–R, Brooke, Churchill, Montgomery, Smuts) (*IWM*)

Montgomery with General Omar Bradley, Commander 1st (US) Army. At that time, as Allied Land Forces Commander, Montgomery commanded British and United States armies in Europe (*IWM*)

In the Ardennes, December 1944, Montgomery's Liaison Officers. (L–R, CM, Eddie Prisk (US Army), Charles Sweeney, Maurice Frary (US Army), Dudley Bourhill, Dick Harden and John Poston (seated)) (*Author's papers*)

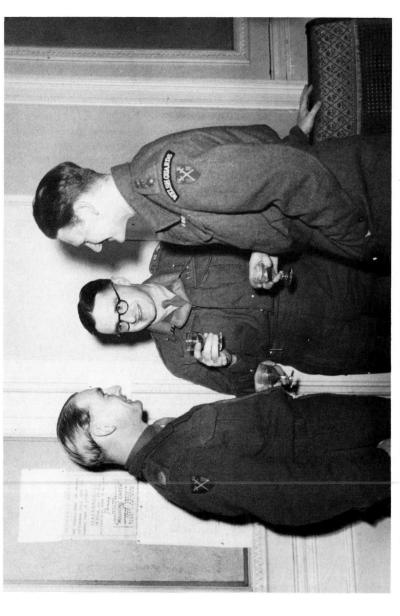

At Tac HQ, Zondhoven (Holland) November 1944. (L–R, Major John Poston, Colonel Joe Ewart and CM) (*Author's papers*)

The Victory Dinner, Brussels 1945. (L–R, Brigadier David Belchem, Lieutenant General Sir Brian Horrocks, Field Marshal Montgomery, Lieutenant General Sir Oliver Leese, Lieutenant General Sir John Harding (back view) and Lieutenant General Sir Brian Robertson) (*Author's papers*)

The Surrender. Luneburg Heath 4 May 1945. (L–R, The German plenipotentiaries, Col. Joe Ewart, Field Marshal Montgomery)

Writing with hindsight, having experienced the trauma of the Cold War, it is easy to fall into the belief which must have been conveyed, I fear, by many passages in these pages, that the Russians were our real enemies. But in 1945 this was not the general perception. Certainly not amongst the public at home nor amongst the average serviceman, who had no knowledge of high-level diplomacy. There was nothing but admiration for the spirit and fighting qualities of the Russians. They had suffered great privation and lost millions of men in the sieges of Leningrad (which lasted 900 days), and of Stalingrad, and the other bitter battles of the Eastern Front. This feeling was of course assiduously fostered by Allied propaganda, but was no less genuine for all that.

Feelings of contempt and disgust were reserved for the Germans, together with their allies and camp followers, who had done so much to bring the whole edifice of European civilisation crashing down, whose grosser acts were past human understanding, and whose lesser activities caused untold suffering to countless millions of human beings. And, now, in their hour of defeat, there was a shrugging-off of responsibility. 'I know nothing of these things', or a lingering air of arrogance, a trait at that time endemic to the German nation. Cruelty, torture and death had been the fate of those who would not bend the knee, as thousands in the concentration and extermination camps would testify. We must be clear, therefore, who was considered to be the real enemy in the post-surrender period. It was not the brutal, uncivilised Russians. It was undeniably and unmistakeably our former enemy, Nazi Germany. Nazi sympathisers and activists were to be ruthlessly weeded out by the Allies and those with a criminal record were to be brought to trial and execution, if found guilty. A whole de-Nazification programme was designed for this purpose. The Austrians, I fear, were not exempt from this process, or its consequences.

No '*tour d'horizon*' of post-surrender Austria is complete without a description of the conditions in Styria, over-run by the Russians in their advance and now reluctantly conceded to the British to whom it had originally been allocated. The report, dated 25 July 1945, from which I have drawn these facts, comes from Mr Nicholls, Foreign Office-appointed Political Advisor to 5 Corps (now with 46 British Division).[9]

Nicholls realises that the inhabitants of Graz, to whom he is talking, have an interest in painting the Russian occupation in its blackest terms, the better to ingratiate themselves with their new masters. The

Russians automatically removed industrial plant or equipment whose ownership would in any way be attributed to the Germans (even though 'reparations' in this province were by rights a British one). Almost all the load-carrying vehicles were carried off by the Russians when they left. Sixty locomotives were removed from Bruck just before the British arrived. Almost all the postal sorting vans were removed, and looting by troops in the early days was of course the accepted norm, so long as it was portable. Later, there were reports of looters being summarily shot.

Nicholls adds some current anecdotes on the behaviour of the Russian soldiery.

> 'Watches evidently exercised a peculiar fascination on the Russians ... several of my informants told me that it was not at all uncommon to see a Russian wearing five or six wrist watches and stopping every few yards to listen to the mass ticking ... in another case, a Russian gave a dirty and shabby old coat in exchange for a bicycle, whose disconsolate owner subsequently found four gold watches in the pocket of the coat.'

Cattle and horses were driven off when the Russians left, this was a form of requisitioning for the Russian Army who, by tradition, 'lived off the land'.

But the real dread for the inhabitants of Styria, as for other parts of Austria was the occurrence of rape. It seemed to be considered as part of the traditional 'rights of conquest' by the Russian soldiery, and in Germany was responsible as much as any other cause for the mass emigration of German refugees from East to West. But as always it was difficult to disentangle fact from fiction. First reports in Styria of 60,000 cases of rape proved to be a gross exaggeration, for the official provincial health service had only recorded 5,000 cases in Russian occupied Styria. But a Military Government officer who toured the Eastern districts was told that between 70 and 75 per cent of the female inhabitants had been raped. Age being of no object. Nicholls concludes his report by saying that the opinion of the more unprejudiced of his informants was that the behaviour of the troops, except on first entry and upon departure, might have been worse. Much of the ill-behaviour was by L of C troops of whom a large proportion were Bulgarians and Ukranians; foreign workers, local criminals, and the so-called freedom and resistance movements, also played their part.

'Nevertheless' concludes Nicholls, 'after all allowances have been made, the picture remains a singularly unprepossessing one'.

But compare this with the behaviour of the Nazis in the German occupied countries of Europe, with the mass movement and extermination of Jews, and the events in Austria begin to pale in comparison.

Having dwelt in this chapter on the internal problems of Austria, we must now revert to the circumstances which brought Alexander into Austria in the first place, from the other side of the Alps.

PART TWO

THE SITUATION AT ALEXANDER'S HEADQUARTERS

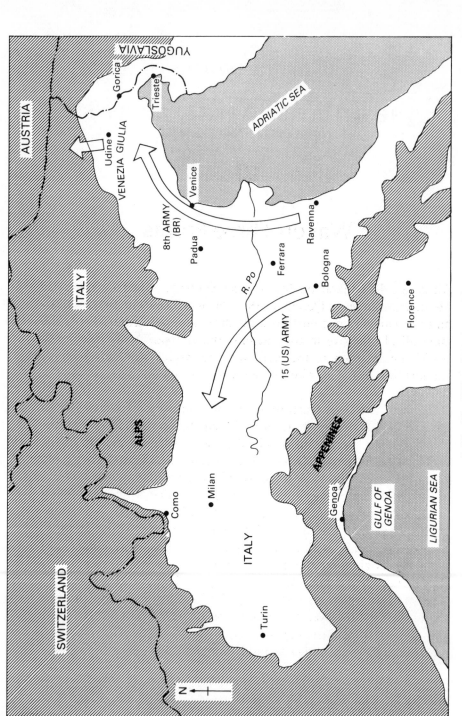

2. The Final Phase in Italy 1945

VI

War on Three Fronts

Alexander had taken up his post as Supreme Allied Commander Mediterranean on 12 December 1944. He was faced with the responsibility of carrying out hostilities on three separate fronts. First, the main allied offensive in Italy against the German Army. Second, a British intervention in the civil war now raging in Greece. Third, support for Marshal Tito in harrying the German forces in the Balkans.

It must have been frustrating, if not confusing for Alexander to have to deal with the situation in Athens before he had taken over command at Caserta and obtained a more balanced picture of the problems in his theatre. Obviously he was no stranger to Italy having already commanded 15 Army Group in some of the toughest battles of the Italian campaign. But he was not so familiar with the situation in Yugoslavia and the tricky relationship with Marshal Tito, which at this stage had reached an all-time low. Greece, whose crisis he had seen so vividly with his own eyes, was to be a continuing thorn in the flesh, right up to the end of the war.

Alexander had a huge task. Not only did he have to oversee and take strategic decisions concerning the battle in Italy. But he was responsible for the eventual occupation of Austria, the Dodecanese and the Istrian peninsula at the head of the Adriatic. His remit also ran as far as Turkey, Bulgaria and Roumania.

He was responsible as Supreme Commander Mediterranean for all questions of supply for British troops and one American Army. He deployed huge air and naval forces to be integrated into his strategic plan, but although the British 8th Army was balanced by the American Fifth Army at the time he took over, four-fifths of the troops were either Commonwealth or British supported.[1] Churchill therefore took a proprietary interest in the events in the Mediterranean. He had not lost his nostalgia for the 'soft underbelly of Europe'. The Combined Chiefs of Staff located at Washington were, however, the authority exercising direct control of this theatre.

Alexander's plans for a dash to Vienna by crossing the Adriatic in a sea-borne operation with Eighth Army, whilst leaving Fifth Army to hold the fort in Italy were thought to be unsound by his superiors, particularly the CIGS, Brooke. This venture was code-named 'Operation Gelignite', and once safely across the Adriatic Sea and onto the Yugoslav shore (with Tito's agreement), he would fight his way to Vienna via the Ljublijana Gap. Though this kind of grandiose plan appealed to Churchill, he realised that the likely timing would be far too late to achieve anything. In any case, it conflicted with the overall policy that the Italian campaign was to be a 'holding operation', and a reservoir from which troops and resources, including landing craft, might well be drawn to bolster the campaign in Northern Europe.

A very similar situation had arisen in Yugoslavia to that which had come about in Greece. The objectives of the Allies and of Tito were of a totally different nature, and it was difficult for the two sides to get on the same wavelength for a proper mutual understanding.

> 'The Allies wished to trap and destroy the German forces in the Balkans so that they could not reappear on the Eastern and Western fronts as soon as Hitler deemed it expedient to abandon the Balkans. The Partisans wanted merely to hustle the Germans out of their country so that they could consolidate Communist power in post-war Yugoslavia. This, as far as they were concerned, was a Balkan war. Berlin, the Rhine and Rome meant little to them.'[2]

Another bone of contention was Tito's rival, General Mihailovic, and his anti-communist partisans named Chetniks. We had virtually abandoned this group in favour of the more effective Tito. But two OSS Missions[3] remained with Mihailovic, and caused Tito deep distrust of Allied motives. Indeed jealousy and suspicion dominated Tito's relationship with the Allies so much that it was doubtful if the effort was worth while. It was not as if we had any say in his military planning. Tito was a client of Moscow and took his orders from Stalin; it is ironic therefore that we poured in equipment and supplies without really achieving our objective, which was to destroy the German forces withdrawing northwards.

Despite all the difficulties recounted above, Tito's Yugoslavs were very much our allies, and such was the favourable light put upon their activities by press and radio, and through the official organs of information, that the public perception was that they were, like the Russians, our brothers-in-arms, bonded together with us in the blood and sacrifice of the common struggle.

It is worth considering for a moment the terrain over which these armies had been fighting. Italy was divided by a huge spinal *massif* which ran the length of the country. This seriously impeded progress to those armies advancing on the Left. On the right the going was just as difficult with dozens of rivers tumbling out of these mountains and into the coastal plain. I appreciate only too well the rigours of the terrain, having walked the length of the Appenines before the advancing armies, as noted in a previous reference.[4] In addition, if this were not enough, the enemy was a tough and resilient fighter clinging like a limpet to his fastnesses, never conceding ground unless forced by military necessity. It was a mean, pitiless campaign not attended by the hope of glory, as with the Armies of the North, for the objective was to pin down and hold as many German troops as possible in the peninsula, rather than to enter into the Third Reich. The campaign had been marked by a series of bitter battles with names to conjure with: the Salerno landings, the battle of the River Sangro, Cassino Monastery and the Anzio beachead.

Alexander tells of two telegrams he received from Churchill about this time. The one:

> 'What are you doing sitting down doing nothing? Why don't you use your armour in a great scythe-like movement through the mountains?'

and another, it must have been about the time of Anzio.

> 'I expected to see a wild-cat roaring in the mountains – and what do I find? A whale wallowing on the beaches!'[5]

But Churchill, for all his *braggadocio*, was the real inspiration for Alexander's Italian campaign. He longed for victories, and he certainly got one on a plate, the capture of Rome, just before the D-day landings. He encouraged Alexander to dream of goals like Vienna.[6]

For as Alexander said:

> 'I shall always believe that the Allied Armies in Italy would have gone forward with a new impetus at the prospect of a wider victory. Instead – as I had to note in my despatch – the state of indecision had a lowering effect on the morale and efficiency of the troops . . . .'[7]

Alexander was fighting with one hand tied behind his back. For the powers that be, and this in effect was the Combined Chiefs of

Staff in Washington, had no intention of letting him have his head. His job was to fight the Germans, without winning the war. For the harder he fought on the spot, the more German reinforcements would be drawn from the vital battles of the north.

The final blow was struck by the decision to mount a sea-borne landing ('Dragoon') in the south of France to join up with Eisenhower's forces in North-West Europe.[8]

For this purpose, seven divisions were withdrawn from Alexander's depleted battle front, and he expected his air strength to be reduced by 70 per cent.[9]

It is worth considering for a moment the total effect of force withdrawals from the Italian Front during the course of the campaign, during the time that Alexander was either the Commander-in-Chief or Supreme Commander. Operation 'Overlord', the Normandy landings, took seven divisions from the Mediterranean theatre.

The next change was, as I have described above, the 'Dragoon' force withdrawals, another seven divisions. This lost to Alexander the invaluable French Expeditionary Corps especially trained in mountain warfare which was so badly needed in the mountainous areas of the Appenines. Then came the withdrawals for the fighting in Greece which, although not technically a 'force level' reduction, did reduce our capability on the Gothic line.

Finally, following the Ardennes offensive, the whole of the Canadian Corps, comprising another four divisions, was sent to bolster North-West Europe, together with the greater part of the US Twelfth Air Force. The deception plan to conceal the movement of 1 Canadian Corps was a masterpiece of its kind. This was at a time when serious doubts began to arise about the Allies' ability to win the war. Alexander saw as clearly as anyone else the vital need to reinforce the northern campaign. It was not so much the effect that these withdrawals had on his ability to hold the Germans in Italy, but the continual and time-consuming re-assessments, re-grouping and re-planning that took the heart out of his campaign.

It is said that Alexander became more withdrawn from the Italian campaign as the planning for the final offensive approached. That there was no firm guiding hand, that his directions were couched in terms more appropriate for a discussion than for actual orders. And this was the strange thing about the man. Although a fighting soldier *par excellence*, he was at the same time strangely withdrawn.

Alexander's detachment from the spring offensive is noted by Jackson in his history of the campaign, but he points out that:

'Between 29 January and 28 February when the most important planning decisions were being taken, Alexander was only in his office at AFHQ for five days: Athens, the Argonaut conference at Malta and Yalta, and the visit to Belgrade and the Russian front occupied the rest of his time.'[10]

Alexander's dislike of paperwork was notorious. He liked to paint with a broad brush and let his Chief-of-Staff work out the details. This characteristic was shared by Montgomery who even exiled his staff away from his own small headquarters. Monty maintained that 'a commander must have time to think' and this was impossible surrounded by the clutter and activity of a huge headquarters. I often wonder whether there is a lesson to be learned here for politicians!

The next distraction for Alexander was the Crimea Conference. Even before Christmas, Churchill had been brooding over the Allied failure to make any real progress in the war. He was intensely depressed. The Ardennes offensive concentrated his mind on the need for a Summit Conference of Allied Leaders.

An immediate cause for concern was the situation in Poland. The Polish Government in exile was located in London. On 5 January, Stalin, against the undertakings he had given previously, now recognised the so-called 'Lublin' Government in Poland which had become a puppet of the Soviet Union. Affairs in Poland, over which we had gone to war, clearly had to be thrashed out.

The final overthrow of Japan was perhaps a more crucial issue. John Colville, late private secretary to Churchill put it this way:

'It is often forgotten that a primary objective of the British and Americans at Yalta, in days when the successful development of an atomic bomb was still far from certain, was to induce the Russians to join in the war against Japan. It was feared that this might last another eighteen months or two years and cost half a million Anglo-American casualties when the main Japanese Islands were assaulted.'[11]

As a matter of routine, the usual protocols for the exchange of prisoners of war were drawn up. The document[12] which was not special in any way, provided for the care, segregation and repatriation of each other's nationals over-run by the other party. It allowed for Soviet officers or British, to visit the camps of their nationals. It forbad hostile propaganda to be directed against the contracting parties or against any of the United Nations.

It was greatly in the interests of the Western Allies to have this guarantee as to the care and return of prisoners. Britain signed its own agreement on behalf of, and in consultation with the other Imperial governments, of Canada, of Australia, of New Zealand, of the Union of South Africa, and of India, with whom there was no disagreement. The United States signed its own similar agreement with the Soviet Union.

There was only one article in the nine Articles of the Agreement which could be interpreted in any way as '*force majeure*', and that was Article 7 which laid upon both parties that 'they undertake to use all practical means to transport liberated citizens or subjects to places to be agreed upon where they can be handed over to the Soviet or British authorities respectively'. But after all, this was the whole object of the Agreement.

Churchill persuaded a reluctant Roosevelt to agree to this Summit at Yalta, and for the British and American delegations to meet a week in advance at Malta on 2 February.

Alexander was in attendance at Malta, and the Yalta Conference. He did not have much to do, and it was a time-wasting exercise so far as he was concerned. At Malta he suffered an extraordinary rebuff from CIGS Brooke whose critical comments on the Mediterranean Theatre have already been remarked. It all arose out of the appreciations on the Greek situation put together jointly by Alexander and Macmillan, and sent to Churchill. Brooke disagreed strongly with such proceedings, holding that the Supreme Commander's views were his alone and should not be adulterated by the Resident Minister Macmillan. In any case, Alexander was too much absorbed in the affairs of Greece, so Brooke thought. Jackson describes the incident in Brooke's own words: 'Some of us', he records himself as saying, 'had doubts as to whether Macmillan or Alexander was Supreme Commander of the Mediterranean'.[13]

It would be tempting to follow the war leaders, Churchill, Roosevelt and Stalin over to Yalta, and like a fly on the wall be a witness to these imponderable matters. It was held in the former Tsar's summer palace at Livadia on the Black Sea Crimean peninsula amid every evidence of war-time splendour and *bonhomie*. But it is not part of our story, and it is necessary to follow Alexander back to his theatre of war, and his impending visit to Tito.

One thing however, did impress Alexander which he recalls in his memoirs:

> 'Stalin made one significant reply to a question put to him by the Prime Minister. He said "we have already lost four million soldiers on the field of battle, and the war is not yet won – and they are human being you know".
>
> Four million dead! It was so. When I got back to my headquarters in Italy I asked for the War Office estimate of the Russian losses up to date, and the answer was "anything up to four and a half million".'[14]

VII

Final Phase and Surrender.

Before we follow in Alexander's footsteps, to see Tito in Belgrade, let us look at the key issues which took him there in this final phase of the fighting.

From Alexander's point of view, it was vitally necessary for him to secure his 'line of communication' for the onward march across the River Po and into Austria. This lay through the province of Venezia Giulia at the head of the Adriatic Sea. This was disputed Italian territory, claimed by Tito. It was inhabited by a mixture of Slovenes, Austrians and some Croats, the Italian population being in the minority. Tito had further territorial ambitions in the direction of Carinthia in Austria, where there was a Slovenian minority. But in order to take a view of Alexander's strategy, we must understand the geography of this region, which stated in simple terms is as follows: Venezia Giulia covers the head of the Adriatic and acts as a bridge between the Balkans and Italy. Hanging from it, like a bunch of grapes, suspended from Trieste on the left hand, and from Fiume on the right, is the peninsula of Istria, dangling, as it were, over the Adriatic Sea. At its point is the port of Pola, which, together with Trieste, form the two main supply ports which Alexander required. To the north of Venezia Giulia lies the barrier of the Karawanken range, an outlier of the Alps through which Alexander must pass to reach the Austrian towns of Villach and Klagenfurt, and north-eastwards, the road to Vienna.

At his disposal are a number of tortuous passes winding up the ragged mountain ravines. From left to right, these are as follows: the Tarvisio Pass running from Tolmezzo in Italy to Mauthen in Austria; the Predl Pass running from Gorizia to Villach; the Wörzen Pass, again descending on Villach; and the Löibl Pass between Ljubljana in Yugoslavia and Klagenfurt. All these passes, as I subse-

49

quently discovered for myself, have their own individual characteristics, but the best one available to General McCreery of the 8th Army in 1945 was the Tarvisio.

After leaving the Yalta Conference (5–19 February 1945), Alexander began his talks with Marshal Tito on 21 February. Alexander was a modest man, but one who knew how to lay on a good show in the best traditions of the Brigade of Guards, if the need arose. When Tito visited Alexander at Lake Bolsena in the summer of 1944 he was accompanied everywhere by a bodyguard of partisans armed to the teeth. Jackson tells us that on this occasion Alexander decided to reply in kind and brought with him for his visit to Yugoslavia an escort of 16 enormous guardsmen, which deeply impressed the Marshal.[1]

Tito's interest in these talks was to secure Allied support for his spring offensive to clear the Dalmatian Coast of the German Army.

As a result of his pleas, the 4th Yugoslav Army was to receive from Alexander not only a complete wing of the RAF and naval support but tanks, guns, food and battle-dress clothing for the army's nominal strength of 50,000.[2] Alexander thought this worth his while if he were to negotiate successfully for the Venezia Giulia lifeline.

But on this Alexander had his hands tied. For the Allied governments had been totally unable to agree on a joint policy, the Americans being adamant that the whole of the province of Venezia Giulia must be occupied, whereas the British side were quite happy to agree to a share-out with Tito, pending a peace conference. This disagreement between the British and Americans reached a complete *impasse* so that Alexander could only insist on his right of free passage from Tito. But when he explained that to take the province by force, would mean shooting, he received no reply from his superiors.

One thing did become clear to Alexander on this visit, and that was Tito's territorial ambitions in the name of the Slovenes, which extended right into Carinthia. And Tito's offer of Yugoslav troops to help liberate and occupy Austria was a warning of things to come.

Whilst in Yugoslavia, Alexander expressed a wish to meet Marshal Tolbukhin on the Eastern Front, against the time when their two armies would be side by side in Austria. Alexander described him as an elderly, heavily built man, but certainly an impressive figure. Whilst they were left alone for a few moments before dinner, 'the Marshal noticed that among my medal ribbons I had the old Tsarist Order of St Anne with crossed swords. As he put his finger on it he sighed 'I have that, too, but I'm not allowed to wear it'. During the First World War, Marshal Tolbukhin had commanded a battalion in the old Imperial Army'.[3]

The picture at the beginning of March 1945 was this. All quiet in Greece but British troops not yet out. In Italy, the Allies improve their positions in preparation for the offensive to crush the German armies south of the River Po. In Yugoslavia, the Dalmatian offensive by the 4th Yugoslav Army about to begin. But no agreement on the disputed territory of Venezia Giulia.

Meanwhile mysterious discussions were going on in Germany between *Oberstgruppenführer* (Col-General) Karl Wolff, the senior SS Commander in Italy, an Italian industrialist, Baron Parilli, and an emissary from Allen Dulles, one Gero von Gaevernitz.[4]

The Germans had planned to lay waste the land in a 'scorched-earth' policy before they withdrew from Northern Italy. This *'Herbst-nebel'* was carefully organised to allow nothing of value to remain. The Wehrmacht were to be responsible for military targets, bridges and the like whilst the SS, under Wolff, were to destroy civilian targets, power stations, water supply, factories and plant. It was fortunate for the civilians that Wolff intervened with his surrender proposals.[5]

Before concluding the two campaigns in which Montgomery and Alexander predominated and the problems they faced together (discounting for a moment the American contribution), it may be opportune to take note of CIGS Brookes's opinion of these two men.

As David Fraser shows in his biography of Lord Alanbrooke,[6] the Alanbrooke papers reveal his inner thoughts on his subordinates at crucial stages in the contest.

Just before the Sicilian landings at the joint allied headquarters in Malta, Brooke complains of 'bearings being inclined to heat already; the root of it all is the personality of Monty', and reporting a meeting at Algiers with Montgomery, he says in his diary:

> 'He required a lot of education ... to make him see the whole situation and the war as a whole outside the 8th Army orbit. A difficult mixture to handle, brilliant commander in action and trainer of men but liable to commit untold errors due to lack of tact, lack of appreciation of other peoples' outlook. It is most distressing that the Americans do not like him, and it will always be a difficult matter to have him fighting in close proximity to them. He wants guiding and watching continually and I do not think Alex is sufficiently strong and rough with him.'[7]

I can hear the Public School ethos coming through very strongly in these words. The team captain is at his best in dealing with these recalcitrant fellows.

On Eisenhower and Alexander he harbours very serious misgivings. Brooke wrote in a note later:

'It had been made quite clear up to date that Eisenhower had not got the required ability to ensure success in this theatre. Alexander, his deputy had many very fine qualities but not strategic vision. He has been carried by Montgomery through North Africa as regards the strategic and tactical handling of the situation. Monty was now far from him and Anderson [Brit. First Army] certainly had not got the required qualities to inspire Alex . . .'.[8]

And later on, meeting Alexander (who was then commanding 15 Army Group in Italy), Brooke confided to his diary.

'Charming as he is [he] fills me with gloom. He is a very, very small man and cannot see big . . . I shudder at the thought of him as Supreme Commander.'

Brooke was fond of making such withering comments.

But, on one occasion, however, Brooke was present when Churchill belaboured both his Field Marshals, Alexander and Montgomery, in front of the Cabinet. Brooke sprang to their defence and had a blazing row with the Prime Minister.

VIII

War and Blood in the Mountains

We have only had a brief encounter with the Italian Partisans in a previous chapter. No account of the period would be complete without describing their activities. Unlike the Yugoslav and Greek partisans, who had been conducting desultory warfare against the occupying German forces for many years, the Italian partisans were latecomers to the scene, for the simple reason that Italy only changed sides in the latter stages of the war. Indeed although Archie Hubbard and I had heard of various fugitive groups on our long trek south, as we escaped from prison in the autumn of 1943, we never encountered any. In fact, we studiously avoided contact in case such bands contained latent fascists who would betray our whereabouts. It was therefore with some scepticism that I later heard stories of effective Partisan operations.

THE PATRIOTIC WAR OR *SECONDO RISORGIMENTO*

But I was wrong, for those Italian patriots played a notable role in the Allied war effort. In the end, they had developed into a fully fledged liberation movement. They took the surrender of German forces many times their own size. Never more than about 145,000 strong, they are reputed to have sustained not less than 50,000 casualties during the 19 months from October 1943 to May 1945.[1] In the three months, September to November 1944, they are estimated to have inflicted over 6,000 casualties on German and Italian Fascist troops.[2]

Alexander was first given responsibility for the Partisans in July 1944 when he was commanding the Fifteenth Army Group. He took a great interest in their activities from the start, perhaps recalling the group of irregulars he commanded in the Baltic campaign. The

53

Partisans were helpful in a number of ways. Some acted as couriers, intelligence gatherers and guides to the armies in the field. Others played a notable part in the liberation of Rome and of Florence, but perhaps the most effective were the northern groups who made their special targets the German communications in the rearward areas. Signals cables, roads, railways and bridges were harried by them.[3]

Towards the end, where previously 20 trains had passed in one day, en route for Austria, now only one got through. This effectively cut off the German life-line. It is claimed that the 'Italian Patriots, tied down some 23 enemy divisions in the northern part of Italy'.[4] None of this would have been possible without the help and support of the British and American liaison missions parachuted in behind the lines. British SOE teams (No. 1 Special Force) sent in over the last six months of the war amounted to 96 separate missions, and no doubt the American effort was on a similar scale. But the demands on Allied supply aircraft were enormous and at one point were drastically scaled down. At least one Allied commander, Air Marshal Slessor, thought the operations in northern Italy were a wasted effort, aircraft losses were high and few stores dropped in the right place. But the sorties continued.

In November, as winter was approaching, Alexander decided that the operations should be scaled down, that the Partisans should go into 'winter quarters'. In a message broadcast in his name, he explained the reason why supplies would have to be reduced, and suggested that the resistance should spend the winter months in gathering intelligence. This dropped like a lead balloon on the beleaguered Partisans and seriously damaged their morale.

But there was another reason for it, as Macmillan explains in his diary.

> 'Unless we are very careful, we shall get another EAM/ELAS situation in northern Italy. The operations of SOE in arming nearly 100,000 so-called Patriots will produce the same revolutionary situation, unless we devise a system for ... taking them into either our or the Italian Army. Then, in return for pay and rations, we may be able to get hold of their weapons. The lesson of Greece is that nothing matters except "disarmament". The political questions are the excuse for retaining armed power.'[5]

However, Macmillan was at great pains to bring 'the Patriots' into the Allied fold. To honour and reward them for the work they had done, and to bring them into local government. Like most other resistance movements the communist faction predominated, and it was touch and go whether the communist groups, fully armed and organised, would not stage a violent coup, with the possibility of Italy splitting into two. Macmillan's role in steering Italy through these troubled days, and his skill as a diplomat and statesman has not been fully recognised. In his memoirs he pays tribute to the British and American Liaison Officers behind the lines and concludes:

'Italy owes a great deal to the moral, as well as material, aid which we gave her tortured people when the great day came. The proof of our success is to be found in the subsequent political history of the country. It was the last great achievement in this field of Anglo-American organisation.'[6]

At the time these events were going on, Macmillan was also shuttling backwards and forwards to Greece as nursemaid to the fledgling Greek democratic government. The justification for Churchill's posting of a resident minister to the Mediterranean Theatre was now becoming apparent.

Kesselring had placed Wolff in charge of anti-partisan operations north of the Po and was told to use 'the utmost severity'. These instructions were faithfully carried out by 16 SS Panzer Grenadier Division in the area north of Pistoia.[7] In the Friuli area north of Venezia Giulia, in the alpine foothills, the Patriots reported a campaign of rape and pillage by 'Mongols' or 'Tartar hordes' unleashed by the German high command. A huge area was being cleared and houses ransacked by these people. There were two distinct offensives[8] to clear the countryside of all civilian inhabitants, who were forced to abandon their homes.[9]

'TEMPO DI COSACCHI'

Pietro Menis, the author of a book of this name, was living in the town of Buja (Buia), and kept a tiny diary during the Cossack occupation in which he recorded all the events which took place under this eyes, and his record therefore has a direct impact on our story.[10]

'In many villages in the foothills, the Germans had placed large groups of Cossacks, with all the characteristics of nomad tribes ... They had committed every kind of violence and robbery against the local populations, who were often at their mercy ... Near Gemona there was one of their bishops, living in a tent ... At Tarcento they were camped along the banks of the river Torre, and they were seen bathing there naked, men and women together, under the benevolent eyes of their priests.'

The activities of the Partisans brought down the wrath of the Germans supported by their Cossack mercenaries in a *'rastrellamento'* (lit. 'coming through' an area).

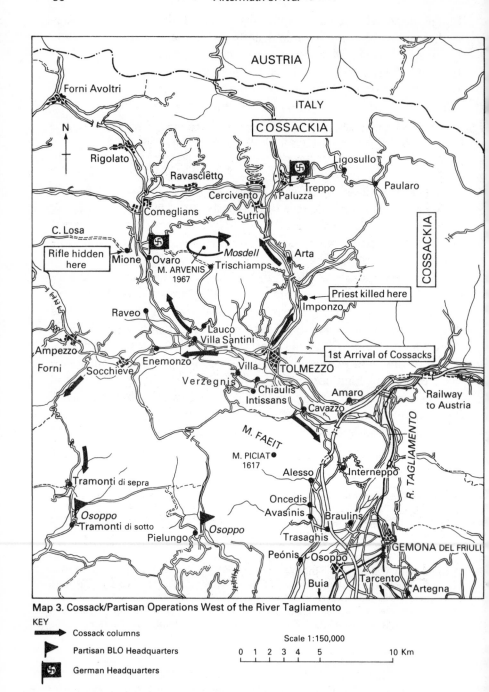

Map 3. Cossack/Partisan Operations West of the River Tagliamento

KEY

➤ Cossack columns

◢ Partisan BLO Headquarters

卐 German Headquarters

Scale 1:150,000

0 1 2 3 4 5   10 Km

3. Cossack Partisan Operations West of the River Tagliamento

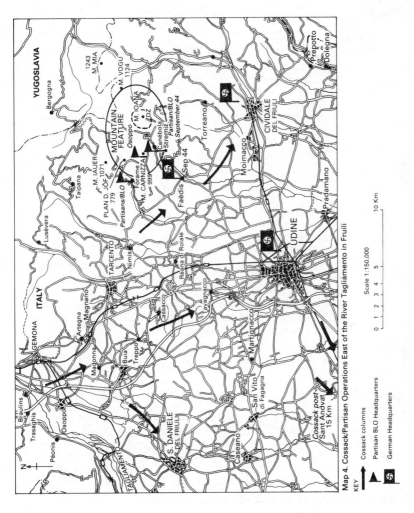

Map 4. Cossack/Partisan Operations East of the River Tagliamento in Fruili

KEY

Cossack columns

Partisan BLO Headquarters

German Headquarters

4. Cossack Partisan Operations East of the River Tagliamento in Friuli

On 13 September 1944, five Germans were killed at S. Floriano and there followed 'a furious *rastrellamento*'. Three hundred people were brought from the villages to the *piazza delle scuoli* in Buja, there they were lined up in the square before the coffins of the five dead Germans and told that ten of their number would hang if they did not reveal the names of those responsible for the killing. Nobody spoke. Later all were released except 30 men who were sent off to Germany ...

On 4 October two more Germans were killed near S. Floriana. The response was swift,

> 'Germans and Cossacks came flooding in from Osoppo and Artegna. By mid-day the sky was full of black smoke ... the evacuated population was assembled at the place of the crime, and meanwhile specialized troops ransacked the villages.'

The German commander now called for a large contingent of Cossacks to be sent in, for he himself with his few troops was unable to cope.

> '5 October: And here they are!
> At the head of the procession are 4 horsemen, followed by the Prince, dressed in black, on a black horse, protected by a platoon of youths.
> The rest of the procession arrives, dragging behind them those typical primitive carts, falling to pieces, pulled by all kinds of horses. These carts are full of all kinds of stuff, and are followed by a most nauseating smell ... The men wear uniforms which seem to come from every European army. As they pass through the villages, they enter every open door and ask for wine: many are already drunk ... at three in the afternoon the procession is over and in the deserted street all you see is dung, straw and rubbish. In the evening all around the village are hundreds of campfires: those poor ragamuffins are cooking their food, in their tents or sheltered by their carts ... and the drunks are singing songs from the steppes.'

Then on 6 October they re-appear, knocking on doors,

> 'asking for wine, but no one opens ... wine has been scarce for a long time, and these savages would drink it by the bucketful, then they become violent and threatening. They aim their guns at you or take grenades from their pockets as if it were the most natural thing in the world.'

More and more refugees poured from the villages to make way for the Cossacks. It is like a gypsy invasion 'the hills, fields and meadows, even gardens are full of their horses grazing ... drunken Cossacks have committed violence everywhere'.

But according to the diary the Partisans are also spiteful, capturing Cossacks to beat them up, strip them, even to kill them, throwing their carts into the ravine.

By 14 October, more rumours have spread with refugees arriving from the far side of the Tagliamento. Frightened, confused, 'telling of horrors'. They say that all of Gemona and the Ferro valley will have to be evacuated to make room for more Cossacks arriving from Austria. By 20 October, now it was getting colder, they began to come into the houses. Once they were in 'they were the bosses'! No-one dared raise their voice.

Pathetic incidents were reported. On 27 October, the Cossacks were alarmed by German target-practice, thinking it was the Partisans:

'They ran towards Colosomano, beating everyone they met on the way. They stopped Enrico Alessio, who was coming back from the fields, beat him with their rifles and then, as he was walking away, shot him in the back, seriously wounding him. Not content with this, one of them followed him home and shot him to death on his own doorstep.'

And then on 29 October four girls were going to get bread at Madonna, when the Cossacks shouted at them to stop:

'One ran away, was shot and died 1 hour later. (Nives Sant, 19 years old.)'

The Cossack women do not escape censure either,

'The Cossack women have been shouting for bread at the bakery. And yet they always seem to be eating, even in the streets. And drinking! How they drink! They drink any kind of alcohol and when they are drunk they get violent, they threaten and beat people.'

Then the *diarista* (the diarist) adds:

'There is a tremendous difference between the officers and the men: the former are usually intellectual and speak other languages, while the latter are the typical serfs. They are only the same when they drink.'

These isolated incidents may seem like the small change of war, but repeated and compounded over a wide area they amount to a holy reign of terror.

No wonder our narrator writes:

'25 November. *Te Deum Laudamus*! The Cossacks have all left. Even the Germans have celebrated with wine and singing. After 2 months of oppression, theft and bloodshed, they have finally gone away ... you would have to see the schools to believe the dirt and disorder that the Cossacks have left behind them.'

They had left Buja, but it would be many more months before they left the Friuli and Carnia.[11]

THE ROLE OF THE BLO'S AND THEIR ITALIAN COUNTERPARTS

Who were these people who were unleashed on a peaceful countryside? They were Domanov's Cossacks (and some Caucasians) who had been sent from Poland to serve under the SS Commander and Police Chief *Gruppenführer* Glöbocnik of the German Adriatic Littorale Command. They had recently been incorporated into Himmler's SS and had all taken the personal oath of loyalty to Hitler, apparently with enthusiasm. They were now to operate against the Italian Partisans, and had been granted a new national home or *Stanitsas* in Carnia, an area which the Germans intended to annexe. The idea being that here they could practise all the traditions of their native culture under their own leader or *Ataman*[12]

Now let us see this occupation from the view-point of the Italian Partisans and their BLO's.

A British Liaison Officer with the Italian Partisans at that time, Patrick Martin-Smith, explains that the Friuli area was a strategic hub for the German forces now withdrawing on the Eastern Front. The Adriatic *Littorale* was doubly important as forming the 'right' of the final defensive line for the Reich, and guarding Kesselring's vital communications between his armies in Italy and Germany proper. Furthermore Rosenberg of the *Ost Ministerium* (Ostmin) and Himmler (Reich Marshal SS) had a joint interest, he writes:

> 'The former needed to compensate his *protégés* those Cossacks who had aligned themselves with Hitler, the latter needed to reinforce his SS subordinate in Italy [*Gruppenführer* Glöbocnik]. It was arranged that over 20,000 Cossacks and Caucasians should be brought into Friuli in order to drive the partisans out and, more important, prevent them returning'.[13]

Another British Liaison Officer, Lionel (Pat) Mosdell, who had been 'dropped' about that time, writes:

> 'It appeared that a large scale *rastrallemento* had taken place on 4 October prior to which time Carnia had been a free zone in which the partisans could move freely with transport if they so wished. During October and during the *rastrallemento* the Cossacks arrived and were placed as garrisons in practically all the villages and towns in Carnia. Many partisans had dispersed.'[14]

Martin-Smith also gives an account of these offensives.

> 'By October the Germans were ready. Cossacks and SS swept out of Tolmezzo, cleared the road to Austria and fanned out into the lateral valleys to meet columns coming from the west. Hostages and forced labourers were seized ... the Republic was destroyed and in a second offensive the Free Zone was overrun. The SS withdrew, the Cossacks remained in occupation of the valleys and villages. 41 Cossack settlements were superimposed on 38 communes; 80,000 Italians spent a miserable winter.'

Speaking of the area East of the River Tagliamento, around Mount Giovanni (M. Ionna) the DZ (or dropping zone), just north of the town of Cividale, another BLO, Major Ronald Taylor, writes of the great courage not only of the Partisans accompanied by the *missione inglese*, but also the civilian population, the *Friulani*.

> 'Surely they suffered not only in their daily lives but also through the terrifying visits and actions of the Cossacks. No home was safe, no woman or child respected. Anyone known or suspected of supporting our cause would be dealt with in brutal fashion without mercy. Yet not once were we betrayed but always made welcome in the poorest homes with the richest reception.'[15]

In a letter from Ronald Taylor, I learnt that:

> 'In the areas immediately East and West of the river Tagliamento there was a strong Cossack presence. At one time our partisan group captured some 100 or so in the Nimis area.
>
> After the war I was sent to Tolmezzo where I "took charge" pending the arrival of "AMG". I was shown a book some 1½ inches thick reportedly documenting atrocities attributed mainly to the "Cossacks".'[16]

What were those Cossacks like when one met them face to face? The bullet was the usual greeting for the captured Partisan, as this adventure of Gianandrea Gropplero di Troppenburg shows.[17] After parachuting into the Friuli area his party (which included a young girl of 18, Paola del Din ('Renata'), who had taken the place of her brother Renato, a Partisan killed by the Germans), they began their operation. The first thing that '*Secondino*' (alias Dumas Poli the wireless operator), did was to broadcast the special coded message, *War and Blood for the Partisans of the Mountains*, which meant that the mission was now operational.

The idea was that Troppenburg would form a new brigade of Partisans, recruiting dissident members of the Osoppo Division and the *Garibaldini*[18] which had been active in the area. In April 1945, he decided to move the brigade from Buia to Mels. Three of them were doing a reconnaissance of Mels by bicycle when they were surprised by a Cossack patrol. After a short fight and sustaining some wounds they were overpowered. They were disarmed and tied up by dozens of Cossacks and taken in a horse-drawn cart to the Cossack post which was under command of an SS captain. A lot of people were standing by and Gianandrea just had time to yell out 'Tell the Partisans that Freccia and Secondo are in the hands of the Cossacks'.

> 'There the SS captain and three Cossacks began the interrogation. They wanted to know all about us, the partisan movement in general, the names of our leaders and how strong we were. They got nothing out of me, so they started to hit me in the back and re-open my wounds. I suppose this could have been called torture but, with fresh wounds, it did not seem to hurt and I held out.'[19]

All three were interrogated again, and sentenced to death by firing squad.

'We were taken to the courtyard of the house. The firing squad was already in position. Suddenly a Bixio mortar was fired into the courtyard sending the enemy scattering – the Partisans of the Italian Brigade of the Osoppo Division had come to save us. The SS captain ordered the execution to be postponed and for us to be taken to the fortress of Osoppo to be shot.

Then fate intervened. A crazy escape followed.

'We were tied up and thrown into the cart to start our final journey. At a certain point along the way, the convoy was attacked by the Partisans of the Osoppo and Rosselli Divisions, who wanted to free us. The Cossacks positioned themselves along the side of the road with their machine guns, leaving us on the cart, unguarded. The horses bolted at the sound of the bullets and mortars and galloped away across the fields. I managed to get loose and grabbed the reins to stop the horses. Then a Partisan came running towards us and untied us and we set off for the cesspit near his home – our hiding place. We had to disinfect our wounds with *grappa*.'[20]

Secondo (Dumas Poli) who was also one of the three, was surprised that on first capture,

'The behaviour of the Cossacks was over-careful, and the lack of the *coup de grace* which we were expecting, their savageness being well known in the area, seemed strange to us. Even the Germans considered them to be unnecessarily cruel and later we heard that a short while before they had begun firing at us, they had shot, with no motive at all, a peasant who had been pruning a tree.'[21]

Meanwhile 'Renata' was doing her best to establish order among the various units 'acting with great courage and generosity'.[22]

And here it is worth recording the role that the women played in the patriotic war, as Martin-Smith records.

'I recall not only the courage, endurance, cheerfulness and comradeship of the Partisans, but also the kindness, patience and sheer long suffering of the country people of Carnia and the Prealpi. Nowhere can women have payed [sic] their part more fully – they provided the supply column that fed 60,000 people. Few things have done more to elevate the status of women in post-war Europe than the contribution of women to the resistance.'[23]

As a former fugitive in the Appenines, I can endorse the statement. We owed so much to these unknown people which it proved imposs-ible to repay.

PART THREE

THE VENEZIA GIULIA CRISIS

IX

Tito Moves In

Cease-fire has come to the Italian front before that in North-West Europe. The rout of the German armies in the valley of the Po has been dramatic. Alexander, bled white by the demands of the Western Front, has turned the tables and achieved the first surrender of a German Army Group. Now he had to see to his lines of communication, through the disputed territory of Venezia Giulia, into which Tito had already infiltrated.

Under the armistice agreement signed between the Western Allies and Italy, Venezia Giulia was recognised as an Italian province and its immediate occupation was envisaged. The Americans insisted that we should forthwith occupy and impose our rule over the whole of Venezia Giulia, whereas the British were thinking in terms of an arrangement, *pro tem*, with Tito pending the Peace Conference. Alexander pointed out that occupation of the whole area would mean the use of force against our Yugoslav allies, to which means the Americans reluctantly agreed.

Alexander's reaction to the American agreement was a realistic one.

> 'If I am ordered by the Combined Chiefs of Staff to occupy the whole of Venezia Giulia by force if necessary, we shall certainly be committed to a fight with the Yugoslav army, who will have the moral backing at least of the Russians.'

And he added his disquiet about the possible reaction of his soldiers who had,

> 'a profound admiration for Tito's Partisan Army and a great sympathy for them in their struggle ... we must be careful therefore before we ask them to turn away from the common enemy to fight an ally.'[1]

Churchill agreed that,

'Tito would not withdraw his troops if ordered to do so, and the Russians will never tell him to.'

Meantime, Alexander had informed Tito that Allied formations were nearing Trieste, and that he intended to establish his lines of communication from Trieste to the British zone of Austria, through Venezia Giulia, in accordance with their verbal agreement at Belgrade. Tito's reply was predictable, but full of foreboding. The situation had changed since their meeting. His troops were already in control of Venezia Giulia and his civil government had been set up. Possession was evidently nine tenths of the law, as far as Tito was concerned, but he did concede that at least the Allies should have right of passage and use of the port of Trieste.[2] By 3 May, the situation had taken a turn for the worse. Tito demanded an explanation as to how British forces had entered a region already liberated by the Yugoslav Army.[3] He then demanded the withdrawal of British troops behind the Isonzo River. The same day, Alexander replied with some indignation that Tito was apparently prepared to renege on the Belgrade agreement, by denying the right of British troops to enter the area, and he added

'I have thus fully kept my promise to you and I still believe that you will keep yours to me.'[4]

No wonder Alexander was so concerned. Trieste and its hinterland was his life-line, the most sensitive spot in the whole Allied operation to secure Austria and prevent it falling into the hands of a usurper. So direct a threat from the Eastern powers was a most untoward event, particularly since those powers were our closest allies, whom we had been aiding and succouring during the long years of the war. And so the wheels were turning furiously in the West in an effort to re-assess this new situation.

In his latest communication to Churchill on 5 May, Alexander questioned whether Tito's hand had not been strengthened by his recent visit to Moscow, hence his new intransigent attitude. He will allow us 'user rights' only, claims Alexander. But once we have gone he will step in.

Churchill's reply on 6 May scolds Alexander for his implied belief that a deal should be done with Tito, but leaves no doubt that a show of strength is now necessary.

'There is no question of your making any agreement with him about incorporating Istria or any part of the pre-war Italy in "his new Yugoslavia". The destiny of this part of the world is reserved for the peace table, and you should certainly make him aware of this. In order to avoid leading Tito or his Yugoslav commanders into any temptation, it would be wise to have a solid mass of troops in this area ..."⁵

The imminent collapse of German Army Group E under General Löhr was a further reason for anxiety for this would put further troops at Tito's disposal.

General Löhr, who was now *OB Sudost* (Commander-in-Chief South East) was unable to stop the advance of the Yugoslavs on Fiume. 97 corps of Army Group E was trapped and soon had to surrender to the Yugoslavs. Army Group C had capitulated, so General Löhr's western flank was completely exposed. He therefore made urgent representations to Dönitz, who by this time had succeeded the dead Führer, that he should be allowed to surrender to Alexander. It was lucky that Dönitz had been able to prevaricate with the West at the time of Luneburg for this enabled some two-thirds of Army Group E to cross the Austrian border. When the instrument of unconditional surrender for all German forces was signed at Rheims on 8 May, Löhr unwisely re-crossed the border back into Yugoslavia, and himself negotiated the surrender of the remaining 150,000 German troops to Tito. But he was to pay for it. In 1946 he was brought to trial for shooting Partisans and was duly executed.⁶

The disposition of allied troops backing up the Venezia Giulia operation was therefore as follows: The New Zealanders were in Trieste. The 91 (US) Division was in the Gorizia, and 56 British Infantry Division was forming a bridge between the two, all under command of the 8th Army's 13 Corps. Sitting in reserve and waiting to advance into Austria, around Udine and Cividale in the Friuli area, was 5 Corps under General Keightley (see Map I).

On 6 May Alexander reported, via the Cabinet, to the Combined Chiefs of Staff in Washington, and the British Chiefs of Staff in London, that in his estimation the Yugoslavs would make every effort to obtain a boundary approximately along the River Isonzo (west of Trieste) and would themselves control the line of our L of C up to the frontier.

'Estimated strength Fourth [Yugoslav] Army now about 60,000 in Trieste and to the North. Every day Yugoslavs are strengthening their hold right up to R. Isonzo and even West of the river with our troops looking on.

All Italians of any standing in Trieste except Yugoslav sympathisers are being arrested. Complete control of activities being taken over by Yugoslavs. Banks forced to hand over their securities today. All manpower between ages 18 and 60 being conscripted, Italians for forced labour, sympathisers of military age being armed. Rifles actually seen being issued to batches of men. Requisitioning of grain and other supplies by Yugoslavs on a big scale, is taking place even west of R. Isonzol. Archbishop of Gorizia and other Priests believed arrested and many others threatened ... quite impossible to set up any form of AMG [Allied Military Government] in Venezia Giulia. In fact in Eastern part Udine Yugoslavs are endeavouring to set up Civil Control. Relations between our troops and Yugoslavs remains satisfactory and no incidents have yet occurred but Yugoslav policy is to commandeer all large buildings and post sentries in Trieste, all seven Barracks are denied to us.'[7]

To which the following response came from Churchill on 7 May.

'Personal and Secret from Prime Minister to Field Marshal Alexander:
   Am much concerned about all this. Pray let me know whether any lack of authority is hampering you. Meanwhile surely a steady gathering of British controlled forces on this front if you can spare them is most likely to maintain peace and most convenient if any unpleasantness arises. Let me know what you are doing in massing forces against this Muscovite tentacle, of which Tito is the crook.'[8]

To which Alexander replies on the same day that he has acted and is acting as if he had full powers and does not feel hampered in any way. But that he is dealing with Tito as C-in-C of the Yugoslav forces and not as Prime Minister. He concludes:

'The situation is undoubtedly tricky. But I do not repeat not believe it will come to a shooting match providing that we do not fire the first shot ... Personally I am not repeat not too sure that Tito has the full backing of Moscow and I think he will agree to my proposals in the end.'[9]

So by the end of the first week of May 1945, the Allies have achieved an unconditional surrender of German armed forces on all fronts. But in the Mediterranean theatre as a whole, we are not secure, for we can feel the 'Muscovite tentacle of which Tito is the crook' (as Churchill so aptly put it), groping blindly around us.

X

Crossing the Alps

It is now vital that the British should get into Austria before the arrival of Marshal Tolbukhin and Marshal Tito. Intense parleying takes place with representatives of Lieutenant General Löhr, commanding Army Group South East, who still considers himself bound by oath of loyalty to Hitler and cannot give himself up, even though the Führer is now dead. But the threat of the British artillery proves a great persuader and Löhr, on 7 May, sends one of his Corps Commanders, Lieutenant General Felmy, to negotiate a ceasefire for the next day in accordance with Admiral Doenitz's declaration. After that there is little difficulty.[1]

On 8 May, the Welsh Guards received orders to move into Austria directed on Villach via Cividale and Caporetto.[2] The Battalion War Diary takes up the tale.

'Bn moved at an early hour 0300 hrs and move went up on time. The drive was an exquisite one, winding up over alpine passes, first in darkness, then through a mere glimmer of dawn and then through the pine-scented woods and alpine pasture land with the snow-capped mountains suffused in early sunlight. Bn stopped off the road in convoy short of TAVISIO where breakfasts and brew ups took place ... After certain delays and parleys Bn moved into Austria over frontier at THORL and one's immediate impression was an unexpectedly sullen population in marked contrast to the handkerchief waving Italians. This was due to bewilderment rather than to any disaffection.'[3]

Carinthia, which they were just entering, was an over-whelmingly Nazi province. Hence the sullen reception was not to be entirely unexpected.

On 6 May, 36 Infantry Brigade had been about to embark on an encircling movement of the strong German position between Tarvisio and Tolmezzo, with some apprehension as to its feasibility. For although the war was officially over, this German Corps evidently did not accept it. However, when they reached the environs of Tolmezzo, they found the enemy had fled and the Argyll and Sutherland Highlanders occupied the little alpine town with no difficulty. The Brigade War Diary continues:

'Meanwhile, on the northern route, the Queen's Own had met no opposition. Their progress was more like a peacetime drive through the very beautiful scenery just SOUTH of the Austro-Italian border. From here we caught our first sight of Austria and read the first German names on the signposts. Here too we encountered a scene that might have been transplanted from comic opera. At FORNI AVOITRA (0678) the Queen's Own were surprised to find a battalion of Georgians living peacefully in the town. Their relations with the local Italian population were of the friendliest, but there had been trouble between the Georgians and the Cossacks. The latter had raided their compatriots, killing many. These Georgians were an aristocratic throwback to the days of Tzarist Russia. Their officers, 10 of whom were Princes, were arrayed in glittering uniforms and treated their soldiers like serfs. Many of them had been taxi-drivers in PARIS before the war. (Just after the arrival of 6 RWK there was a sound of shots in the town and all the civilians ran for cover; it was discovered that one of the Georgian officers had shot another in a duel). The Georgians were ready and willing to surrender themselves to us. As they explained, they had no quarrel with the Western Allies, only with the Soviet Union, an argument we were soon to learn by heart. It seemed however, that their surrender had been accomplished without the cognisance of their commanding officer. Later in the day the CO came down from the mountains and raised hell with the Princes for surrendering without authority. Perhaps it should be mentioned in passing that the CO, unlike many other COs we have known, more's the pity, was a beautiful Princess. The daughter of the "King of Georgia", who had been killed in an air-raid on BERLIN, she had taken over command of her people. Clad in buckskin trousers she presented a striking and commanding figure as she demanded to see the British general. She was escorted to Bde H.Q. where terms of surrender and disposal were determined. This was the first of our many dealings with the Russian Army of Liberation of General Vlassov. Composed of turncoat Red Army men, displaced civilians turned soldier, and Tzarist exiles, they numbered in all something like 150,000 men.'

The diary noted that there were still large and disorganised bodies of Russians in the vicinity, but in the town the Italian Partisans were in control, *Garibaldini* and *Osopini* working side by side.

'Many of these men were arrested by us in mistake for Vlassov's Russians. An international incident was avoided when the Italians assured us that these Russians, who were led by a very able young man of 20, had been fighting on their side, and the situation was smoothed over with several glasses of cognac all round.'

The existence of a guerilla group comprised of loyal Soviet citizens fighting with the Italian Partisans, having escaped from German prisoner of war camps, gives some idea of the confused situation which the Allied armies were discovering. It would prove extremely difficult to sort out the exact allegiances during subsequent screening processes. The Soviets automatically treated any of their returned prisoners of war as suspect, if not traitors, if they were considered to have given 'aid or comfort to the enemy'. If the men of the 'Stalin Battalion' found their way back to the USSR they are likely to have undergone a prolonged period of 're-education'.

We now hear of a considerable number of Azerbaijanis, presumably recruited from that 'Soviet Republic', into one of the L of C '*Ost battalions*'.

'The general feeling of uncertainty was still acute however, due to time factors. Firstly, there were large numbers of Azerbaijanians, civil and military, of both sexes who had fled from the Partisans and were now roaming about the hills. Some of these were apprehended at ARTA where they were concentrated and evacuated to UDINE, but the remainder were potentially a constant source of trouble, inasmuch as the Partisans were eager to pay off old scores, thus causing the clashes we were anxious to avoid. It should be mentioned here that the Partisans were nevertheless remarkably well disciplined.'

We now catch up with General Domanov's Cossacks who have left their so-called German implanted homeland in the Carnia area and are fleeing west before Tito's Partisans, although they could well have proved a match for them.

'Another disturbing factor in this somewhat tense situation was the arrival in TOLMEZZO of a delegation from the Cossack commander, General Domanov, who had under his command a division of 16,000 men, Don, Terek, and Kuban Cossacks, with their attendant women and children numbering 7,000. Domanov was willing to surrender himself and his division unconditionally. Previously in the TOLMEZZO area they had retreated over the frontier to MAUTHEN (C2386) in AUSTRIA in order to avoid conflict with the partisans. The Italians were not their only worry. There was no love lost between Cossacks and Germans, and the latter had already ordered the arrest of General Domanov and condemned him to death in absentia for disobedience to their instructions. The plight of the Cossacks was indeed pitiable. Harried on all sides, with all their hopes of conquest disappointed, they now faced the certainty of return to the Soviet Union as traitors. But they would have been still a force to be reckoned with if they had refused to capitulate and until that capitulation was complete we could not feel secure.'[4]

So eventually General Domanov was called to meet Brigadier Musson[5] at Mauthen at 9 o'clock the next morning to discuss terms of surrender. General Domanov was himself a former Red Army officer so would have been extremely keen to surrender to the Western Allies. His division also included White Russians. An additional surrender was also concluded by Musson for 4,000 Caucasians under Sultan Klyshgirej who was their tribal chieftain.

'They were even less of a military body than the Cossacks and were composed entirely of voluntary refugees from the Caucasus during the German retreat from Stalingrad. When the preliminary parley was over, the Cossack envoys moved off under armoured car escort to rejoin their division, the escort being necessary to protect them from the Partisans. All this happened on May 8 and it was in the afternoon of this day that we heard that the war in Europe was over. It is remarkable how little we were affected by this news. We have already celebrated our own victory and it had been obvious for some time that complete victory was at hand. When it came we were too busy with our own problems to pay much attention. On the morning of 9 May, the day on which all fighting in Europe officially ceased, the Bde moved into AUSTRIA. The dramatic surrender of General Domanov and Sultan Klyshgirej had been completed at MAUTHEN and the Bde Commander had given his orders to them to concentrate all their forces in assigned areas, when the head of the Bde column wound its way up over the PLOCKEN Pass and crossed the frontier into the Reich, two and a half years to the day after it had first gone into action on the shores of N. AFRICA."[6]

Posterity is greatly indebted to the authors of these war diaries whose accounts are as fresh and vivid as the day they were written. The contrast presented to the desert army as it emerged from the dust-covered plains of Italy into this alpine wonderland, where first encounters were with these extravagant characters from another age, is a story not likely to be repeated.

XI

Cleaning-Up

In order to capture the atmosphere of those first days in Austria, let us have recourse to Brigadier Gerald Verney's account written shortly after he left that country.[1] He was commanding 1 Guards Brigade, which was then under General Horatio Murray's 6 Armoured Division. It must be about 9 May, and they had just crossed the Alps and descended into Villach. He calls it an ugly little town, in a lovely situation.

As soon as he stepped into the centre of the town he was surrounded by people asking questions. A man whom he took to be an Austrian 'collaborator', a Count 'somebody or other' introduced to him a German General, who turned out to be a Russian in German uniform wearing an Iron Cross. The General was a man of forbidding appearance. 'This creature was in command of the Cossacks', writes Verney, 'who were fighting against the Russians and had I known what a terrible record they had in various parts of Europe, I should have acted differently. ... I ought of course, to have arrested him, as he must have been a war criminal, but I did not fully appreciate who he was'.

History does not relate who 'this creature' was. General Domanov's Cossacks had come over the passes which led to Villach. Domanov was a Red Army turncoat, conceivably it could have been he, but whoever it was, he evidently created a very unfavourable impression with the commander of 1 Guards Brigade. The Mayor's secretary then came forward with wine and bread and butter for the officers, as if to symbolise his country's surrender. But, more carefully, he produced a very full statement of the town's resources and condition. Verney was met with a plethora of problems, deputations, complaints and suggestions:

'In many ways it was worse than the war, and by the end of a couple of weeks

73

some of the Brigade Staff were "out"; the Brigade Major, indeed, had to have two days in bed. Everything came at us helter-skelter, in such bewildering confusion, that few of us even had the time on that first afternoon to listen to the Prime Minister's broadcast telling us that we had won the war. . . . It is interesting to record that we had no instructions whatsoever as to what one does when one occupies an enemy city under such circumstances. We got occasional orders about what to do with prisoners and with certain categories of German, but for the most part we just worked at what seemed most important at the time. Looking back on it, it seems that we did all right, in spite of the fact that we always had far too few troops for the many jobs on hand. . . . The matter of first importance was to clear the streets of German uniforms. There were thousands of armed men in and around Villach, but when we came to sort them out we discovered that there was virtually not a single organised unit among them. They were all individual refugees from the Italian, Jugo-Slav and even Russian fronts, men on leave or just out of hospital, and many who lived in this part of Austria and genuinely believed that now the war was over they were free to return to their own homes.'

Villach had been one of the principal German supply bases for the Italian campaign. Guards had to be provided for road blocks and supply dumps of all kinds. The railways were still in working order; hospital trains, goods trains, passenger trains and refugee trains were continually arriving, adding to the congestion of the town to an alarming degree.

Verney's account continues:

'So much so that I decided to stop any more trains from coming in. The only way to do this was to have sections of the line taken up some miles out of town. This raised a great moan from the German Army people. They pointed out that in the case of the line running from Jugo-Slavia the Jugs were in pursuit and would murder the German wounded in the stranded hospital trains. What, they said, was to happen to the poor wounded who could not walk? Verney icily replied it was a pity they invaded Yugoslavia in the first place.'

Allied prisoners of all kinds began appearing. British prisoners were evacuated as soon as possible:

'We soon got our own prisoners to the airfield at Klagenfurt; as already stated, their condition was good, but the lot of the prisoners of other Allied nations was very different. On the first evening at Villach an emaciated figure dressed in thin, striped overalls had walked into Brigade HQ, and speaking perfect English, had introduced himself as Louis Balsan, head of a department in the French Ministry of Finance. For two years, he and six hundred of his compatriots had been interned in a concentration camp on the Loibl Pass, where they had been mercilessly bullied, starved and over-worked; many had been shot or allowed to die for want of medical attention. The day before our arrival the German guards had fled, and the prisoners had seized a train which they managed to bring to a station on the outskirts of Villach. We gave them a lorry-load of captured food, and to many we also gave British uniforms. Balsan was made a temporary Lieutenant in the British Army. All but he went off to Italy, but Balsan remained behind in order to bring his tormentors to justice. He had brought with him detailed records of their crimes, copied at dead of night and at the risk of his life from the SS records in the camp. And now, unrecognisable in his British battledress and dark glasses, he would tour our vast camp at St. Andre and Arnoldstein, looking closely into the face of each man and occasionally pausing to point out an individual to his British escort. *"Et voila un autre"*. He was never wrong.'

The next passage in Gerald Verney's account conjures up a picture of the extraordinary enmities which had arisen between Hitler's former allies:

'There seemed to be no limit to the number of nationalities who appealed to us for protection. The Germans wanted to be safe-guarded against Tito, the Cossacks against the Bulgarians, the Chetniks against the Croats, the White Russians against the Red ones, the Austrians against the Slovenes, the Hungarians against everyone else, and vice versa and contrariwise all through the list. This part of Austria had become the sink of Europe. Not only was it the refuge for many Nazi war criminals, but also of comparatively inoffensive people fleeing from the Russians or Tito, unwanted and all but persecuted wherever they went.'

The following message received on 14 May from Divisional Headquarters gives some idea of the problem:

'Three hundred thousand Germans and two hundred thousand Croats, the greater part of them armed, are moving across the Jug border, although they have all nominally surrendered to Tito. They have with them only enough rations for 48 hours, and are accompanied by thirty thousand horses and two thousand motor vehicles. Eighth Army have been urgently asked for a decision whether we are to accept the surrender of these forces or oblige them to return to Jugo-Slavia. Pending the decision you will hold them South of the Drava.'

Contained in this passage was the clue to much of the subsequent story. It had been agreed between the Allies that surrendering enemy should only be accepted by the armies whom they were facing (and by inference fighting). It was therefore entirely right and proper that as they had formally surrendered to Tito, but preferred the custodial arrangements of others, they should be returned to him.

Another unexpected problem is the surrender of the Hungarian Army to 1 Guards Brigade. An officer arrived one day and said they would like to surrender. As it was very hot, the Brigadier and his staff captain only wore shorts and shirts. Rather reminiscent of the scene at Luneburg Heath, the Hungarian staff were dressed most formally. 'About a dozen Generals being present, all in their best clothes, field boots, high collars, gloves and medals'.

At about this time, Gerald Verney was becoming quite exasperated by the multitude of problems he had to face. He wrote home to his wife,

'It is becoming a sort of nightmare life. The size and number of the problems are immense and increasing, and what makes it much worse there appears to be no settled policy up above. We had about 5 or 6 changes of plan yesterday. As a result my staff, the CO's, Adjts and Coy. Comds, who are being worked to the bone anyhow, and are so "bobbery" that they are almost impossible to deal with.'[2]

The roads were another problem. For he tells us in his account that 'the roads were littered with thousands upon thousands of weapons of all calibres, abandoned by the retreating Germans and their satellites'. This was the very same scene that Macmillan had witnessed many years before in the Winter War, in Finland.[3]

Let us end on a more cheerful note, Verney pours out his admiration of the English soldier in another letter home to his wife,

'I visited the most lovely castle overlooking the river, and had a wonderful view up and down the valley and across to the Yugo-Slav mountains. With my glasses I could see all the Tit vehicles, and also see the Guardsmen standing about like London policemen eyeing the Tits and ready to say "you can't do that there 'ere". What this country, England I mean, owes to the ordinary English soldier and his young officer is realised by few people. They, and they alone, are responsible for the fact that we have not had a second Greece, or out and out war with Jugo-Slavia. If the Foreign Office foresaw the problem, they certainly did nothing about it, and we never had the slightest warning of what was in store for us from Udine onwards. I hope you will propagate this among all our friends.'

There is one salutary fact about Gerald Verney's account. There is no mention of the repatriations in which his brigade were involved. Perhaps we should take cognizance of this fact, and put the repatriations in the context of the times, and understand who our enemies really were.

But Gerald Verney was not unconcerned about the operation that his guardsmen had to undertake. Thanks to the researches of Tony Cowgill, the diary of Major Mennell, GSO2 HQ 6 Armoured Division, has come to light.[5] Mennell had been to see the embarkation of Yugoslavs at Rosenbach Station, with an officer from 5 Corps. On arrival at HQ 3 Welsh Guards, he met a worried Brigadier Gerald Verney who handed him a questionnaire, which ran as follows:

'Where do British hand-over Croats to Tito, and where does British responsibility end?
(Answer: *As soon as train leaves they are his.*)'

'What action is to be taken by British troops if Croats object to entraining or embussing and Titos use violence?
(Answer: *Try and persuade, if no use do nothing.*)'

'Are British troops to stand by and see women and children killed?
(Answer: *Obviously not and very unlikely to arise.*)'

'What action is to be taken by British troops if Croats refuse to embus to RV with Tito?

(Answer: *Persuasion but no force*.)'

Mennell, presumably provided the answers, and noted with some relief at the end of the passage,

'In point of fact the whole thing went off without any trouble at all.'

So now let us follow the fortunes of Brigadier Musson's 36 Infantry Brigade.

XII

The Melting-Pot

We left 36 Infantry Brigade on 9 May, as the head of the column wound its way over the Plöcken Pass, into Austria. A minor pass over the Carinthian Alps but none the less an impressive one. The two ridges making up the pass are separated by a broad valley through which runs the River Gail, close by the little town of Mauthen. As you climb up the second ridge, it becomes a spectacular winding road. A typical alpine pass, with on the lower slopes, beech trees, and as one goes higher, spruce, then sheer rock and snow.

After entering Austria, the next few days were spent in settling in both themselves and the surrendered Russians, the companies in the little villages which abounded in this area, and the Cossacks and Caucasians in the fields outside the villages. Brigade Headquarters was set up at Oberdrauberg.

As they wound down into the broad valley of the River Drau, they would have seen in front of them a wall of snow-capped mountains, the Hohe Tauern Alps in East Tirol, culminating in the massive Gross Glockner group – as dramatic an arrival as one could possibly imagine.

The 36 Brigade diarist tells us:

'The part of AUSTRIA we were occupying was by nature very much the same as those northern boundaries of ITALY we had traversed during the previous week, but there the similarity ended. It was not difficult to realise that one was in a different country. The people were blonde instead of dark, the houses were built in a more modern, less enduring manner, the churches were much less ornate and more recently built. The general air of cleanliness about everything, the people, the houses, the streets, was very foreign to the Italian scene. Where we had been accustomed in ITALY to living in the splendour of a mansion or the squalor of a cottage, we now found ourselves occupying buildings similar to those we had known at home. We felt that we were now in a "civilised" country according to the town dweller's idea of civilisation. The general air of tidiness, however, was marred by the countless hundreds of displaced persons, both civilians and soldiers, who, overtaken by our victorious advance, were now a source of constant worry to us. Most of them were German soldiers who could be dealt with comparatively easily. Prisoner of war cages were set up locally in which they were impounded. At LIENZ we found the Franz Josef Barracks where about a thousand men from almost as many different units were formed into a composite battalion. At MAUTHEN, a divisional prisoner of war cage capable of taking 5,000 men was opened. Every available vehicle was commandeered to evacuate prisoners to these cages. Several thousands had thus passed through our hands when supply overtook demand and we had to call a temporary halt to evacuation. This still left us many hundreds of unemployed German soldiers whom we were obliged to maintain and administer. Within the Corps a great deal of sorting out and transferring of German units took place, and an enormous amount of staff work was involved – much of it to very little purpose.'[1]

Their task was greatly helped by 'the German's own native ability to organise and be organised', so that by the end of the month matters were well in hand. But they had a greater problem in sorting out the hordes of foreign civilians, who now seemed to be concentrated in this part of Austria.

The diarist gives a vivid picture of this melting-pot of broken armies and countless refugees.

'Civilians of almost every European nationality were an even greater problem. There were many such displaced persons (DP). Civilians are of course an AMG responsibility, but as yet no AMG had been set up locally. The whole burden of responsibility thus fell on our shoulders. Much of this burden we were able to shift on to the Teutonic shoulders of the local *burgomeisters*, but with each individual civilian considering himself or herself a special case and giving a far from brief outline of his or her life story to prove a point, our time was fully occupied. What made our task more difficult was that it was not enough to know a man's nationality to decide how to deal with him. Was he a Jugoslav? Then he might be a Serbian Chetnik who had fought against Tito, but professed undying love for ENGLAND. Or he might be a Tito Partisan, captured by the Germans but now escaped and trying to make his way back to JUGO-SLAVIA. Or again he might be a member of Pavelich's infamous *Ustachi*, who would no doubt attempt to conceal his identity. Was he a Russian? Then he could be a runaway Cossack, or an escaped Red Army prisoner, or a Latvian who left LATVIA before it became part of the Soviet Union, or a displaced Soviet citizen who just did not want to go back home. Was he Italian? Then was he a Fascist or a Democrat, a patriot or a traitor? And so on ...

The one category of DPs we were able and glad to deal with straightaway were those of our own prisoners whom we found in the area. These amounted to several hundreds who were quickly despatched home by bomber. There were also many hundreds of Frenchmen who had been in captivity since the fall of FRANCE; many of them had been working on the land. The treatment of these prisoners received seemed to vary according to their accounts, but there could be little doubt about the treatment meted out to the unfortunate Russian and Polish prisoners who formed the vast majority of Germany's slave-workers. And there could be little doubt of the apprehension with which the local Austrians viewed the release of these victims of their oppression. Nationals, other than British or French, were for the most part difficult to evacuate immediately, and DP camps were set up at LIENZ and SPITTAL (X 1600), where this unfortunate human jetsam awaited repatriation to a country many had not seen for five years. With these enormous numbers of people of all nationalities moving around in the area there was bound to be a percentage of wanted men – men whose continued freedom would be a menace to the Allied Armies of Occupation. Among these could be classed all civil and military members of the SS, all German Intelligence personnel, Gestapo, Todt organisation workers, paratroops, and of course any high members of the Nazi Party. All such, when apprehended were evacuated to ITALY where their cases could be investigated at leisure. Naturally, enough, these men knew they were "wanted" and took every precaution to avoid arrest.' [2]

This gives some idea of the size of the task facing 5 Corps who were at that time very thin on the ground.

Some graphic evidence of conditions in Carinthia at that time was heard in the Court case Aldington v Tolstoy and Watts, from two former British Officers. [3]

John Stanley Shuter (a retired Crown Civil Servant) had been a captain in the Royal Horse Artillery in 6 Armoured Division, and had been based with his regiment in the area north of Klagenfurt. He was asked by Mr. Gray, Counsel for the Plaintiff (Lord Aldington) for his recollections on conditions in Carinthia, and he replied;

'Well, it appears to me that the area was one of great surprise. We had been fighting a war against a simple enemy, so far as we knew. We arrived in Klagenfurt in the province of Carinthia to find an extraordinary melting-pot of displaced persons of one kind and another. The villages we ourselves occupied had French and Belgian, some English, some South Africa, prisoners who were more or less anxious to get home. The whole area was very deeply involved with German Army wounded. An enormous number of amputees. The whole of the lake district outside Klagenfurt was a convalescent area. It was a very sad sight to see thousands upon thousands of young German men with an arm or a leg missing.

The Austrian population itself was in a very poor state. There were practically no young adult men: there were boys and there were old men and women, but there were no others. They were very short of physical labour. They were short of fuel. All their inter-structural machinery, their water supplies were very much in need of maintenance. There were many Ukranian prisoners who had been working on the farms who had been very happily established there who, again had to be gathered together. The whole area was an absolute "melting-pot" and must have been an administrative nightmare.' [4]

Shuter's evidence, conjures up an extraordinary picture of those days. Now let us see what a former staff officer at 5 Corps HQ has to say. His job was to deal with all personnel matters. Major Taylor (now Judge Taylor) is being cross-examined by Mr. Gray. Gray again asks him to describe the conditions in Austria and if he had encountered the Titoists. Judge Taylor:

'I heard they were in Klagenfurt and so I went to have a look. Klagenfurt was at that time a most extraordinary place. It was full of civilian people milling about, not very sensibly, in every different direction. There were Yugoslav troops, male and female, carrying out some form of patrol. The males had their rifles slung over their shoulder and the females had grenades tied to their belts, each of them that I saw had two grenades on their left hip and two grenades on their right hip. There was a placard, which I saw, which was interpreted to me. I cannot tell you what it means. It was a placard or proclamation by some-body, I have forgotten who, saying Carinthia belongs to the Yugoslavs and "Long Live Tito".'

'What were your personal problems? What where you having to tackle?'

'After fratting had gone [the non-fraternisation policy], the next question was the one the last witness mentioned, medical. You see underneath everything was the question of leave. People wanted to get home but anything came on top of that. There was a perfectly frightful business. Somebody complained that there was a frightful smell on the road going into Klagenfurt. So we sent the hygiene man. He said it was gangrene, and so it was. The last witness had got it exactly right, there were several houses full of German soldiers who had their legs amputated, whose doctors had gone and left one or two medical orderlies who were doing the best they could. Brigadier Bailey, the DDMS said that something had got to be done about it and indeed of course it had. And everything had to be stopped while those who could be saved were saved and those who could be attended to were evacuated. Bang goes transport!'[5]

Then the regular peacetime administrative procedures had to be attended to. Enemy action of course meant the automatic 'write-off' of any equipment, but any other kind of loss had to be accounted for, hence the use made of the invaluable enemy shell!

'On top of it all was the anxiety about the Russians. They had come further than they were supposed to come. They showed no inclination of coming any further, thanks I think almost entirely to General Charles Keightley, but they showed no indication of going back. Then on top of it all there came a day when the Russian came in to claim his prisoners. I have forgotten his name but it is in the log which I saw, but you will remind me about that later.'[6]

Taylor is asked how many men there were in the Corps, and he guesses 25,000. How many of those men were on guard duty? He could not tell the figure, but from the observations he got from division and elsewhere, a very substantial proportion. The fact that there were only 25,000 men in the Corps available at that time for disarming and guard duties should not be lost sight of. Alexander had despatched a skeleton force to occupy Carinthia, it being vital to prevent the consolidation of Tito's forces and any further incursions by the Russians. At a conservative estimate, there were a million people for Keightley's men to feed and guard, which largely explains Alexander's subsequent actions.

What about the operational position as regards the Titoists? It was not strictly his business but he knew enough about it,

> 'To describe our position as very shaky indeed. We were as it were at the bows of a ship. On our right hand side were the Yugoslavs who, if they had come into our territory could I think have easily overwhelmed us.'

Half left, in front, there were the Russians who were further forward than they should have been. They showed no sign of coming further forward, but they showed no sign of going back. Taylor concluded:

> 'I rather suspected that the Yugoslav's would do what the Russians told them rather than what we asked them, but I would describe our condition as shaky.'[7]

Of course there were degrees of perception as to what was happening. The public at large in Britain, and probably in the United States, felt very strongly attached to our allies, Russia and Yugoslavia. They were heroes and they had been standing shoulder to shoulder with us against the hated common enemy. The newspapers had told them so, and they could see with their own eyes what catastrophe might have befallen without our allies. Maybe they were communists, but that was something for 'after the war'. It was the same by and large with the troops, for they it was who had at long last joined hands with our allies and cemented the longed-for union.

At the other end of the scale was quite a different perception amongst those who had the responsibility for conducting the war and who had to deal with these 'allies' on a day to day basis. They were under no illusions as to the 'nature of the beast'. Here was a wolf in sheep's clothing who was every bit as dangerous, if not more so, than our former adversary, Nazi Germany.

XIII

Sorting Out the Armies of Europe

At the time of these events, Brigadier T P D Scott was commander of the 38 (Irish) Infantry Brigade. The Brigade War Diary is an outstanding example of the concise but intelligible military record. But alas space forbids access to this source of knowledge.

However, the personal account written by Scott himself shortly after these events were over must rank as one of the classics of war and peace in those turbulent days, somewhat reminiscent of Captain Gronow's escapades in the Peninsula war.[1] I am indebted to the Regimental Museum of the Royal Irish Fusiliers for being allowed to quote from it.[2]

First of all a little scene-setting. It is 9 May, 38 Brigade are now advancing into Austria, and they receive new orders from the Corps Commander. Scott is told that he will do well if he gets his brigade concentrated round Wolfsberg by the following evening.

> 'We Settle Frontiers
> The only people to the east of us at the moment were the 27 Lancers [an armoured car regiment], under Andrew Porter. Their RHQ, was at Wolfsberg, and they had squadrons reaching out toward Graz. They had contacted the Russians. Our job was to come in behind them and stabilise the situation. To do this we would obviously have to push out quickly in all directions in order to contact the Russians on all likely lines of approach ... our task was to make contact with the Russians, a problem we didn't know much about; to get some order out of chaos ensuing from the retreating Army Group South-East, and Army Group East, and to disarm its assorted membership, and to deal with the "Jugs".'

Once at Wolfsberg and in contact with the Lancers, he realised that the trouble was further south:

> 'We never had a moment's difficulty with the Russians: everything was done most correctly and with the minimum waste of time.
> As soon as the "Faughs" [Royal Irish Fusiliers] got to St. Andra they collected up 1,200 SS troops. These were the only sort we really bothered much about. All other types were just more or less shuffled backwards under their own steam,

but the SS were given a special form of treatment all to themselves. They were the one type that we were definitely not prepared to have running spare about the country, either now or in the future. The SS were to be eliminated for all time.

There was one very difficult principle that we were up against which I did not really know about to start with, and that was in accordance with the general surrender everyone was supposed to surrender to the Allied Army against whom they had been fighting. Everyone in this part of the world had obviously been fighting against either the Russians or the Yugoslavs, but the devil of it was that they were prepared to do anything rather than surrender to either of these armies.

When I got to my new Headquarters, which was an imposing-looking building in the middle of the town, several deputations were already waiting there. There was a German Corps Commander, a Hungarian Divisional Commander, and a number of other erstwhile centurions. I did not know about the Hungarian Army – apparently that was in our midst too.

While I was dealing with these people I got word that the Bulgarian Army was bearing down on us. There was word of a Croatian Army doing something somewhere, and there were a lot of Cossacks alleged to be running wild to the south-east. Which sides all these people belonged to I had some difficulty in determining. The Bulgarians turned out to be Allies, and the Croats and Hungarians were enemies, as, of course, were the Cossacks, who had changed sides when things had looked black for Russia.

I told the Hungarians to say where they were and look after themselves, which they seemed quite willing to do. I told the Germans to push off to the west, and then devoted my attention to the Bulgarians.'

The Bulgarians were surging along in a westerly and north-westerly direction. At Lavamund, a platoon of 'Faughs' had been placed to try and hold the fort. The whole village was seething with Bulgarians who were terrifying the local populace.

He found in the village inn the Bulgarian Corps Commander and a Divisional Commander.

'In the village, too, were about a hundred British prisoners of war who had been in a prison camp there. As soon as the Germans had gone, these fellows, under command of three of their sergeants, had organised themselves into a company in the most businesslike and efficient way, and had promptly proclaimed the town to be British. These lads were worth their weight in gold. They knew the local form, and several of them were first class interpreters. I got a rough picture of what was going on from them, and then took one of them to the inn in the hopes that the Bulgarians would talk some known language.

Eventually the Bulgars produced somebody who spoke German. Talking through two interpreters can be a very slow and irksome business, especially if a large part of the time has to be spent in exchanging windy compliments on the magnificence of each others' Army, and the pleasure both sides have in meeting on this auspicious occasion. The trouble was that the last thing they wanted was to meet other people. They wanted to get as far as possible and collect up as much loot as possible before they met anyone likely to stem their tide.'

The Bulgars were cagey about establishing mixed road posts as had been done on equally embarrassing occasions with the Yugoslavs. 'They were a small country and unfortunately had not had an opportunity of studying the culture of the great nations like England and America', said the Bulgars. Therefore 'mixed road posts' were off! Scott then larded them with further compliments, but as he wrote:

> 'All this was a little far-fetched as none of us had even heard of them two hours before, and if we had we would probably have mistaken the side on which they fought.'

They were then packed off in a car to see the Corps Commander Keightley.

> 'As soon as they had gone, I was set upon by all sorts of people in the street: Hungarians wanting to be taken away by us; civilians who had been experiencing some of the fruits of victory at the hands of the Bulgarians; Germans who were begging to be removed; Yugoslavs who were trying to get through and were being stopped by the Bulgarians; Bulgarians who complained that they were about to be attacked by 5,000 Cossacks; and our own prisoners of war, who had the Cossacks all round their camp. There was the father and mother of a "party" going on.'

These Cossacks must have been General Von Pannwitz's 15 Cossack Cavalry Corps which had been fighting on the Yugoslav front against the Titoists. Scott now had the ingenious idea of trying to make the Bulgars (whose responsibility it really was) take the surrender of the Cossacks:

> 'Earlier that day I had had an order from 6 Armoured Division to disarm and accept the surrender of 21,000 Cossacks, who were reported to be near Dravograd, further to the east and well inside Yugoslavia. I supposed that these were part of the contingent in question, if not the whole lot. 6 Armoured Division, of course had never heard of the Bulgarian Army. Further enquiries revealed that these Cossacks were a real menace to everybody, and that unless something was done, and done quickly, there was going to be no ordinary shambles in the midst of this representative body of nations. There was a German SS battalion offering fight also.
>
> I asked the Bulgarian, therefore, in whose area these Cossacks now appeared to be, if they would be good enough to disarm them and remove them quickly. This they said they were quite unable to do, as the Cossacks would resist them, and they had not enough men for a fight. I do not think that "fighting" was item No. 1 on their agenda at that moment anyway! They thought it would be an excellent idea if I disarmed them. There was only Murphy Palmer [CO of the "Faughs"] and myself, with a couple of drivers and a platoon of "Faughs" somewhere scattered about in the village, so that if strength of arms was required to deal with the Cossacks, the Bulgarians compared very favourably with us. The Bulgarians' only real worry concerned the final destination of the Cossacks' arms. I said I did not care a brass button what happened to the arms, and that they could have them if they liked. As soon as the Bulgarians saw the

way the wind was blowing over the matter of this booty, they implored me to disarm the Cossacks before everybody got killed by them.'

Scott now sets off for the Cossacks camp with Murphy Palmer to take the surrender of these desperate echelons single-handedly.

'One of the prisoner of war sergeants knew where the Cossacks were, so I told the Bulgarians that I would disarm them and give them the weapons provided they guaranteed that the Cossacks should pass through them to the British area. This they were only too keen to do. Murphy and I accordingly got in the jeep and drove up to the Cossacks' camp, leaving word for any of the "Faughs" platoon that could be spared to come along up there and join us.

We arrived in the Cossack camp, where there was an incredible array of cut-throats all armed to the teeth, some in defensive positions around the perimeter of their camp. We drove straight past all these to what appeared to be their Headquarters and summoned the head boy.

I asked him if he proposed to surrender to the Bulgarians in accordance with the terms of the general surrender.

This, he said, was quite out of the question. All his men would fight before doing that.

I told him that he would be outlawed if he did not surrender.

He said he was quite prepared to surrender, provided it was to the British.

I therefore accepted his surrender and told him to get cracking straight away, and in a very short time all his warriors were filing past outside the house putting their arms in a heap, but as there were 5,000 of them it was nearly dark before they had finished. I thought that if we tried to get them through the Bulgarians in darkness there would be certain to be a row, so I decided to put off their march to the west until the next morning.

They complained that they would be attacked by the Bulgarians during the night.

I assured them that they would not, and that I had an adequate guard to stop that. The adequate guard consisted of about eighteen "Faughs", who were now peacefully "brewing up" in the middle of the party, not bothering their heads about any of the strange nations that were surrounding them. The amazing thing that one discovered at this time was that one British soldier was quite enough to restore order and prevent one of these nations attacking another. The one thing nobody was prepared to do was to have a row with the British.'

Scott soon discovered that most of the Cossack senior officers were Germans, one of whom had a nice red-setter bought in Dublin before the war, upon which he cast envious eyes. 'Looking back on it I think I was a fool. The dog was bound to be taken off him before long'.

He then deployed the 'Faughs' platoon between the Cossacks and the Bulgarians for the night and left them to it, expecting the Cossacks to be marched out under British guard at 5.30 a.m. the next morning. Nothing happened. 'Had the whole place gone up in smoke or what?' wondered the Brigadier. All was well, after a slight delay, the Cossack column came marching through Lavamund with one 'Faugh' on a horse at their head. This was quite sufficient to ensure that both sides did what they were supposed to do!

The Corps Commander arrived just as the Cossack column was beginning to show up, and said that by agreement with the Russians, the Cossacks should have been handed over to them and the Brigadier's action might therefore produce some international incident. The Bulgarians, however, later admitted that they were under Russian command, and they had no authority to hand them over, but they had done it on their own to save an 'incident'. The Bulgarians got their 'loot', but they greedily demanded the Cossack horses too. On this Scott was adamant. If the Cossacks had no transport they wouldn't be able to march!

An interesting summary is given at the end of this section of his journal showing the kind of problems which a British brigade had to deal with during those first few days of 'peace'.

> 'Apart from prisoners on the move, we had on our ration strength on the 14th a fairly representative cross-section. They were:
>
> 17th Field Regiment Area. – 7,000 Cossacks, 3,000 369th Croat Division, 700 Army Group "E" Headquarters, 300 42nd Jaeger Division, 1,100 miscellaneous.
>
> London Irish Area. – 7,000 Laszlo Hungarian Division, 400 Hungarian Cadet School, 2,000 2nd Hungarian Corps, 700 Croats, 1,600 SS.
>
> Royal Irish Fusiliers Area. – 1,300 wounded on hospital trains, 10,000 miscellaneous.'[3]

In addition to the above there were a fair number of what we have already come to know as 'displaced persons'. Scott's maxim for a DP is characteristic of him. A displaced person, the journal recollected 'is merely somebody who is in his wrong country through no apparent fault of his own'.

PART FOUR

HOW WE ALMOST STUMBLED INTO WORLD WAR THREE

XIV

The Crisis Deepens: Is Russia Backing Tito Or Is It All a Bluff? 9–11 May

We have had a vivid impression in the last chapter, from the pen of Brigadier Pat Scott, of the turmoil which existed in the little province of Carinthia in the first few days after the war was over. Now let us renew our acquaintance with diplomatic channels where the wires have become red-hot.

On the morning of 9 May, the British Ambassador in Rome was reporting to the Foreign Office remarks made by the communist leader Signor Togliatti to the effect that the Allies would not stand up to Tito as the latter had Russian support. And at the meeting of Italian Ministers the previous night he had declared, that the Allies must have come to some agreement with Marshal Tito recognising his territorial rights; and if the Allies knew Tito had Russian backing they would not resist his demands.[1] Although our Ambassador was somewhat sceptical as to Togliatti's information, the latter was a trained communist with a foot in either camp and was in as good a position as any to assess communist intentions. So this was the crucial question. Was Russia backing Tito? Or was it all a bluff?

That evening Macmillan telegraphed the Foreign Office.

'*Important*
    In addition to trouble over Venizia Giulia Tito is engaged in a scamper into Austria and [Yugoslavs] are generally engaged in an attempt to make good their claims by *de facto* possession. As you know these include the Klagenfurt area. Situation is becoming very embarrassing to local British commanders ... some clear instructions must soon be issued as to whether he [Alexander] is to order 8 Army to close Austrian frontier to Yugoslavs and eject them from the positions they have infiltrated.'[2]

Macmillan ended by saying that the Field Marshal and he, felt that Carinthia was in a different category to Venezia Giulia. For the former, agreement between the four powers on occupation had been reached, but there had been no such agreement about Italian territory.

Events now follow thick and fast, and as far as possible I follow the course of events in date order.

10 MAY 1945

The first telegram of any significance comes from Lord Halifax, our Ambassador in Washington, to the Foreign Office, where it would have been immediately transmitted to the Foreign Secretary, Anthony Eden. It was copied of course to all other interested missions, Belgrade, Moscow, Caserta.

> *'DIPLOMATIC (SECRET)*   1.37 pm.
> (This telegram is of particular secrecy and should be retained by the authorised recipient and not passed on).
>
> I am informed in confidence by State Department that United States Government takes a very serious view of the attitude of Yugoslav Government, not only in regard to Venezia Giulia but also Klagenfurt area. They are of course conscious that Yugoslav Government would not be acting in this manner without feeling sure (rightly or wrongly) of tacit Soviet support.
>
> United States Government are therefore now prepared to take a very much stronger line than has hitherto seemed likely and I understand that a message from President to Prime Minister to this general effect will be going off very soon.'[3]

A follow-up telegram, at 3.10 pm. follows, from Foreign Office to Caserta, 'Please ensure that Field Marshal Alexander sees.'

This later message crosses with the following from Macmillan (No. 844) to Foreign Office dispatched at 3.50 pm., reporting results of Alexander's Chief of Staff, General Morgan's visit to Marshall Tito in Belgrade to put forward a *modus vivendi* for the Venezia Giulia confrontation. The following is an extract.

> 'Following is General Morgan's report of his final interview with Marshal Tito.
>
> Marshal Tito said that he was sorry he could not accept Field Marshal Alexander's proposals. His reason for that was that as his troops had liberated the territory, which is Slovene, he considered that they had a right to occupy it as an Allied army on account of their services and sacrifices in the Allied cause. He further mentioned that at the peace conference he would claim the territory to the west of the Isonzo. In view of this he pointed out that the matter had taken on a predominantly political significance.
>
> He offered Field Marshal Alexander the full and unrestricted use of the port of Trieste and the communications he required, and he considered that this should meet all reasonable military requirements.'[4]

Tito then went on to suggest other facilities that the Allies might have, but he insisted that he alone should exercise civil control over the province, for which he now claimed areas west of the Isonzo River.

Later that afternoon Alexander explains this latest development in a signal (F.73280), to the CIGS Brooke.

> 'Personal for CIGS from Field Marshal Alexander. Morgan has just returned from BELGRADE. Tito has refused my proposed agreement and put forward counter proposals of his own from which it will be seen that the whole argument has now been lifted from a military problem to a political issue . . . [as] a responsible commander, I can NOT accept Marshal Tito's proposals since they deny me full control and responsibility for my own L of C which is obviously an impossible position over a long term.'[5]

The Foreign Office (and this will be Anthony Eden) now sends a sharp note (Telegram No. 546) to Belgrade at 11.25 pm.

> 'Please address the following communication to Marshal Tito.
> "As one of the steps required to implement the Moscow Declaration of November 1st, 1943, about the re-establishment of a free and independent Austria it has been agreed that Austria, within her 1937 frontiers, will be jointly occupied by British, American, Russian and French forces. The British zone of occupation contains the territory bordering the 1937 Austro-Yugoslav frontier. British troops have entered Austria and are in the process of taking up their positions in the zone allotted to them. His Majesty's Government must ask that all Yugoslav forces which are at present in Austria should immediately be withdrawn and that the Yugoslav Government will respect the 1937 frontier as the provisional boundary between Austria and Yugoslavia pending the final settlement of frontiers at the peace table." '[6]

This was not quite an ultimatum. There was no time limit, nor was the telegram signed by Eden, but it was the usual diplomatic way of implying that there would be more pressure to come if Tito failed to respond. It was the first round only.

11 MAY

Churchill has been ruminating meantime on the latest developments and at 56 minutes past midnight he sends this message. Personal, Top Secret to Field Marshal Alexander. 'Would it help if I sent the following message to Marshal Tito?' asks Churchill, and then gives his draft.

> *'PRIME MINISTER TO MARSHAL TITO*
> 1. I have received a lot of telegrams from Field Marshal Alexander. I earnestly and devoutly hope you will not take any action which leads your troops into armed conflict with ours. Field Marshal Alexander has been instructed to make a heavy concentration of all arms upon the British front facing your men in Venezia Giulia. It would be a great mistake I am sure for you to make an

attack upon him. In such circumstances he has already the fullest authority to reply.

2. I see no reason why this trial of strength should take place because all questions of sovereignty in this area are reserved for the peace table and may be settled there harmoniously after all claims have been taken into consideration. As I gave you all support at our disposal in the days of your weakness and tribulation, I greatly hope that you will not try to anticipate the decision of the Great Powers at the peace table by violent local action, for which we are none-the-less fully prepared both in willpower and in arms.

Message Ends.'[7]

This message is never sent to Tito, but shows what was going through Churchill's mind at the time. It is marked GUARD which means that it is not for American eyes.

At a quarter to six in the morning Alexander sends a routine message to the Combined Chiefs of Staff in Washington and also to the British Chiefs of Staff in London reporting Morgan's visit and Tito's counter proposals. Morgan is convinced that Tito will not give way on the issue of sovereignty in the area and considers his own plan perfectly workable. Morgan believes that this question is now outside the military realm and should be taken up by Allied Governments. If the governments intend to reject Marshal Tito's proposals, they should certainly be prepared to use force, with all its implications. At the end of this message Alexander repeats the last message he has sent to Tito which terminates. 'Meanwhile I propose to use the Port of Trieste to maintain my forces in north east Italy and Austria. I trust you will take steps to ensure that no regrettable incidents occur.'[8]

General McCreery, commander of the 8th Army is now getting gravely concerned about the situation and the effect it will have on British prestige and at 10 o'clock in the morning sends a message to Alexander. His first concern is the depredations being made by Tito's Yugoslavs on food for the civil population in the Trieste area. The Yugoslav armies are 'living off the country' and large scale requisitioning is taking place. It is known that 2,000 tons have been moved from the Udine area. He feels that 'our troops cannot stand by and see civilians without food'.

Allied Military Government is being flouted in certain areas, most seriously in the Cormons and Tarvisio areas where our posters are being torn down.

'My considered opinion is that unless we can support AMG in these areas by force it necessary we must withdraw rather than be flouted. Tarvisio is a key point in our L of C.'

Finally General McCreery considers that the area of operations is too big for the British 8th Army only, which should be responsible for Austria with American 5th Army taking over Venezia Giulia.[9]

At 6.30 pm Alexander sends him a sharp reply. Personal for General McCreery from Field Marshal Alexander.

> 'I have seen your telegram. I am afraid you do not realise the serious implications behind this affair. At this very moment I am in direct communication with London, Washington and Belgrade. This affair is now on the highest level. Macmillan will explain it to you when he arrives.'[10]

Alexander is obviously fussed about drifting into hostilities with Tito before his own state of readiness, and the full implications have been assessed. This message presages a forthcoming visit by Macmillan to 8th Army to brief McCreery on these matters.

At 8.35 pm Macmillan reports to the Foreign Office an added twist to the situation, that Tito has entered Austria and already occupies a number of points, furthermore that Tito informed Morgan that he had made an official request to the Great Powers, to be allowed to share in occupying Austria which had received a favourable reply from Moscow. Had a formal reply been dispatched to Tito by 'Allied Governments', refusing this request? A Foreign Office internal memorandum comments that both Macmillan and Alexander must think that 'this has been put into a pigeonhole and forgotten', but in point of fact HMG had already made its attitude clear by demanding the withdrawal of the Yugoslavs from Carinthia.[11]

At 9.00 pm on this exceptionally busy day, 11 May, Macmillan sends an important telegram to the Foreign Office (No. 853) on possible courses of action, which is the subject of several exchanges over the next few days. He first refers to the British and United States Ambassadors' (in Belgrade) joint proposal that Tito should be issued with a 'virtual ultimatum'. Macmillan proposes four possible courses of action,

(a) to issue an ultimatum referred to above,

(b) to accept Tito's proposals and withdrawing most of our forces west of the Isonzo River,

(c) to concede Tito as a partner in occupying ex-enemy territory under certain safeguards. If not accepted by him the United States and United Kingdom Governments would withdraw their ambassadors as an act of disapproval. They would not attempt therefore to expel Tito by force. And the fourth proposed course,

(d) to attempt a settlement for part of the disputed territory and dispose of the remainder in six months.[12]

Macmillan's immediately following telegram (No. 854) contains his comments on the above in a rather long rambling dissertation. The only points of which we need take note are in his preamble. First, he mirrors Alexander's views concurrently being expressed to the Prime Minister, about the state of mind of the troops. For goodness sake, he seems to say to the Foreign Secretary, take into consideration all implications over here and at home.

> 'We might find ourselves involved in open hostilities with Jugoslavia, and it is more than doubtful if either British or American troops would, after so many years of weary warfare, embark on a new campaign except with extreme reluctance. Many months of pro-Tito propaganda have convinced Allied troops generally of the genuineness of his cause and of the great service which he has rendered the Allies. It would be difficult if not impossible to persuade them that Tito had suddenly changed his colour and was no longer the paragon he had been so consistently painted. Nor must we forget President Truman's warning that he does not want to see United States troops involved in the Balkan arena.'

Second, he speculates as to whether Tito is bluffing.

> 'Of course, Tito may be bluffing. It is evident that his political as opposed to his military entourage are nervous. Mr. Stevenson [UK Ambassador Belgrade] who is in a position to judge on the spot, clearly believes, with his United States colleague, that Tito will yield if his bluff is called. Nevertheless it is dangerous to make this assumption unless we are in practice in a position and willing to go to extremes. It would be fatal to attempt a counter-bluff. Strong action should not, I think, be contemplated until you have seen the Field Marshal's military appreciation ... this appreciation must, of course, be based on the assumption of no direct military support from Russia.'[13]

XV

History Repeats Itself
12–13 May

There was a chilling similarity between the situation now developing and that over which we originally went to war, five years previously. Both periods were marked by territorial aggression. Both dictators used hapless minority peoples as their pawns. Tito and Hitler both subscribed to the theory that 'might was right'. But Tito had an immensely powerful backer in Stalin. Any sign of weakness or appeasement on the part of the Western Allies might simply lead to further demands and goodness knows what else. The only difference between 1945 and 1939 was that then we had enjoyed peace for 20 years. Now our fragile peace had not yet lasted 20 days. The period immediately after the end of hostilities is a blank on the map of history. How little we know of the political and military manoeuvrings of that time. For the war was over and the curtain rang down on that stage. The new scene was switched to home events and the birth pangs of a new social and economic order. Even the war in Japan was to fizzle out quite soon, as it proved to be. But let us follow the sequence of events to their conclusion.

12 MAY 1945

Shortly after midnight, Macmillan at Caserta sends the Foreign Office a routine situation report. 5 Corps have two brigades established forward in Austria, one in Klagenfurt, the other in Villach, a third brigade is sitting astride the border at Tarvisio. The Yugoslav 14 Division has about 4,000 men over the Austrian frontier and moving north-west towards Klagenfurt and Villach. [1]

This is followed shortly afterwards by another from Macmillan announcing:

'At Field Marshal Alexander's suggestion I am making a short visit to 8th Army Headquarters and 13 Corps tomorrow in order to put Generals McCreery and Harding fully in the picture. I hope to be back ... [undecipherable] ... on morning of May 13.'[2]

At nine o'clock in the morning another message is sent by Alexander to Tito, this time about Yugoslav troops in Austria. He sets out the position reminding Tito that he has been ordered by the British and United States governments to occupy and administer the Austrian Provinces of Styria and Carinthia. His troops have occupied Villach and Klagenfurt and also made junction with the Russians. His Allied Military Government has been proclaimed. After referring to Tito's request for an occupation zone in Austria he then demands that Tito, 'forbid your troops to move over the Austrian frontier and to withdraw any who have already crossed'. Alexander concludes his *démarche* by reminding Tito that Yugoslav forces are already west of the Isonzo river and are pillaging the Udine population of foodstuffs. 'I trust that you will order the requisitioning to cease immediately and will withdraw these forces.'[3]

The word 'immediately' implies a time limit. Hence this demand must be considered an ultimatum as it comes from a military commander who can immediately dispose of armed force.

Now let us see what is happening on the ground. This is explained in a signal from 5 Corps Commander, Keightley, which reaches his superior, 15 Army Group Commander, Clark, early in the morning of the same day. It is copied to General Morgan, Alexander's Chief of Staff at AFHQ, so that everyone is in the picture.[4]

Charles Keightley reports that he is containing approximately 500,000 enemy troops and refugees in the areas north of Klagenfurt and Villach. This huge number is causing acute guarding and control problems. (Keightley has still only about 3,000 infantry in this area at his disposal). But there is a report from the Tito Army Headquarters that the Yugoslavs are getting worried about what they have taken on and will withdraw south of the Austrian border on 12 May. Keightley casts doubts on the reliability of this information. Meantime, he says that the Russians and the Bulgarian Army under Marshal Tolbukhin's command are still advancing and infiltrating between the main roads on our side of the Austrian border. The Bulgarian Commander insisted that he had been ordered by Tolbukhin to seize the town of Volkermarkt inside the British zone.

Now a signal of considerable importance goes from Alexander to the Combined Chiefs of Staff in Washington.[5]

It was dispatched on 11 May and is now being circulated to Alexander's generals. It contains the Supreme Commander's assessment as to his needs *vis à vis* Tito. It boils down to the broad choice as to whether or not force is to be used. If force is not to be used there seem to be two alternatives. One, to enter into a signed agreement with Tito on the lines of telegram NA957 which will really concede what Tito demands or, two, simply to continue on an *ad hoc* basis. If either of these two alternatives are to be taken, then certainly the Port of Trieste alone will be too unreliable for supplying his armies, and alternatives will have to be found. (He even considers the ports of North-West Europe, with an L of C across the Alps.) If however force is to be resorted to, the resources required will depend on whether or not the Russians back Tito. Alexander estimates:

> 'In view of the great quantities of arms, ammunition and warlike stores which have fallen into Tito's hands …and the fact that he would be able to employ captured German specialists and technicians, I consider that even if the Russians did not give him material support, but that nevertheless he decided to resist us by force, I should require a total of eleven divisions.'[6]

This would have to include, Alexander informs the Combined Chiefs of Staff in Washington, all naval forces in the Mediterranean, and the Desert Air Force or its equivalent.

Then he adds the *caveat* over which Churchill is already fulminating, but which nevertheless he finds it necessary to repeat.

> 'The foregoing is based on the assumption that my forces would display the same fighting spirit and high endeavour in battle as hitherto. In view of the announcement of VE day and the long publicity given to Tito's operations in and of the Allied cause, I am doubtful whether in fact this would be the case. In my view, both US and Brit. troops would be very reluctant to engage at this stage of the war in a fresh conflict against the Jugoslavs.'[7]

If, on the other hand, the Russians decided to support Tito, such support might vary between open hostilities and the provision of volunteer formations operating under Tito's command. In either case, 'it is impossible to estimate the resources that would be required. This would clearly be beyond all that I have available in this theatre.'

Then Alexander enumerates the number of divisions he has available: seven US divisions, four British divisions, one New Zealand division, one South African division, two Indian divisions, two Polish divisions, one Brazilian division, total EIGHTEEN DIVISIONS. Of these, four divisions are required for the occupation of North-West Italy, and two to control the large number of surrendered enemy personnel in this theatre. Furthermore, the two Indian divisions are now being concentrated for deployment in the Far East. This reduces the number of divisions available for operations in North-East Italy and Austria to ten divisions, assuming compliance of their respective governments. Under current directives United States forces also could not be employed. If the Naval and Airforces are to be found, then present intentions regarding disbandment and redeployment would have to be abandoned or drastically modified. [8]

By the time the Combined Chiefs of Staff receive this not very sanguine appraisal, they will have already discussed Truman's message to Churchill, which puts a different complexion on the affair. Truman's message is robust.[9]

> 'I have come to the conclusion that we must decide now whether we should uphold the fundamental principles of territorial settlement by orderly process against force, intimidation or blackmail. It seems that Tito has an identical claim ready for south Austria, in Carinthia and Syria and may have similar designs on parts of Hungary and Greece if his methods in Venezia Giulia succeed. Although the stability of Italy and the future orientation of that country with respect to Russia may well be at stake the present issue, as I see it, is not a question of taking sides in a dispute between Italy and Yugoslavia or of becoming involved in internal Balkan politics. The problem is essentially one of deciding whether our two countries are going to permit our Allies to engage in uncontrolled land grabbing or tactics which are all too reminiscent of those of Hitler and Japan.'[10]

Truman understands that Alexander is prepared to go ahead 'if we agree', and proposes a stiff note to Tito. 'If we stand firm on this issue', he concludes, 'as we are doing on Poland, we can hope to avoid a host of other similar encroachments'. Alas, Poland was not to be a very good example!

This response from Truman was a breath of fresh air, not least to Churchill. Here was an untried and untested President who demonstrated a clarity of vision surpassing that of Roosevelt. Churchill, greatly heartened, replies.

> 'I agree with every word you say, and will work with all my strength on the line you propose ... If the situation is handled firmly before our strength is dispersed, Europe may be saved from another bloodbath.'[11]

Churchill finally suggests that he and Truman issue a standstill order on all their armed forces in Europe before re-deployment to the Far East or demobilisation begins to disperse their strength.

Churchill hastens to confirm with Alexander the robust and encouraging telegram he has received from the President.

> 'Of the eighteen divisions concerned, you could, I should think count on all. The six British and British-Indian divisions are under Imperial orders. I should

Italian Partisans (*IWM*)

Three Cossack soldiers and a German NCO (*IWM*)

A Chetnik officer (*IWM*)

Chetniks beg a lift (*IWM*)

With the surrendered Hungarian Army in Austria – camp followers (*IWM*)

Marshal Tito in his mountain hideout (*IWM*)

General Mihailovic (R) with a veteran Montenegrin leader (*IWM*)

A typical operational scene. Brigadier Pat Scott (38 (Irish) Infantry Brigade) (centre, with pipe) and Lieutenant General Sir Charles Keightley (Commander 5 Corps) (right) discuss the difficulties of disentangling the armies of Europe (*IWM*)

Crossing the Wörthersee by launch. Field Marshal Alexander and Lieutenant General Keightley during the Field Marshal's visit to 5 Corps in Italy 4–6 June 1945 (*IWM*)

Field Marshal Alexander with Brigadier Verney (1st Guards Brigade) during his visit to 5 Corps 4–6 June 1945 (*IWM*)

think it likely that the Brazilian division would act with the seven Americans. I should imagine the two Poles [Polish divisions] would like [nothing] better.'

And he brushes aside Alexander's doubts about the will to fight.

'The fact that Great Britain and the United States are acting together should make the matter clearly comprehensible to the troops.'[12]

A telegram from Halifax in Washington confirms that the President consulted the United States Chiefs of Staff before dispatching his message. A 'healthily-worded' document was now to be issued to the Press. This was no moment for 'pussyfooting' was the current American view.[13]

Corroboration for this line comes from Rome that same evening of 12 May. Sir N Charles, the British Ambassador, is worried about Italian public opinion should we weaken. The public is becoming daily more tense. He fully appreciates the arguments for compromise seeing that the Americans and British people would be opposed to antagonising Russia 'who has done so much to win the war while Britain would no doubt much rather offend the Italians than risk starting a war with Jugoslavia'.

Nevertheless the British envoy supports Macmillan's Course 'A'. (see page 95). The feeling in Rome is that the 'Russians have promised Tito moral, though probably not concrete, support'.[14]

Ten minutes later Sir N Charles sends this follow-up.

'My immediately preceding telegram. Italian press contains daily reports of increasing acts of violence on the part of Yugoslavs against Italian population in Trieste and Gorizia. Arrests, executions and mass deportations are apparently being carried out with the object of eliminating all Italian influence and resistance in anticipation of a plebiscite which in such circumstances could hardly fail to be favourable to the Yugoslavs. Fact that this is being done almost under the noses of Allied troops inevitably saddles us with a certain responsibility and places the Allied (and especially ourselves as it is British troops who are involved) in a most embarrassing situation towards the Italian Government and people both now and in the future.'[15]

13 MAY 1945

On the following morning, Sir Orme Sargent (Permanent Head of the British Foreign Office) sends a memo to Churchill on the two telegrams from Rome. He suggests that if we and the Americans jointly approach Tito, then we ought to let the Italians know, in order to calm their fears. Churchill marks the paper:

'I should not worry too much about this. The dog will know soon enough who has given him the bone.'[16]

Back at the scene of action Keightley informs 8th Army that the Commissar of the Yugoslav Fourth Army complains that we are taking the surrender of enemy troops who had surrendered to Tito. 'I confirmed that any fmn. wrongly surrendered will be returned to Tito,' signals Keightley. The commissar coolly told Keightley that two divisions of Fourth Army had been ordered into Austria from the south. Keightley asks for 'earliest directions on attitude to be adopted towards these two divisions.'[17]

A whole series of comments is now coming through from British Missions on Macmillan's 'options'. Our Moscow Embassy thinks we ought to say something to the Soviet Government, if we are to adopt Macmillan's Course 'A'. British Ambassador Roberts in Moscow is not aware at this stage that a note is now in course of preparation. Roberts is inclined to think that the Russians' predilection for Yugoslavia and the importance to them of establishing a reliable Slav satellite in the key port of Trieste will out-weigh any consideration of reactions in Italy. As they have occupied Poland however, they might be prepared to do a deal over Venezia Giulia.[18]

The British Ambassador in Belgrade now comes up with his own comments on Macmillan's 'options' – clearly in favour of the 'Ultimatum' route, with which his United States colleague is fully in accord. Although events have now over-run the 'go it alone policy' envisaged in the Macmillan proposals, by the new Truman-Churchill initiative, these comments from the opinion-formers in our key posts abroad do show the way in which minds were working.

But Churchill now suspects 'a somewhat violent internal reaction at Washington'. The isolationist faction in the United States reacts strongly against the 'bold' message from Truman to Churchill. Churchill ruminates in his History of this period on the 'isolationist' factor. And he sets out his belief that the withdrawal of the United States from the League of Nations, through the pressure of isolationist sentiment, undoubtedly led to the Second World War.[19] It was now to play almost as deadly a part, says Churchill, at a moment when the future hung in the balance.

14 MAY

Truman's reply to Churchill on 14 May made clear that unless Tito did attack, it was impossible to involve the United States in another war. Back home the pressure is clearly on. So here is the situation. Churchill and Truman both believe that the time for prevarication or appeasement is over, but Truman is temporarily constrained from doing what he knows is right by reactionary opinion in the United States. We have been here before. We know the results of appeasement of dictators.

But another thought occurs to me. This is the second time in the space of five years that we have been on the brink of war with Russia. The first time, as I have pointed out in an earlier reference, was the War Cabinet plan for a landing near Murmansk during the 'winter war' of 1940. Now we have the threat of war with Russia on the Balkan front.

It is idle to speculate what might have happened if we had forcibly ejected the usurpers. Would the Russians have backed their ally Yugoslavia? Could we have sustained another major war? Could the Russians, numerous but exhausted, themselves have sustained such a conflict? All we now know, because we only have to 'read the book', is that from that moment on we became involved in a 'cold' or underground war which lasted for 45 years and in which very few parts of the world were unaffected. The weapons of this conflict were psychological warfare, subversion, terror and threats which eventually stabilised into a nuclear stalemate, or as some would have it 'a balance of terror'. It was immensely expensive, draining the resources of West and East alike. Should we have taken time by the forelock? Should we have gone on, whilst we were still able, and pre-empted the dictators? Thus forestalling a new ice-age in Europe? This is a question that even the history books have not answered. Nay, barely have they addressed the question.

XVI

'The Klagenfurt Conspiracy': The Dog That Didn't Bark in the Night 13–14 May

Macmillan's visit to Klagenfurt on 13 May has been dubbed the 'Klagenfurt Conspiracy' in a recent book by Nikolai Tolstoy.[1] According to the author, Macmillan entered into a criminal conspiracy with 5 Corps Commander, General Keightley, allegedly with the intention of sending 70,000 Cossacks and Yugoslavs to a certain death. Brigadier Toby Low, (now Lord Aldington) formerly BGS HQ 5 Corps was later named as an accomplice and described by Tolstoy as 'a major war criminal whose activities merit comparison with those of the worst butchers of Nazi Germany or Soviet Russia'. In a libel action brought by Lord Aldington in 1989, his name was completely cleared of such slanders and he was awarded substantial damages. This does not entirely remove the stigma remaining against the names of Macmillan and Keightley, both now deceased. As the Trial Judge[2] reminded the jury at the beginning of the case, the trial was purely about the libellous statements concerning the plaintiff (Lord Aldington). It did not include wider questions of the honour of British arms or armies. This argument the judge considered would continue for some time to come.

What therefore is the story behind Macmillan's visit to Klagenfurt? Why was it supposed to be so sinister? What ulterior motive lay behind? The reader must judge for himself or herself if any such motive existed. I can only tell the story as I saw it happening. But perhaps one word of explanation is necessary. Military command in war, for those unfamiliar with the system, and as practised at the time, was for the widest possible dissemination of information amongst all commanders and staff concerned. Even those not directly involved in a particular operation must know what is going on upon their flanks. Information flowed up the chain of command, and it flowed down, it percolated laterally so that every one concerned knew exactly what was happening. It is therefore unrealistic to suggest that a 'conspiracy' could have taken place between Macmillan and Keightley without everyone knowing all about it. For a number of staff officers including the head of Military Government were present at the 'Klagenfurt Conference'. The truth, as so often proves to be the case, was prosaic and unexceptionable. So those looking for sensation will not find it here. I think this was a case of 'the dog that didn't bark in the night'.

Macmillan's original intention, as foreshadowed in his telegram of the previous day, was for a visit to McCreery at 8th Army headquarters (Treviso), and Harding at 13 Corps headquarters (Monfalcone). The object of the visit, as explained by Alexander to Churchill, was 'to put Generals McCreery and Harding in the picture', to brief them upon the politico-military crisis and to warn them not to provoke any shooting incident *vis à vis* the Yugoslavs in the highly tense position that then obtained. As Macmillan explains in his diary, whilst he was with McCreery:

> 'I summed up the political and military situation; the problems confronting the Field Marshal and HMG and the equivocal and uncertain attitude of the Americans. I had brought all the files, and showed them the most recent interchange of telegrams from different capitals of the world. I think this did a lot of good from the psychological point of view and put the general and his staff thoroughly "in the picture".'[3]

But when he went on to visit Harding, whom he described as 'a very firm, confident and stalwart character, as well as a very clever professional soldier', he found the morale higher there than at General McCreery's, who seemed worried and somewhat sore that Alexander had kept him in the dark about what was really going on.

Whilst in northern Italy, he decided to pay a visit to General Keightley at 5 Corps Headquarters at Klagenfurt on the next day 13 May, to complete the briefing and get a first-hand impression of his problems. This would complete his tour of the forward areas. He left Caledon Camp (Alexander's forward headquarters) early that morning accompanied by Brigadier Floyd, BGS 8th Army, 'Con' Benson, head of Allied Military Government 8th Army and one or two other Army staff officers: Macmillan recalls 'a truly wonderful flight ... an absolutely perfect day. The flight across the Alps was really magnificent. The Appenines seemed like modest hills in comparison with these tremendous mountains, with their great jagged peaks and cliffs, some still snow-clad.'[4]

> 'We landed safely at Klagenfurt airfield about 10 am. The field is a grass one, small and rather bumpy, but the DC3 machines land well in such circumstances. We were met by General Charles Keightley (Fifth Corps) and some of his staff. This officer, whom I have met from time to time, is an admirable soldier and a very level-headed and sensible man. He is well suited for his difficult and embarrassing task.'[5]

Remarkably enough, Macmillan had never been to Austria before, 'had no real picture in my mind what Klagenfurt and the district would be like. It is really a beautiful Alpine valley, of fair size with lakes, etc. and Alpine fir plantations.'[6]

After recording in his diary the difficulties that Keightley is encountering with the Yugoslavs, he goes on to say:

> 'Moreover, in addition to the Yugoslavs, to the order of 30,000 to 40,000, General Keightley has to deal with nearly 400,000 surrendered or surrendering Germans, not yet disarmed (except as to tanks and guns) who must be shepherded into some place or other, fed and given camps, etc. On his right flank Marshal Tolbukhin's armies have spread into what is supposed to be the British zone in Austria, including the important city and road centre of Graz. With the Russians are considerable Bulgar Forces. Moreover, among the surrendered Germans are about 40,000 Cossacks and "White" Russians, with their wives and children. To hand them over to the Russians is condemning them to slavery, torture and probably death. To refuse, is deeply to offend the Russians, and incidentally break the Yalta agreement. We have decided to hand them over (General Keightley is in touch and on good terms with the Russian general on his right), but I suggested that the Russians should at the same time give us any British prisoners or wounded who may be in his area. The formal procedure is that they should go back through Odessa (which I understand means great hardship). I hope we can persuade the local Russian to hand them over direct (we think he has 1,500–2,000) and save them all this suffering, in exchange for the scrupulous adherence to the agreement in handing back Russian subjects.'[7]

Macmillan in this passage blurs the difference between 'White Russians' and 'Russian subjects'. At that moment there was no difference, in the eyes of the participants, in the exact racial or other origin of these people. They were all in German uniform and had been fighting on the German side. They were part of the problem which now had to be dealt with as a matter of urgency. Macmillan further underlines the general confusion which reigned.

> 'To add to the confusion thousands of so-called Ustashi or Chetniks, mostly with wives and children, are fleeing in panic into this area in front of the advancing Yugoslavs. These expressions, Ustashi and Chetnik, cover anything from guerilla forces, raised by the Germans from Slovenes and Croats and Serbs to fight Tito, and armed and maintained by the Germans – to people who, either because they are Roman Catholics or Conservative in politics, or for

whatever cause are out of sympathy with revolutionary Communism and therefore labelled as Fascists or Nazis. (This is a very simple formula, which as a modified form is being tried, I observe, in English politics).

We had a conference with the general and his officers covering much the same ground as those with Generals McCreery and Harding yesterday. He gave us his story and we gave him ours. I feel sure it was useful and helpful all round.'[8]

These two diary passages tell us all we need to know about the motives for the repatriations. There was nothing sinister in Macmillan's journey, or the conference. It would have been foolhardy to have risked, what the Russians would have considered an unfriendly or hostile act, in refusing to return their prisoners in accordance with the Yalta agreement. As we have already seen, Keightley signalled Eighth Army on 13 May in the early hours, reporting that the Commissar of the Yugoslav Army 'complains that we are taking surrender of enemy tps who had surrendered to Tito. I confirmed that any fmn wrongly surrendered would be returned to Tito.'[9] So it was entirely proper that we should have returned all those fighting against our Allies into their custody, particularly if they had surrendered to them in the first place.

Furthermore, it might have jeopardised the return not only of our own prisoners 'who may be in the area' but thousands of others who were now behind Russian lines. Macmillan was surrounded by senior staff officers and commanders and he would have had explained to him the military consequences of refusing to move these surrendered prisoners. In the minds of those present, the likely sufferings of our own men in Russian hands, as against the men in German uniform, must have tilted the scales decisively.

But out of this meeting did not come an executive decision. Macmillan had no authority to issue instructions. It was 'a recommendation' which yet had to be endorsed by Alexander and his staff. And soon it came from AFHQ in the form of the 'Robertson telegram' the following day, 14 May.

To 15 Army Group, Main Eighth Army, Distone.
From Chief Administrative Officer AFHQ.
'1. All Russians should be handed over to Soviet forces at agreed point of contact est by you under local arrangement with Marshal Tolbukhin's HQ. Steps should be taken to ensure that Allied PW held in Russian area are transferred to us in exchange at same time.
2. Movement to Italy of all Germans is NOT acceptable because it would cause serious blockage on our L of C. SS and other arrestable categories will be disarmed and evacuated to DISTONE ...'[10]
3. All surrendered personnel of established YUGOSLAV nationality who were

serving in German forces should be disarmed and handed over to YUGOSLAV forces.'[11]

Major General Brian Robertson,[12] far from being a remote and uncaring figure sitting back at Caserta with no idea of the consequences of his instructions, was on the contrary a kindly and considerate man, everyone's idea of a 'favourite uncle', who would not have sent orders such as these without consulting Alexander, or Alexander being well aware of what was intended. But Robertson was a realist, as we all had to be in those days, for ultimately it was our own men's lives we had to think about. A brilliant administrator, Robertson had been one of Montgomery's *protégés*, of whom the latter held a high opinion. An ideal anchorman whose shrewd advice was widely sought.

And let us not be too mealy-mouthed about 'the Russians' as described in the telegram.[13] Until a bare week ago, they were in German uniform, some bearing the dreaded insignia of the SS who had sworn personal loyalty to Hitler. They had been 'the enemy', now they were 'the surrendered enemy'. But they were foolhardy in the extreme, in joining the German Army and fighting against their country, (even 'the emigrés' knew this). They were taking an enormous and calculated risk. For if they were caught or fell into the hands of their compatriots (many Cossacks were fighting on the Soviet side) they would be as good as 'dead men'. Nevertheless, they backed Hitler. I am afraid they backed the wrong side.

But if those responsible *knew*, had proof (not mere surmise as in Macmillan's diary note), that they were to be going off into slavery, torture and probably death would the Allies have acted in the way they did? This is a question which I shall attempt to answer in a later chapter.

XVII

Pre-Requisite for War –
A Question of Morale
15–16 May

Churchill is beginning to champ at what he considers to be a craven attitude by our men on the spot, for Alexander's latest message (NAF 960), is in similar vein, to that of Macmillan's (sent on 11 May). Alexander signals:

'If I am ordered by the Chiefs of Staff to occupy the whole of Venezia Giulia by force if necessary, we shall certainly be committed to a fight with the Jugoslav Army who will have the moral backing, at least, of the Russians. Before we are committed, I think it is as well to consider the feelings of our own troops in the matter. They have a profound admiration for Tito's Partisans, and a great sympathy for them in their struggle for freedom. We must be very careful therefore before we ask them to turn away from the common enemy to fight an ally.'[1]

Churchill's reply was blistering. Sent on 14 May it was marked Personal and Top Secret and carried the suffix Guard. Churchill refers to Alexander's NAF 960.

From the Prime Minister to Field Marshal Alexander.

'The wide circulation given to your Para 5 . . . has done much harm.
   I hope that in the changed circumstances produced by the President's telegram No. 400 you will find it possible to give me the assurance that the Army you command will obey your orders and [sic] its customary sense of duty and discipline.
   I have been much distressed by the paragraph and wish that, so far as the British troops are concerned, it had not been given such a wide circulation'.[2]

And Churchill follows this up on 16 May with:

'I have just received the telegram in my immediately following from the Foreign Secretary who had long interviews with the President yesterday. You will I am sure be grieved to see how much the reference to your doubts about the reluctance of your troops to do their duty when ordered by their Governments and their Commander has counted against the pursuance of a firm policy. Mr. MacMillan's telegrams are also mentioned as a cause of doubt in the State Department.'

And then more in the tone of a father addressing a wayward son, he continued,

'I supported you, as I always have, in the very strong line you took with Tito at the outset. I was angry at the rebuffs you received from him. I was surprised that you did not welcome more ardently the all powerful backing I have been gathering for you.'

Churchill continued to cast aspersions on Alexander's leadership qualities which would have rocked a less impassive man, and which clearly bears the mark of the midnight oil.

'I should have thought that you would have found it possible to give plain assurances to the Combined Chiefs of Staff about the moral state of your command which would enable the joint policy of the two governments to be carried out. If the Western Allies cannot now resist land-grabbing and other encroachments by Tito, and have to put up with some weak compromise, this may well breed a danger far greater than we now face at the head of the Adriatic. I am very anxious about the general attitude of the Russians, especially if they feel they have only war-wearied armies and trembling administrations in front of them.'[3]

Churchill expressed the hope encouraged by Truman's recent reaction that the United States would not sail away and leave us to face the overwhelming might of Russia without any adequate solemn settlement, for if we did not show will-power at this present time, we should be driven from pillar to post.

Churchill's last sentence was more confident.

'I hope that a growing concentration of troops on the Yugo Slav front will be effected for I do not believe that Tito or Russia behind him will provoke a major collision while the American armies are in Europe.'[4]

Alexander's reply to Churchill's earlier telegram sent on 14 May is dispatched the following day, 15 May.

'I regret if paragraph 5 of my NAF 960 has caused any misunderstanding. My military appreciation of the situation to the CCS would not have been complete if I did not take into account the morale factors involved. I specifically mentioned US as well as British troops after discussion with General McNarney[5] who agreed with me. I am sure our soldiers will obey orders, but I doubt that they will re-enter battle, this time against the YUGOSLAVS, with the same enthusiasm as they did against the hated Germans. I trust and hope that guidance will be given to the Press and Radio to present our case in the right light . . . .'[6]

A rather poignant note in Alexander's private papers is added by his pencil notes on the back, for the draft of this reply. They are written in a firm clear hand with no alterations.

The British Foreign Secretary, Eden, now reiterates, (from the United States), the unease that these telegrams on the state of mind of the troops, have caused. In a message to the Prime Minister sent on 16 May in the early hours he says that the Americans have not yet finally made up their minds about the next step to be taken if Tito does not respond to Anglo-American demands.

Eden's impression was that they were reconciled to the fact that in the last resort force would have to be used.

> 'They have been shaken by Alexander's reference to effect on British and American troops of action against Yugoslavia in general, and advice they have received from their political Advisor in Caserta repeating Macmillan's views.'[7]

In a corrupted passage (in the telegram) he then refers to a meeting that morning with Grew and State Department officials who read out the offending passages concerning morale in the American text. Eden then follows this up with a special message for the Prime Minister, which reflects the American view, and in which appear the enigmatic words.

> 'War would not be declared nor would force be used to expel the Yugo-Slavs from any area to which they had infiltrated.
>
> We would for the present accept our troops equivocal position and allow matters to develop and the public to become informed.'

Did Alexander and Macmillan make a misjudgment about the troops' readiness to fight the Titoists? Here is one piece of evidence which contradicts their view. It comes from a young Guards officer in 5 Corps:

> 'At the outset, our higher commanders apparently believed that our men would not be eager to take up arms against the Partisan soldiers who had fought so bravely in the common cause, but they soon appreciated the real feeling of the troops. The Welsh Guardsmen without exception from the outset regarded the Partisans with utter scorn and fierce dislike. As most of our soldiers came from a political environment as far left as Red Clydeside, this was surprising. But they just hated them, and were constantly asking me and other officers when they would be allowed to boot them back where they came from.'[8]

Whilst not being conclusive proof that Alexander was wrong, this comment at least shows which way the wind was blowing.

XVIII

On the Brink 14–16 May

So let us take stock once again of the traumatic events that are now unfolding, on a wider scale, before delving once more into the secrets of the past, now surviving as so many scraps of paper in the dusty archives.

We are still at war with Japan. The armies of the Western Allies, now at their greatest strength, are poised facing the Soviet armies. For how long will the Allies be able to maintain this stance in face of the greater demands of the unfinished war and general demobilisation? The new President, at once so refreshingly forthright, is coming more and more under the influence of the Washington establishment which wishes to be rid of the entanglements of Europe and the Balkans in order to deal with the threat from Asia. Very soon the United States is to pull out of that mass of Central Europe (centred round Leipzig and Erfurt) which had been gained by force of arms, thus yielding a huge tract of territory to be absorbed into the maw of the Soviets, under the stamp of the Iron Curtain. And this without any *quid pro quo*, or deal over Poland or Austria or Venezia Giulia. As we have already seen, Poland did not get its free democratic elections, as promised at Yalta, and is already sinking beneath the red glow on the Eastern horizon.

Frequently Churchill speaks of the Third World War,[1] which he now fears to be inevitable. At home in Britain, the hard-tried nation longs to be reunited with its loved ones. The soldiers, disorientated by the thoughts of home, find it hard to concentrate entirely on their military duties. We have seen this happen in occupied Germany. We now see it happen in Austria. Home leave and release are on the minds of all, but at the same time everyone is wryly aware that the war is not yet over.

14-16 MAY

General Keightley faces the sober fact that in a few days he may find himself in open warfare with Yugoslavia. His headquarters and subordinate formations are well into the planning stage of 'Operation Beehive' (to clear Austria), the codename suggesting at once the danger of the angry bees who might have to be ejected from the territory over which they have swarmed, and the irritation of the rightful owners of the property!

On 14 May, just after midnight, he informs his superior headquarters of the dilemma he faces.

> *'Personal Army Comd. from Corps Comd.*
>   Present situation approx. 300,000 PW surrendered personnel and refugees in Corps area further 600,000 reported moving NORTH to AUSTRIA from YUGOSLAVIA. I am taking all possible steps to prevent their mov along rds but this will NOT completely prevent them as they are short of food and are being harassed. Should this number materialize food and guard situation will become critical. I therefore suggest that all possible steps are taken to dispose soonest of all surrendered personnel in this area whether GERMAN, AUSTRIAN or RUSSIAN by moving them to Northern Italy or their homes whichever may be the policy. Certain SS tps already causing trouble but this being dealt with. On advice MACMILLAN have today suggested to SOVIET General on TOLBUKHINS HQ that COSSACKS should be returned to SOVIETS at once. Explained that I had no power to do this without your authority but would be glad to know TOLBUKHINS views and that if they coincided with mine I would ask you officially. Cannot see any point in keeping this large number SOVIET nationals who are clearly great source contention between SOVIETS and ourselves. This area now becoming clearing house for all stragglers straggling fmns and refugees of all nationalities who require food and shelter. Understand reason for this move due to NO org in YUGOSLAVIA to deal with them.'[2]

This signal was later repeated to Clark at 15 Army Group, and General Morgan, Alexander's Chief of Staff at AFHQ.

The crucial thing to notice in this signal is the fact that these ex-prisoners and refugees amounting to almost a million people will completely paralyse the road system in southern Austria, rendering military operations impossible. Much of the strength of Keightley's divisions will be taken up by guard duties and the essential administration of these unmanageable hordes. Given the directive under which he is working, it is essential, therefore, to evacuate this huge body from the area as swiftly as possible.

Both the Cossacks and the Chetniks are considered to be 'collaborationists' in the language of the day, but in plain terms, traitors, as far as the Russians and the Yugoslavs are concerned, in that they have fought with the enemy against their own country. At this stage, Cossacks are considered to be Russians and all eligible therefore, for repatriation under the terms of the Yalta agreement. The multiplicity of national groups is confusing to the Allied soldiers who had little idea that they were going to have to deal with such a variety of races, tribes and factions.

Keightley continues his situation report with the information that although there is no great increase in Yugoslav infiltration, at the same time there are rumours of large concentrations of Titoists south of the Austro-Jugoslav border, ready to move north into Austria. The good news is that the Bulgarian army under Marshal Tolbukin's command, who had been pursuing two Cossack divisions of the 15 SS Cossack Cavalry Corps, commanded by the German General von Pannwitz, into Austria at Lavamund, had now withdrawn back to the Yugoslav frontier. The two Cossack divisions were allowed to surrender to the British, presumably because the Bulgars had not the means to secure and feed them. With Marshal Tolbukin, Keightley established a most friendly relationship 'with much interchange of whisky and vodka.'[3]

We now get a closer glimpse into these huge bodies of men, surrendered armies, who are now approaching Austria from Jugoslavia. They are still south of the river Drava (or Drau) which runs just south of the border, 300,000 Germans and 200,000 Croats who have been fighting with them. These formed part of German Army Group E and their Chief of Staff says he is powerless to prevent them crossing into Austria. He has tried to contact Tito's headquarters on frequent occasions but has received no acknowledgement, presumably to arrange surrender terms. McCreery signals to Clark that he has authorised Keightley to take over formed bodies and disarm them as they cross the border, working through the German command. 'Please ask AFHQ to ask Tito how many enemy he eventually wishes to retain. Suggest Croats become Tito's show', signals McCreery.[4]

This last sentence couched in the vernacular of the day is taken by latter historians to signal some evil intent, for the Croats met with an unhappy fate when they eventually fell into Jugoslav hands again. The fact remains however that all these people, under command General Löhr in Army Group E, had helped the invaders of Jugoslavia and had been locked in mortal combat with our ally, Tito's Resistance. It was in the interests of these people to surrender to the British rather than their enemies the Yugoslavs. It may also have been in the interests of Tito to have the British, in the territories he coveted, fully engaged and overwhelmed by sheer numbers whilst he, his hands no longer tied, quietly infiltrated more deeply into Austria. But there is another scenario now revealed following recent research into Yugoslav archives.[5]

> Marshal Tito to Yugoslav First Army, 13 May.
> 'A group of Ustachi and some Chetniks, a total of over 50,000 men, is reported by Third army in the Konjice-Sotanj area towards Dravograd. It includes Pavelic, Macek, the Croatian Government and a huge number of criminals. They are attempting to cross at Dravograd and give themselves up to the British. ... You must move your forces most urgently from the Celje area in the direction of Sotanj-Slovenjgradec in order to concentrate for an attack aimed at the annihilation of this group.'[6]

And then, a little later, from Marshal Tito to all Yugoslav Army headquarters:

> 'Take the most energetic measures and at all costs prevent the killing of PoWs and those arrested by units, organisations or individuals. If among the PoWs and arrested people are persons who could be responsible for war crimes, they should be turned over with due acknowledgement to military courts for further treatment.'[7]

The Croatians referred to in the first of these two signals were responsible for horrific atrocities against the Tito side, soon to be avenged. But Tito, in his message to all Yugoslav Army headquarters, is anxious that indiscriminate killings of PoW should not take place, in case the evidence of war crimes is also destroyed.

On 15 May, Marshal Tito sends the following signal to 3rd Yugoslav Army.

> 'Received authorisation from the Soviet Government for our units to occupy a part of the Austrian territory. These are my instructions:
> 1. Occupy the part of the Austrian territory designed [sic] by Marshal Tolbukhin.
> 2. Your occupation force stands under command of Marshal Tolbukhin.
> 3. The HQ should be located at Leibnitz.
> 4. Confirm that the instructions have been carried out by 24 hours, 16 may ...'[8]

This shows two things. First, that the Yugoslav 'occupation' forces are clearly under Soviet command. Second, that the Russians have directed them to set up their headquarters at Leibnitz, south of Graz on the border between the British and Soviet occupation zones.

So although this information would not have been available to the Allied higher command at the time, it shows that the pressure on Alexander was Soviet directed and controlled. Therefore the Western Allies had very good reason to fear that Russia would back Yugoslavia in any conflict arising.

A further message on 15 May is from AFHQ to MACMIS (Brigadier Maclean's mission to Tito). This refers to the 200,000 Yugoslav nationals (amended from 'Croats' in signal text) who were serving in the German Armed Forces and who have surrendered to Commander of Allied Troops in Austria (McCreery).

> 'We would like to turn these over immediately to Marshal Tito's forces and would be grateful if Marshal Tito would agree to instruct his commanders to accept them and arrange with GOC 5 Corps the rate at which they can be received and handing over point on Austrian frontier south of Klagenfurt for return to Yugoslavia.'[9]

This came from Alexander's headquarters and he would have been well aware of its contents.

The Foreign Office will meantime have been reminded of the situation back in Italy by her prime minister, De Gasperi. The Italian Ambassador in London has been directed to make Italy's anxiety known to the British Government.

De Gasperi to his ambassador:

> 'I ... request you to inform them there that the situation locally [Venezia Giulia] has become worse in recent days. The régime of terror has increased. 4,000 persons have disappeared from Gorizia, 700 are said to have been shot in Trieste. Jugoslav partisans, to whom it is difficult to attribute the character of organised troops, have also crossed the line of the Isonzo. British and American troops for the present stand passively by.'

De Gasperi stresses,

> 'State once more that Venezia Giulia question and the events now occurring profoundly affect Italian internal situation, which is today passing through a particularly delicate phase and they are disturbing and complicating it in serious manner.'[10]

A War Cabinet Briefing Note for the meeting on the situation in Venezia Giulia and Austria, to be held on 16 May, gives the potential enemy strength as follows.

Venezia Giulia area approximately 34,000 Jugoslav regular Army troops with some guns and tanks behind the Isonzo line. North and East of Udine is another additional force estimated at 14,000. In Southern Austria, Jugoslav Partisan forces have thinned out from Klagenfurt and the South-East, but are said to be only waiting for further troops from the South. The strength immediately available in North-West Jugoslavia is approximately 157,000. Forces elsewhere in the country amount to approximately 150,000 only some of which are likely combatants. (See Map II).

Then the note ends with a War Office assessment of the Jugoslavs. I wonder whether the troops on the ground would have been quite so dismissive?

'Despite the rapid development of the Yugoslav Army during the past year into a relatively compact National Army, it is still only a lightly armed force, with very little artillery or mechanised transport. The Jugoslav Air Force is a negligible factor.'[11]

But the above figures give a British equivalent of some 23 divisions, a force not to be discounted. A force indeed greatly in excess of what was immediately available to Alexander.

XIX

'I Must Clear the Decks'
16–17 May

On 16 May, an important meeting took place at HQ 5 Corps on the Wörthersee between BGS Toby Low and a Yugoslav officer. The officer concerned was Lieutenant Colonel Hocevar, described as senior officer of Yugoslav 4th Army Troops (who were illegally occupying this part of Carinthia).

Low was a brilliant young staff officer who had already made his mark in the Western Desert as a fighting soldier. Hocevar made several unacceptable claims. First, that they had joint control with the British of all surrendered personnel. Second, that Carinthia was not part of Austria, and therefore was not covered by the Moscow declaration. Third, that he was under orders to establish military government in the province. The Croats having nominally surrendered to the Yugoslavs, Low agreed, in accordance with General McCreery's wishes, that Croats should be returned as soon as possible to Yugoslavia and that Yugoslav officers might visit the camp but control must remain in British hands.[1]

Meantime the situation in the town of Klagenfurt is to say the least confused. The Yugoslavs are sticking up proclamations, some ordering the population about, others adjuring them to observe the British curfew. During the night of 15 May, it was believed that the Yugoslavs brought in an extra 1000 reinforcements, making a total of some 2,000 in the provincial capital. There were reports that some Yugoslav columns were moving south across their border, whilst others are entering Carinthia and moving north.

An interesting footnote to this information passed by Low to 8th Army (and of course copied to AFHQ), was that a large column of Croats had surrendered to Tito troops near Bleiburg (near Dravograd), after mediation by the Commander of 38 Irish Brigade.[2] The other group of Croats located in the Viktring area south of Klagenfurt included several members of the Croatian 'quisling' government.[3]

General Morgan, Alexander's Chief of Staff, who happened to be visiting 5 Corps, then sent off a personal report to his master.[4] He explained that 5 Corps' situation was difficult owing to very widespread commitments and the guards required for prisoners and surrendered personnel. These totalled about 220,000 of whom 109,000 were Germans, 15,000 Hungarians, 46,000 Cossacks, 25,000 Croats and 25,000 Slovenes. In view of this, Morgan considered that SHAEF (Eisenhower's command) should be asked to take over 5 Corps front from their positions further to the west.[5]

At about this time on 16 May Lieutenant Colonel Bill Cunningham, Alexander's Military Assistant prepared a telegram (MA 1099) for Alexander to send to Churchill, which set out the problem in stark terms:

> 'My administrative problem is a big one as we have about one million prisoners in the VILLACH-KLAGENFURT area to look after so I am trying to get SHAEF to accept them, but so far without much success. I must clear the decks in this area. Pressure is already having its effect and latest reports indicate that Yugoslav forces west of ISONZO are withdrawing behind the river. I am now awaiting instructions from CCS as to future operations.'[6]

This need to 'clear the decks' and to remove all obstructions to free manoeuvre in the operational area is now to dominate forthcoming events in Carinthia.

Some two hours later, Alexander follows this up with another signal (MA 1100) to Churchill. He notes that in President Truman's telegram he uses the words 'if Tito takes hostile action and attacks our Allied forces any where, I would expect Field Marshal ALEXANDER to use as many troops of all nationalities in his command as are necessary'. Alexander explains that his own situation is a *modus vivendi* only, and cannot last either satisfactorily or peacefully. By which he means that his multi-national force is only held together with the political will of the nations concerned. If Tito refuses to withdraw, it will inevitably lead to armed conflict. Accordingly he proposes to take what action he considers fit 'to carry out my duties and responsibilities' which includes the removal of Tito proclamations and the imposition of his own military government.[7]

But the rift between Alexander and Churchill is not yet healed and in a following telegram Alexander deems it necessary to eat humble pie, in response to Churchill's earlier strictures (MA 1102).

'Personal for PRIME MINISTER from Field Marshal ALEXANDER. I am very distressed if you feel that I have let you down. I only hope you realise that I did what I considered was my duty and if my appreciation to the CCS has had unfortunate repercussions I hope you will approve my latest telegram to them. I am most grateful for all your support not only in this affair but throughout the long period I have had the honour of serving you.' [8]

Alexander here clearly adopted the tones of a subordinate, which if he had realised it, would only have encouraged the irascible Churchill. The end of this saga, which has its place here, is a letter from CIGS Brooke. It is a personal handwritten letter to be found in Alexander's personal papers and headed

The War Office   June 1st 45.
Dear Alex,
'I am so sorry not to have answered your letter of May 16 sooner', writes Brooke 'but have been more rushed since the war is over than I was when it was on! What with Tito on one side, de Gaule [sic] in Syria, the Russians in Poland, and a mad election at home which stops all decisions, there are more worries than one wants. ...

I thought you were entirely right in representing the fact that a Yugoslav war would not be popular with the men and would require putting very carefully to them. I told the PM that I considered you were absolutely right in doing so and got a thick ear for my trouble! His attitude was tipical [sic] and true to form, he refuses to face any facts that are in any way antagonistic to the plans he has in hand. In any case you need not worry about it as it is all forgotten now. Similarly your objection to having to take Pola is entirely correct from a military point of view as I told him; it was only the political outlook which he told you of which was affecting him.

I am sorry you should have had all these worries with Tito after having had such a glorious ending to your Italy campaign. I hope it may settle down now.

With very best of luck to you. [9]

Yours ever Brookie'

But Churchill, childlike and disarming as ever, soon dispels the gloom and in a few days it is all forgotten, and he ends a personal message to Alexander: 'Always count on me should trouble arise.'[10]

In response to Alexander's request for Press guidance on the Venezia Giulia crisis, Churchill responds as follows, on 17 May:

'I asked Bracken to examine the Press and the following is his minute together with a string of quotations which you will see are very different from our Greek experience although this turned out all right in the end.
Minute from Mr. Bracken to the Prime Minister.
Begins:-
"I entirely confirm your impression of strong reaction of the British Press to Marshal Tito's encroachments in the Venezia-Giulia. From my contacts with the Press, I know that with the exception of the '*Daily Worker*', all newspapers are united behind the Government on the necessity of being absolutely firm in this matter. I applaud your proposal to reassure Field Marshal Alexander on this point. I am enclosing examples of what the principal London Newspapers

have said about the Trieste dispute during the last 2 days. Last week also there was no sign of any hostile reaction to Government policy (always with the exception of the '*Daily Worker*').''

With press and public opinion at home thoroughly 'on side' for the need to deal with Tito, and with the distribution of copies of the British newspapers to the front-line troops, the scene is now almost set for action.[12]

There are now only two flies in the ointment. First, the attitude of the United States is still uncertain. And second, Alexander's prospective theatre of operations and his lines of communication are completely paralysed. Clearly it is most urgent that the vast number of surrendered personnel and refugees must be evacuated or repatriated. His deadline is 1 June. He has barely two weeks to do it in.

Alexander therefore sends this signal (NAF074) to General Eisenhower at mid-day on 17 May.

'Personal for General Eisenhower.

Information Combined Chiefs of Staff and British Chiefs of Staff, 15 Army Group Main, Eighth Army.

1. Situation regarding surrendered enemy forces and refugees in my area of Austria has two aspects, operational and administrative.

2. Precise information regarding numbers is not obtainable. Large parts of Army Group South East are still endeavouring to move into this area to avoid surrendering to Tito. Moreover, forces which have surrendered to Tito are being turned loose again by him after being stripped of their equipment. Latest report indicates that prisoners and surrendered personnel total about 220,000 of whom 109,000 Germans, 46,000 Cossacks, 15,000 Hungarians, 25,000 Croats, 34,000 Slovenes. Croat and Slovene refugees still pouring into my area number about 200,000.

3. *Operational Aspect*. With possibility of hostilities in Austria against Jugoslavs it is essential to free my L of C immediately from this embarrassment. Operational efficiency of my troops is already gravely prejudiced, both by necessity for controlling these multitudes and also by general congestion of the area. It is further essential that military supplies, especially ammunition, should be built up to support possible operations. It is impossible to do this and feed vast numbers mentioned in paragraph 2 simultaneously.

4. *Administrative Aspect*. I fully appreciate that you also are faced with immense administrative difficulties. My situation, however, in Austria is one with which it is impossible for me to deal. Enemy dumps are quite inadequate and have been largely looted by Jugoslavs etc. In present political situation and in view of bad state of communications it is equally impossible to expect that German administration can supply that area from stocks or indigenous resources in other parts of Austria. Local resources in the area are inadequate to feed its own population and I am already faced with necessity for importing supplies on this account. It is not practicable to move all this personnel into Italy. Such mass movement would paralyse my L of C, nor would I feed them in Italy when they arrive there. My food stocks in Italy are already severely strained by presence of 425,000 PoW and surrendered German forces. Moreover, as you know, it has always been planned that surrendered enemy personnel should

be fed by German administration from German resources. To move large numbers of surrendered Germans from Austria to Italy would violate this principle and constitute unwarrantable drain on Allied food stocks.

5. Appreciate that it would not be reasonable to ask you to accept Croat and Slovene refugees, nor Austrian and Hungarian military personnel. I will deal with these classes to the best of my ability with my own resources.

6. My earnest appeal to you is to come to my assistance as regards surrendered German armed forces including Cossacks. I request urgently your agreement that these surrendered forces other than Austrians, Hungarians and arrestable categories be transferred to your area soonest at a point agreeable to you in status of surrendered personnel. The only alternative is that as matter of operational and administrative necessity I shall be compelled to disband them, which would produce confusion in contiguous German territory under your command.'[13]

Here again Alexander states his chief concern. As he points out, 'with the possibility of hostilities in Austria against the Yugoslavs, it is essential to free my L of C immediately from this embarrassment'. And he is asking Eisenhower, the 'Supremo' in the West to relieve him of this burden of massed humanity. And he suggests to Eisenhower in his final paragraph 6 that he may be compelled to disband them as a last resort producing 'confusion in the contiguous German territory under your command'. For these people would surely have made their way further west out of reach of the Muscovite tentacle. Such roaming bands would be a considerable embarrassment to Eisenhower.

This telegram gives the full explanation of the dilemma in which Alexander was placed, and it is the clue to all subsequent events. As we have seen, Eisenhower had already been approached by Alexander before on his refugee problem, but had not given any clear response. The attitude of the Americans on the repatriation issue was somewhat different to that of the British. A series of communications between the United States Resident Minister, at Alexander's headquarters, Alexander Kirk, and Washington make this clear. This was Kirk's interpretation of the dispute in a message sent to Washington on 14 May.

'Re the handing over of Cossacks and dissident Yugoslav tps with exception of Chetniks without reference to US Government. CAO [Robertson] expressed disappointment that we did not seem to agree on this point but added that he was faced with a grave problem with hundreds of thousands of PoW's on his hands and could not bother at this time about who might or might not be turned over to the Russians and partisans to be shot. He would have to send his telegram in spite of our non-concurrence. Department's views would be appreciated urgently.'[14]

It must be mentioned that this was a specifically British problem as all these people were concentrated within the British zone of Austria. Kirk's opinion however was endorsed by Washington in a reply on 15 May in which they appeared to believe that the repatriation of Yugoslav dissidents to Tito was against British Foreign Office (and Macmillan's) policy, which of course had been the case at an earlier date.

> 'We are strongly of the opinion that such contemplated violation of agreed Anglo-American policy cannot be justified on grounds of expediency.'

As far as the Cossacks were concerned, assuming they were Soviet nationals, they saw no objection to delivering them to the Russian forces in accordance with the Yalta agreement.

The difference of opinion was solely on the grounds that the Yugoslavs were not covered by Yalta. The State Department had found it impossible to adjust to the imminent war situation developing in the British Zone of Austria, which events had taken place since this policy was originally agreed.[15]

Indeed tension was mounting in Trieste also, as this extract from General Harding's (13 Corps) situation report shows:

> 'SITREP Part 1. Tension amongst TRIESTE CIVS due to continued removal of CIV prisoners from TRIESTE. Estimated sufficient FLOUR in city to suffice 3–4 days. Mobilisation orders NOT yet published in TRIESTE but reported total make population OPPICINA U. 8377 already called up. Many trains passed over TRIESTE-MONFALCONE rls during last 24 hours. JUGOSLAV ARMY mov on br at 680000 estimate 2–3000 each way in past 24 hrs . . .'

Arrests of so-called Fascists and Nazis amongst the Italian population are evidently proceeding apace. Call-up of all-male population has begun. The looting of food stocks by Tito's troops is widespread, a later passage records the Yugoslav army taking 5 tons of sugar and 1 ton of marmalade, and the civilian food stocks are on a hand-to-mouth basis. The signal goes on to quote exorbitant Black Market prices for these days: 1 tin of bully beef equals 1200 lire, 1 cigarette 10 lire.[16] The signs of preparation for war are now unmistakable, and these signs will be ignored by the Allies at their peril.

On the same day, 17 May, another signal goes from Alexander to Eisenhower (No.FX77363), and is a follow-up which reports further deterioration in Austria and asks for a change of boundary to reduce 5 Corps area.

But the message which starts the wheels humming, albeit very slowly, is Alexander's (NAF975) to the Combined Chiefs of Staff in Washington, and to the British Chiefs of Staff in London. This asks for positive instructions for disposal of the enemy personnel:

'To assist us in clearing congestion in southern Austria we urgently require direction regarding final disposal following three classes:

(a) Approximately 50,000 Cossacks including 11,000 women, children and old men. These have been part of German armed forces and fighting against Allies.

(b) Chetniks where numbers are constantly increasing. Present estimate of total 35,000 of which we have already evacuated 11,000 to Italy.

(c) German Croat troops total 25,000.

In each of above cases, to return them to either country of origin immediately might be fatal to their health. Request decision as early as possible as to final disposal.'

This telegram seeks approval for the action which has already been ordered by Morgan on behalf of Alexander, and apparently endorsed by the only political authority in the area of operations, Harold Macmillan. But in cases of operational necessity Alexander already has full Cabinet authority to take whatever measures he deems fit.

XX

The Turning Point
18–19 May

On the 18 May, Macmillan writes a long discursive letter to the War Minister Sir James Grigg. His tone is somewhat deflated:

> 'Venezia Giulia. Since I last wrote this problem has become acute. I feel a little distressed that we have let it run on so long without a definite plan ... During the last fortnight we have been thinking about and working on little else than this problem, which has rather taken the gilt off the gingerbread of victory.'

He is afraid Alex 'feels it rather' because he really deserves a certain amount of rest after his labours. Then he describes his visit to Klagenfurt.

> 'I must say the troops are behaving with amazing self-control and good humour in a very difficult situation; but I think something must be done soon to bring it to an end – I mean at any rate within the next three or four weeks. Otherwise the temper of the troops will be too hardly tried. The utter confusion in these areas is really astonishing – I suppose in Germany it is much worse. In Austria one British corps seemed to be charged with:
> (a) Disarming, shepherding and feeding about 400,000 Germans.
> (b) Dealing with the White Russians and Cossacks, together with their wives and families, serving in these German forces.
> (c) Dealing with Ustashis, Chetniks and other Yugoslav refugees, deciding which, if any, are to be handed back to the Tito troops etc.
> (d) Standing their ground against a very large force of Yugoslav troops and partisans who have invaded Carinthia.
> (e) Coming to some arrangement with large Russian armies on their Eastern flank.
> (f) Dealing with considerable Bulgar forces who are apparently co-belligerents with the Russians and more or less under Marshal Tolbukhin's orders.'[1]

But General Keightley did not seem unduly depressed at the size of his problem, and the officers and men were making the best of it in a very splendid way. But, felt Macmillan, the situation was very disagreeable and could not be straightened out without some lapse of time. He had just heard, at the time of writing, that Tito's response to the Anglo-American *démarche* had come. It was a prevaricating and unsatisfactory one.

Then Macmillan ended on a personal note:

'I have been down at AFHQ more than at Rome lately because of the Yugoslav crisis – the Field Marshal likes me to be about so that we can talk things over.'[2]

The very close relations between Alexander and Macmillan, the one the Supreme Commander, the other the Minister Resident with a line to Churchill via the Foreign Office, might have been very difficult with two different characters. But these glimpses of intimacy give the lie to those who charge Macmillan with deceiving Alexander over his Klagenfurt meeting. They had much in common. They had both shared the privations of the First World War together in France. Both shared the mystique of the Brigade of Guards. Both had gone through the agonising 30's and watched the build-up of Hitler's power. They were good friends and close comrades in the great Mediterranean venture, and the idea that one could have deceived the other does not ring true, nor bear thinking of.

In view of impending hostilities, Alexander now deems it timely to send out an Order of the Day to all troops serving under his command, to be used by officers in discussion groups with the soldiers, another innovation in Alexander's technique of command. The idea that orders should be the subject of 'discussion' would have been anathema to Montgomery. But as we have seen, Alexander felt that he had to engage the interest of the troops and explain the reasons why we should enter into conflict with a wartime ally.

He explains that all disputes over territory are to be settled at the forthcoming Peace Conference.[3]

His Special Message declares:

'It is however MARSHAL TITO's apparent intention to establish his claims by force of arms and military occupation. Action of this kind would be all too reminiscent of HITLER, MUSSOLINI, and JAPAN. It is to prevent such actions that we have been fighting this war. We have agreed to work together to seek an orderly and just solution of territorial problems, this is one of the cardinal principles for which the peoples of the UNITED NATIONS have made their tremendous sacrifices in an endeavour to obtain a just and lasting peace . . .'[4]

Meantime Alexander's telegram NAF 975, proposing the repatriations, has reached the Foreign Office where it is the subject of some inter-departmental discussion.

Mr. S M Addis of the Southern Department (responsible for Yugoslavia) minutes that it is for the Northern Department to give a ruling on the Cossacks, but he includes one in his draft note all the same, for that Department's agreement. This note which amounts to the Foreign Office position on repatriation is of some importance.

> 'We agree with the JSM [Joint Staff Mission Washington] that the Cossacks are covered by the Yalta agreement on the reciprocal repatriation of Soviet citizens and accordingly consider it essential that all of them who are Soviet citizens should be handed over to the Soviet authorities in pursuance of our general policy. If we do not do so in the case of these particular people it would be a breach of the agreement and might look like a change of policy in this matter to which the Soviet Government attach great importance and would be assumed by the Russians to indicate hostile intentions towards them. It also might have very unfortunate reactions upon the Russian treatment of our prisoners of war uncovered by them. We suggest that F M Alexander should make arrangements with Marshal Tolbukhin for the handing over of the Cossacks across the temporary occupational demarcation line.'[5]

He then minutes to the effect that the Chetniks in Southern Austria (ex Mikhailovic men) should be treated in the same way as the Chetniks in Venezia Giulia (i.e. placed in camp pending a decision). The Croats are less deserving of consideration than the Chetniks. 'I think we should hand them over to Tito. This would be a useful gesture at this time. However, the Americans are likely to be more tender-hearted ...'[6]

On 18 May, the Cabinet Committee met and considered two telegrams from Alexander, the one to Eisenhower (NAF 974) asking for his assistance in disposing of surrendered German forces, and the other (NAF 975) to the Chiefs of Staff (London) asking for urgent and specific directions regarding final disposal of Russian, Croat and Chetnik troops, formerly part of the German armed forces. The minutes show that:

> 'Sir Andrew Cunningham[7] suggested that Field Marshal Alexander should be instructed to hand over to the Russians all Cossacks prisoners of war, and pointed out that under the Yalta agreement, they would in any event have to be repatriated to Russia.'[8]

Meantime, in consultation with the Foreign Office and War Office, a reply to Alexander should be drafted as a matter of urgency.

This is also being considered by the Combined Administration Committee (CADC) from the Joint Staff Mission in Washington.

It should be noted here that Alexander is pursuing a 'dual-track' policy in that having already ordered repatriation to Yugoslavia and Russia from the British zone, he is at the same time asking Eisenhower to relieve him from this burden.

As can be imagined a certain amount of activity has been going on behind the scenes between Churchill, Truman and Stalin. The Western Allies have been anxious that Stalin should be aware of Tito's continued illegal occupation of Austria and Venezia Giulia. Stalin argues Tito's case, but he may at the same time be leaning on his ally Tito. At any rate this, the series of allied ultimatums to Tito, and their obvious preparations to eject him by force, are having their effect.

Back at 5 Corps, Mr. Nicholls, the Foreign Office 'rep' temporarily attached to this headquarters writes to Mr. Mack, his superior at Caserta, giving his impressions:

> 'German PW, Croats, Cossacks, Slovenes are all over the place, and in say half an hour's drive there will be more of them to be seen than Austrians ...
>
> The politico-military situation is extraordinary and extremely unsatisfactory though we hope about to improve ... the general picture seems to be that Tito controls some parts of our area entirely and others partially; and in both his "Troops" behave in a way which, apart from being very unpleasant in itself, is making our future much more difficult; for they are looting and requisitioning on the grand scale under our very noses. In Klagenfurt itself there are two Military Governments – ours and theirs; and they issue their own ordinances and proclamations just as if we did not exist. The populace are nervous, and completely bewildered by the apparent absence of any reaction from us. So long as the instructions to the Corps Commander are to take no steps which could lead to shooting, I am afraid there is nothing that can be done in this humiliating and damaging situation.'⁹

Nicholls's one concrete suggestion was for the immobilisation of the Tito controlled printing-press, and so cut short the proclamations and propaganda, and force Tito to resort to 'town criers'.

But a change in fortune is not far off. On 19 May, Brigadier Low holds a meeting at 5 Corps headquarters, Klagenfurt with Colonel Ivanovitch, Deputy Commander, 3rd Yugoslav Army, at seven o'clock in the evening. At this meeting the Yugoslav withdrawal is announced. '14 DIV has been ordered to withdraw all troops SOUTH OF YUGOSLAV AUSTRIAN border ... by 1900 hrs. 21 May at the latest' runs the note on this meeting. Furthermore, 14 DIV will be ordered to return all requisitioned civilian property, and cease requisitioning forthwith. All Yugoslav Town Major's and Area head-quarters in Austria will be informed of the orders to withdraw south of the border. An important part of this agreement, in accordance with AFHQ instructions, is that 5 Corps will return all Yugoslav nationals who have been fighting in uniform with the Germans, and their camp followers. These will include Ustachi, Domobrons, Chetniks, Nedics and White Guards (for a description of the Yugoslav groups see Appendix F).[10]

So Tito's bluff has been called. He has tried by aggression to seize territory that was in no way his. He has now been forced to withdraw at least from Austria. But there is a payment to be made and this the Allies, and in particular the British, will find a painful way of restoring the *status quo*.

Confirmation that Tito is in earnest comes from the British Ambassador, Belgrade on the afternoon of 19 May in a message from the Yugoslav Under Secretary of State for Foreign Affairs.

> 'The Government of Democratic Federative Yugoslavia have issued orders to troops of the Yugoslav Army who are NORTH of the Austrian frontiers of 1937 in the area WEST of DRAVOGRAD to withdraw to pre-war boundary line.'

However, the Yugoslav Government reiterated that the presence of their troops on territory occupied by them in the fight against the common enemies in no way prejudiced the final outcome, but were withdrawing to comply to the utmost with the wishes of their allies.[11]

Let us introduce a mundane note here. Looking through 6 British Armoured Division administration papers I see that it was estimated that on 19 May the total feeding commitment, including refugees and prisoners, was approximately 140,000 persons daily, for a division whose own strength was barely 15,000. Ration scales were laid down. For the troops there was 4oz of meat, horse flesh or sausage-meat a day. For all others the ration was 2oz. The slaughterhouse and sausage-making machinery were placed under the charge of a German, Major Reyels, and the necessary horses for sausage meat would be supplied by the division's transport.[12] These details show the extent of the commitment of divisions for feeding the multitude, let alone being prepared for war.

But two signals show more clearly than anything else the parlous state, both in Austria and in Italy, over food and transport. On 17 May, Military Government staff (Austria) signal 8th Army and AFHQ:

> 'Austrian flour situation in present British occupied zone already serious ... Rationing in Austria being cut minimum to support existence ... will be imposs-

ible to feed numbers moving into Austria ... Alternative force back or hand-over
to Yugoslav anti-Tito Slovenes.'[13]

The reply from AFHQ to Military Government staff (Austria) dispatched on 18 May was equally uncompromising:

'Ref your M1015 of 17 May. Appreciate gravity of position and grateful for
information but consider unlikely can accept further refugees Italy. Food can
be made available when transportation possible.'[14]

It was a classic refugee situation. Chronic shortages of food and
transport had combined to create a near starvation crisis. As these
two signals show, it was no good robbing Peter to pay Paul. The
situation was the same in both Austria and Italy and could not be
alleviated without mass evacuation homewards.

On 21 May, the date on which Tito's troops were to be clear of
Austria, a conference was called at Headquarters 5 Corps, to define
which categories of prisoner were to be considered Soviet Nationals
and to be repatriated by 5 Corps. A number of cases were being
raised over whether certain formations and groups should be included.
The full report on conclusions reached, 'Definition of Russian Nationals' under the signature of Brigadier Low, is given at Appendix
D.

This document has become known as the 'Definition Letter' and
was given a certain prominence in the recent Trial. The case advanced
against Low was that he had exceeded his authority in laying down
which groups should be included and which exempted, in that he
had laid down that individual cases should not be considered unless
particularly pressed, and that in all cases of doubt the individual
should be treated as a Soviet National.

Also included in this letter were some rules of residence not strictly
in accordance with the definitive Orders issued by AFHQ of 6 March
and 15 March respectively, implementing the Yalta agreement. This
defined a Soviet citizen as one who had lived in the Soviet Union
before 1 September 1939, and who was therefore liable for repatriation.[15] For all these reasons, Low was accused of issuing this order
without higher authority. Thanks to Brigadier Cowgill's researches,
we now have the AFHQ authority quoted above, and it will be seen
from the letter reproduced in Appendix D that Low's definition letter
was copied to higher authority, that is his immediate superior headquarters, 8th Army. General McCreery was aware of what was going
on.

The definition letter specifically excluded the Russian *Schütz
Korps*.[16] This was reported to be made up from remnants of the old

Imperial Army which had settled in Yugoslavia after the Russian Revolution and who had carried on their traditions by means of schools and training cadres. They had been joined by 'White' *émigrés* from Roumania and Bulgaria, and were under the command of Colonel Rogozhin. The *Schütz Korps* had been moved from the camp at Viktring and were now located at Klein St Viet.

Included in those eligible for repatriation was the Ataman Group (Domanov's Cossacks), the 15th Cossack Cavalry Corps, an SS unit under command of the German, General Helmuth von Pannwitz; reserve units of Lieutenant General Shkouro, also known as 'General Shkouro's Training Unit', he was a former Cossack commander from the civil war; Caucasians (i.e. Christians from the Caucasus and Moslems from Azerbadjan respectively). All these units had of course been fighting on the German side.[17]

The main criticism about the 5 Corps letter of definition has been that there was no individual screening and that they were screened *en bloc* by formations. This is true and under the exigencies of the day with the urgent need to evacuate the area of operations, individual screening would have been quite impossible under the resources and time-scale available. After subsequent and lengthy investigation it was found that the *Schütz Korps* was made up of a preponderant number of *émigrés*, 65 per cent having lived in Yugoslavia before the war, 27 per cent from Bulgaria and others from Roumania. Whilst the groups to be repatriated contained only a minority of *émigrés*.[18]

There had already been substantive representations on behalf of the two groups which were evacuated to Italy. In the case of the former, the Ukrainians, by General Anders Commander of the Polish Corps fighting under Alexander, who pointed out that most of these men were Polish citizens from a part of Poland seized by the Russians and incorporated into the Ukraine after September 1939. In the case of the latter, the *Schütz Korps*, by Colonel Walton Long a retired British Officer now serving with the Red Cross. He had special knowledge of their history having himself served in the British Military Mission to the White Russians in the Civil War in 1920.

And, let us not forget, it was not only former German combatants that 5 Corps had to deal with, but special categories had to be weeded out of the total mass, in order that those guilty of war crimes did not escape the net. Orders issued by 6 British Armoured Division on 23 May categorised the following as candidates for close confinement: Parachutists; all SS units; the Brandenburger Regiment; Sprong Kommando's; Propaganda companies; Naval saboteurs; the Todt (or

Labour organisation) German personnel; the German Secret Intelligence and Secret Police (Gestapo), and Nazi Commissars.

British troops in Austria really had their hands full, even a gigantic colander could scarcely strain the dregs of war.

XXI

The Climb-Down
20–26 May

During this past week there had been a rapid exchange of signals between Alexander and Eisenhower. There were two ways in which Alexander needed help. One, on the disposal of enemy personnel and two, on the reduction of 5 Corps area in the north, in order to free it for possible operations on the Yugoslav border to the south.

The outline operational plan was given in telegram NAF 972 from Alexander to the Combined Chiefs of Staff on 16 May. It included the ejection of Marshal Tito's forces both from Southern Austria and from North-East Italy. General Clark's 15 Army Group would be given overall responsibility for seizing Trieste and securing Allied lines of communication leading into Austria. With 13 (British) Corps he would secure Trieste and the L of C; with his other arm, 5 (British) Corps, he would eject Tito's forces from Carinthia. A part of Eisenhower's 12 Army Group consisting of five divisions (which was to be designated Third Army)[1] was to take over the northern part of Carinthia in the area Judenburg-Leinz and would act in a supporting role.[2]

In order to appreciate the full picture and get a better idea of the sequence of events, we must now deviate from the time-bracket of this chapter, for the situation began to develop on 17 May:

AFHQ to SHAEF

'Refugee and PoW situation in 5 Corps becoming unmanageable and prejudicing operational efficiency of Corps. Essential to clear it immediately in view of political situation. Request your assistance.'[3]

On 17 May, Alexander to Eisenhower.

> 'Can you come to my assistance as regards surrendered German armed forces incl Cossacks.'
>   See page 121)[4]

Again on 17 May, Alexander to Eisenhower.

> '5 Corps situation serious. Can you take on the northern sector of 5 Corps front facing the Russians?'[5]

On 20 May Alexander to Eisenhower.

> 'Much appreciate your prompt assistance. Immediate operational need is to relieve 5 Corps in Judenburg and Leinz areas to enable them to concentrate on Austria/Yugoslav frontier in readiness operations against Yugoslavs.'[6]

Eisenhower to Chiefs of Staff, 20 May.

> 'In entire agreement with FM Alexander ... Taking preliminary steps to concentrate required forces. Have already agreed allow 150,000 surrendered enemy to be moved northwards into my area.'[7]

So far so good. But 8th Army appears to be confused and sends this signal.

8th Army to AFHQ, copy 5 Corps, 21 May.

> 'Is approved policy to dispatch Russians to SHAEF, or to endeavour to secure direct return to Russia by Eighth Army negotiation?'[8]

The answer came next day:

AFHQ to Eighth Army, 22 May.

> '1. All who are Soviet citizens and who can be handed over to Russians without use of force should be returned direct by 8th Army.
> 2. Any other should be evacuated to 12 Army Group.
> 3. Definition of a Soviet citizen is given in AFHQ letter CR/3491/91 (British) of 6 Mar addressed 15 Army Group and 8th Army.'[9]

One must presume that this evident change of policy by Alexander to repatriate Soviet citizens direct to the Russians (instead of asking Eisenhower to accept them), was that he felt the onus was upon him to deal with surrendered enemy who were in his theatre, rather than 'pass the buck' to Eisenhower. For he knew that if he was completely overwhelmed by the task he could count on Eisenhower to help him out.[10]

The definition of a Soviet citizen referred to in the AFHQ letter of 6 March rules that:

> 'Under British law, Soviet citizens are all persons coming from places within the boundaries of the Soviet Union as constituted before the outbreak of the present war. All persons coming from territories west of such boundaries have Polish or Baltic state nationality unless there is evidence to show in particular cases that they have acquired Soviet citizenship by their own voluntary act.

All persons of undoubted Soviet citizenship will be repatriated irrespective of their own wishes.'[11]

The term 'Soviet citizens', as originally defined at Yalta, was intended to deal with such categories only and did not envisage an *émigré* class of Russian who had found his way into a unit predominantly made up of ex-Soviet soldiers or Soviet citizens, such as some groups of Cossacks. The realisation that mixed units was a commonplace occurrence began to dawn on those responsible rather slowly.

An example of this can be seen in the letter which Nicholls (Foreign Office representative attached to 5 Corps) wrote to his superior, W H B Mack at Caserta.[12] One of his concerns was the evacuation of British subjects, former internees etc. Most had been evacuated already and been repatriated to the United Kingdom. But there were a few oddments such as divorcée British-born wives of Austrians, Maltese-British subjects from Tripoli and such like. Then he continues:

'I am being confronted with similar problems; if captured Cossacks fighting with the Germans are to be handed over to the Russians, what should be done with White Russians with French nationality? And so on and so on!'

Clearly the White Russians serving amongst Soviet citizens in the German armed forces were not a problem which loomed very large at that moment. French citizens who had thrown their lot in with the Germans would not have been very popular in France!

The first part of Nicholls's letter, gives a circumstantial report of the negotiations at 5 Corps. It begins:

'My dear Hal
  This is in continuation of the letter I sent you by the hand of my brother. I wrote that on Saturday 19th, while the BGS was sitting with two Yugoslav officers outside his caravan; and by the time I had finished the letter their talk had already made it out of date.'

This was a reference to Low's meeting with Ivanovitch at which the details of Yugoslav withdrawal were settled.

'The two Yugoslav officers stayed to dinner, and the atmosphere was friendly to a degree; they had brought a case of champagne, and in it we exchanged numerous toasts. The Corps Commander has a positive genius for saying the right thing and making it sound completely spontaneous through an interpreter, which is no mean feat; and I doubt if two emissaries sent to climb down ever went away as happy as those two! Yesterday the withdrawal was in full swing, and by tomorrow we should be able to call our zone our own.'

and then he adds,

'The effect of all this on the Austrians is difficult to gauge. They were completely bewildered by our inactivity, but I think the settlement came just in time to

enable us to represent the whole things as a vindication of the British method
of restraint and patience. Feeling apparently varies a good deal from place
to place: in Klagenfurt yesterday the atmosphere was definitely more friendly,
but at Lienz it is distinctly cool and sulky.'

Mack adds an interesting postscript to his covering letter to the
Foreign Office, 'as one would expect in as strong a Nazi a province
as Carinthia.'[13]

The degree of priority given to the White Russian case can be
seen from the fact that although Nicholls' letter was dated 26 May,
it was not received at the Foreign Office until 7 June, well after the
repatriations had taken place.

But do not let us pass over this moment lightly. After all the restraint
shown in the first two weeks of this confrontation; after all the accrued
exertions and exhaustion of the 6 year war; after all the heart-searching
about entering into hostilities against a wartime ally, we have – by
showing some strength and resolution – demonstrated that the very
reasons for which we went to war, namely resistance to the arbitrary
use of force for territorial gain, have not been forgotten. Credit must
go to the leading participants in this business, some to be woundingly
denigrated in later days; to Alexander and Macmillan; to Keightley
his divisional commanders and his Chief of Staff BGS Low. And
behind them the massive moral and political support of Western
leaders Churchill and Truman. But lest I am premature in my conclusions as to Tito's Austrian adventure, let me hasten to add that the
confrontation still continues in the province of Venezia Guilia. And
lest I am accused of over-righteousness concerning this happy outcome of a war within a war, let me take a page from Macmillan's
diary three months earlier which showed that the reason we went
to war, namely over Poland, had now turned to dust and ashes in
our mouths. A sceptic might draw the conclusion that before the
war had ended we had lost the original causes for which we had
fought. Thus Macmillan recorded from Caserta on 17 February:

'Rather a distressing evening. General Anders ... was in a bitter, despairing
mood. The dinner passed off with discussion of trivialities. After dinner Alex
wisely let the General have a fling ... a rather painful discussion – or rather
monologue – in which General Anders said that Poland was finished, betrayed
by her allies. It was now merely a question of time before all Europe would
succumb to Bolshevism etc. etc.'

Returning once more to the main narrative, Macmillan departs
for London on 19 May, having been recalled by Churchill 'for consultation'. Whilst staying at Chequers he is immediately embroiled in
the imminent collapse of the war-time Coalition Government. This

is all the talk at dinner that first night at Chequers. After dinner, Macmillan does attempt to explain the various problems in the Mediterranean, but Churchill's mind is not really on it, 'He thinks and talks of so many things at once.' However, another reason for his recall becomes obvious two days later, when Churchill offers him the Air Ministry, with a seat in the Cabinet. He returns to Caserta, but is now about to bow out. By the 26 May, he has gone. He notes in his diary 'It is the end of a chapter – Mediterranean merry-go-round or from Darlan to Tito.'[14]

PART FIVE

WAR AVERTED – BUT A PRICE TO PAY

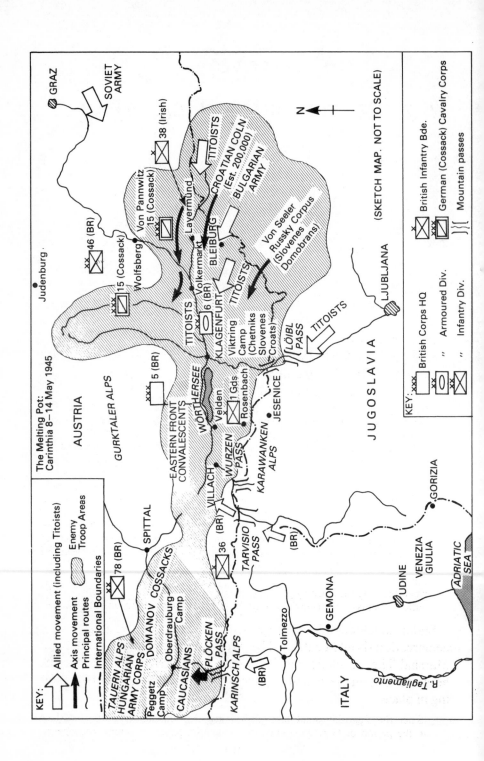

The Melting Pot:
Carinthia 8–14 May 1945

KEY:
⇨ Allied movement (including Titoists)
▲ Axis movement
Principal routes
— — International Boundaries
░ Enemy Troop Areas

(SKETCH MAP. NOT TO SCALE)

KEY:
⬚ British Corps HQ
◎ " Armoured Div.
⬚ " Infantry Div.
⬚ British Infantry Bde.
⬚ German (Cossack) Cavalry Corps
} Mountain passes

GRAZ
SOVIET ARMY
38 (Irish)
TITOISTS
CROATIAN COLN
(Est. 200,000)
BULGARIAN ARMY
Von Seeler
Russky Corpus
(Slovenes)
Domobrans)
46 (BR)
Von Pannwitz
15 (Cossack)
15 (Cossack)
Wolfsberg
Lavermünd
Völkermarkt
6 (BR)
BLEIBURG
TITOISTS
Judenburg
AUSTRIA
GURKTALER ALPS
TITOISTS
KLAGENFURT
Viktring
Camp
(Chetniks
Slovenes
Croats)
TITOISTS
LÖIBL PASS
LJUBLJANA
5 (BR)
WÖRTHERSEE
Velden
1 Gds
Rosenbach
JESENICE
KARAWANKEN ALPS
JUGOSLAVIA
SPITTAL
EASTERN FRONT CONVALESCENTS
VILLACH
WURZEN PASS
(BR)
TARVISIO PASS
(BR)
78 (BR)
TAUERN ALPS
HUNGARIAN ARMY CORPS
DOMANOV COSSACKS
Oberdrauburg Camp
Peggetz Camp
CAUCASIANS
PLÖCKEN PASS
KARINSCH ALPS
(BR)
36 (BR)
GEMONA
Tolmezzo
UDINE
VENEZIA GIULIA
GORIZIA
ADRIATIC SEA
ITALY
R. Tagliamento
N

XXII

Balkan Backlash:
Bleiburg and Rosenbach

The history of the Balkans has been a turbulent one. Yugoslavia, itself created by the Treaty of Versailles out of the broken empires of Austro-Hungary and Turkey, or rather the successor states to the Ottoman empire, that is Serbia, Bosnia and Herzegovina, Montenegro and Macedonia. In the north, the Croatians, Slovenes and Dalmatians were mainly Catholic. The Bosnians were the most northerly outpost of the Muslim world, whilst Serbians and Macedonians were chiefly of the Christian Orthodox faith. There was nothing that united the peoples which became 'Yugoslavs' except that they were all southern Slavs with a tradition of intense racial rivalry and formidable fighting qualities played out against a harsh and inhospitable land.

As Fitzroy Maclean remarked in a report on Yugoslavia written in February 1945, (in preparation for Alexander's visit to Tito).[1]

> 'It is important to remember that in the Balkans – and Yugoslavia has been no exception to the rule – democracy, as we know it, has never existed. Periods of corrupt Parliamentary confusion have been followed by periods of equally corrupt dictatorship. Dynasties and dictators, parliaments and politicians have rapidly succeeded one another and equally rapidly become discredited.'

Maclean pointed out that the ethnological patchwork formed by the frontiers of states and provinces had been an unending cause of external and internal dissension and bloodshed. He doubted whether the Yugoslavs, any more than other Balkan peoples, were in fact capable of government on British parliamentary lines.

But he was quite certain that Tito, the Comintern agent turned Partisan leader, held all the levers of power that would assure him the leadership of post-war Yugoslavia.

141

'Even when the seat of Tito's administration was a cave or hut in the woods, it was clear he was building up an authoritarian system of government on a single party system, and a single party line, with all real power concentrated in the hands of one man.'[2]

It was näive of the Western Allies, in the extreme, to believe that our standards were their standards, or that 'full rights of surrendered personnel' for repatriated dissidents meant anything else than a bullet in the back of the neck. But who are we to judge, from a comfortable posture with the benefit of 40 years' hindsight, what were the true conditions and imperatives of the day. In order to safeguard the British Zone of Occupation in Austria, and resist the bullying of a dictator, we had got rid of Tito, (and his anti-Tito opponents) in one clean sweep, for which the people of Austria should be grateful. But Tito had his pound of flesh. It was inevitable. Only CIGS Brooke was uneasy;

'I cannot help feeling that Maclean is not tough enough with Tito and far too inclined to pander to his whims.'[3]

But even Alexander on his visit found Tito so reasonable. On 28 February he wrote to Brooke.

'I have today returned from a most successful visit to BELGRADE. I found Marshal TITO very friendly, sensible and co-operative. He has agreed to all the proposals I made to him.'[4]

It was in the autumn of 1943 that Britain had decided to switch support from Mihailovic's Chetniks to Tito's Partisans. Mihailovic, who was a former royalist officer, was thought to be getting ineffective. So said reports from SOE Cairo who were controlling resistance operations in Yugoslavia.

In December 1943 the British gave Mihailovic a last chance, when he was asked to blow up the important viaducts on the main railway south of Belgrade. Cairo reported that he failed to do so, and by the end of the year HMG decided to drop him.[5] SOE in Cairo has since come in for a great deal of criticism for allegedly concealing a pro-communist cell, which wrongly influenced HMG against the royalist Mihailovic, and in favour of the communist Tito.

Nevertheless Churchill now became interested in the relatively unknown Tito, and Fitzroy Maclean was sent as Churchill's personal emissary to seek out the elusive Tito and report. Maclean also had a brush with SOE, as he later recalled. Having seen the Prime Minister and been personally briefed by him he was then seeking the good offices of SOE to get him on a plane to Cairo without delay. After much procrastination he decided to see the Minister responsible for

SOE activities, Lord Selborne, who we shall meet in a later chapter. Maclean explains:

> 'I saw Lord Selborne, who was most agreeable, congratulated me on the trust the Prime Minister had placed in me and suggested I should take an oath of loyalty to SOE. I said I would rather not. At this he pointed to the little leather cases on his desk with the letters D.S.O in gold. "That" he said, "is what we do for those who serve us loyally".'[6]

His experiences with SOE in Cairo had made him take an even more jaundiced view of that organisation. Having been dropped into Yugoslavia, he reported positively, on Tito and his partisan organisation. He was accompanied by an experienced fighting soldier, Vivian Street and a Sapper, Peter Moore, also a veteran of the desert. It was this powerful team's report that finally convinced Churchill. It was odd though, that if SOE Cairo had been dominated by such avid pro-Titoists, they had not supported so powerful an envoy, as Fitzroy Maclean, on his mission to their chosen candidate, Tito.

It was in June 1944 that Churchill laid down his strategic goals.

> 'At the present stage of the war in Europe, our overall strategic concept should be the engagement of the enemy on the largest scale with the greatest violence and continuity.'[7]

Tito's group fulfilled this role more effectively than that of Mihailovic. It is not my purpose to enter into the argument concerning the wisdom of switching partisan allies, it was not an uncommon occurrence, as the history of British support for Greek Partisans shows. Our purpose, at that time, was solely to 'win the war' and not to worry too much about the political shape of Europe thereafter. Albeit, by the end of 1944 this attitude had changed dramatically.

But Fitzroy Maclean, writing in 1945, summed up Tito's contribution as follows:

> 'The fact remains that, from the summer of 1941 until the present time, the Jugoslav Partisans, undeterred by lack of supplies, by their own setbacks or by the setbacks of their Allies, alone in occupied Europe maintained constant active resistance to the enemy. During this period, by the successful use of guerilla methods, they succeeded in containing a force of anything from 15 to 20 divisions, which could otherwise have been used against the Allies on another front.'[8]

That Tito used his position, supplied and equipped largely by the British, to improve his internal position and to eliminate his enemies is a matter of history. If the boot had been on the other foot, and Germany and the German sponsored groups in Yugoslavia had ended victorious, then wholesale slaughter of Tito's men would have been the order of the day.

Having received a first impression of the bitter enmity which governed relationships between the two main partisan groups in Yugoslavia, it is not entirely surprising that they should each have acquired allies wherever they could find them. Tito was a communist in close alliance with the Soviets; the Chetniks therefore would have sought support and collaboration from the anti-communist Axis power-base, Germany, once British support was withdrawn.

Croatia was in a somewhat different category, having had their separate nationhood endorsed by the Nazis earlier in the war, when they became a fully-fledged German satellite-state. So much for the politico-military map of Yugoslavia, we must now return to events in Austria.

In Part Four we were dealing with the hectic period in the last two weeks of May 1945. Before finally concluding the events of that month, we must examine an extract from a signal which Brigadier Low dispatched on 17 May from Headquarters 5 Corps to subordinate formations, concerning the repatriation of Yugoslavs. This was in promulgation of the 'Robertson order' (see Chapter xvi), for which Alexander was now seeking retrospective endorsement.

> '*From Main 5 Corps.*
> *Action 6 ARMD DIV – 46 DIV – 78 DIV – 1 AGRA.* . . .
> 0.462 SECRET. All JUGOSLAV nationals at present in CORPS area will be handed over to TITO forces as soon as possible. These forces will be disarmed immediately but will NOT be told of their destination. Arrangements for the handover will be co-ordinated by this HQ in conjunction with JUGOSLAV forces. . . .'[9]

It will be noted that the Yugoslavs to be handed over are not to be told of their destination and this has been seized upon by critics as an act of unparalleled duplicity towards the captive Yugoslavs.

Let us examine this charge for a moment. By this time the dissident Yugoslavs had been fighting in aid of the Germans against our allies, Tito's men, and as such were classed as surrendered enemy personnel. The war was not so remote that normal deception plans should not be used against enemy, or former enemy. Deception was part of a day to day operational resource. But that aside, there was the need to move these numbers, without loss of life either to the Yugoslav dissidents or to our own troops. In fact, deception was essential if our own guards were not to be overwhelmed, or large reinforcements required which would seriously weaken our operational forces now poised to eject Tito's men from Carinthia.

One can imagine that those charged with this responsibility and who had already established relations with the prisoners were loath to tell a deliberate lie to their charges. The official line was that they were simply not to be told of their destination, serious disturbances would have otherwise rendered the operation impossible.

As it turned out practically no force had to be used in the case of the Yugoslav repatriates, and this was the justification for this policy. But was it right to send these people back into the hands of their enemies when they included large numbers of women and children? I think it shows considerable naivety on the part of the British in believing that the Yugoslavs were 'just like us' and that the Tito-ists would honour their obligation to give them a fair trial. The Balkans have traditionally been the scene of internecine warfare of a particularly barbarous type, with inter-ethnic feuds widespread. Many of the dissident Yugoslav leaders were classed as 'war criminals' in the eyes of the Tito régime, or at least as quislings or collaborators. We do not have to go far to see the fate reserved for collaborators. (Even in France, for instance, 4,500 collaborators were officially executed. If one includes those executed by the Resistance the figures may have been as high as 50,000).[10]

Furthermore, the dissident Yugoslavs were all under the command of the German, Oberst von Seeler, who brought them to Viktring camp, and therefore were part of the German Armed Forces. As we have seen, an allied agreement provided that enemy personnel should only surrender to those against whom they were facing, in this case our Yugoslav allies. For although the official policy of the British and United States governments was that the ultimate disposal of those personnel would be decided at national level, this had been over-ridden by operational necessity. Evidenced by General Clark's (15 Army Group) Signal of 7 May (SGS 345) that McCreery should 'accept only those forces in contact with 8th Army. ... Those facing Tito forces i.e. dissident Yugoslavs, must surrender to Tito'. Amplified by General Robertson's AFHQ order of 14 May that 'all surrendered personnel of established Yugoslav nationality who were serving in the German forces (i.e. dissident Yugoslavs at Viktring camp all under Oberst von Seeler), should be disarmed and handed over to the Yugoslav forces'.

Now let us follow the story of the unfortunate Croats. Of all the groups who fought against Tito, the Croats and their 'quisling' government were the hard-liners. The Croatian Ustachi had committed many atrocities against Tito's men.[11]

We remember the signal sent by Marshal Tito to the Yugoslav

First Army on 13 May when he reported a group of over 50,000 Ustachi and Chetniks moving towards Dravograd (see page 115) and his directions for an attack and the annihilation of this group. And then the message from Eighth Army to 15 Army Group on 14 May reporting 300,000 Germans and 200,000 Croats moving towards the Villach-Klagenfurt area, which contained the suggestion that 'Croats become Tito's show' (see page 114). These two messages presaged a major confrontation between Croats and Tito's armies.

On 15 May, 5 Corps signalled 8th Army recording that 200,000 Croats were trying to enter Austria via Bleiburg. Then, on 16 May, 5 Corps signalled AFHQ, 8th Army and its constituent divisions that the Commander of 38 Irish Infantry Brigade had achieved the agreement of the Croat Corps Commander to surrender to Yugoslav forces all the 200,000 men under his command. They were to be assembled and disarmed within the Yugoslav border East of Bleiburg. The signal concluded:

> 'Yugoslavs have guaranteed full rights of surrendered personnel and agreed to trial of nominated war criminals by Allied court. Large train of camp followers to be sent back to Croatia.'[12]

It was at Bleiburg that a major massacre of Croats by those Yugoslav forces was alleged to have taken place, immediately following this surrender, and we will pursue this in a later paragraph.

Let us now return to the crossing points fixed for Viktring camp. The place appointed for handover of the Viktring prisoners was at the branch line stations of Maria Elend and Rosenbach on the Austro-Yugoslav frontier. Here the mountain barrier of the Karawanken range, which rises above these stations out of the plain, was the actual border line. At Rosenbach, the line forked, the left hand route entering a tunnel through the mountains and emerging at Jesenice in Yugoslavia, the other line, which happened to be disused at the time, carrying on until it crossed into Italy.

I do not intend to go into the indiscreet message sent by a staff officer at HQ 1 Guards Brigade, questioning the whole purpose of the repatriations, for which he got 'hauled over the coals' by his divisional commander. It has been covered elsewhere, for this was a task which anyone taking part could not look forward to with great relish.

Brigadier Gerald Verney's views are not recorded. But judging from his letters home he took a harder line towards those he considered Britain's enemies. Describing, in the robust language of the day, how he organised Viktring camp for which the brigade was responsible, he wrote shortly afterwards:

> 'On 12th we were relieved at Villach and moved to Klagenfurt. There we were again overwhelmed with refugees and battered Armies. We formed a huge camp in an open space and collected what we estimated to be about 48,000 people with their cattle, sheep, old folk and children. The camp was run by a German Corps Staff assisted by a Russian Corps Staff, and it went well as they all understood the motto, coined by me, was "no obedience, no food".'[13]

It was the task of the British troops to deliver the Croatians, and later the Slovenes and Serbian Chetniks over to Tito's Yugoslav officers at the crossing points at Maria Elend and Rosenbach. As described above, Tito's Partisans lay concealed until the trains were loaded. When the wretched Croatians realised that they were bound for Yugoslavia and not Italy, there was indeed considerable anguish. Even though the Croatians were deemed to be collaborators of the first degree, and included members of their quisling government, and the Domobrans, who were the home guard or 'resistance', and the dreaded Ustachi, it was not a very nice task for the British troops to carry out. After many conversations with Welsh Guards officers, who were in the first instance involved, it is clear that it was a very distasteful incident, but there was general acceptance that it was 'another bloody job which had to be done'.

But to return to Bleiburg once again. There is now less certainty that the massacres at Bleiburg did take place. Previous writers did not have access to the material which has subsequently come to light. There is no mention of these happenings in Brigadier Scott's War Diary of 38 Infantry Brigade or in his personal account of events. Since the castle dominated the plain upon which the killings are alleged to have taken place, it is strange that there are no British eye-witness accounts, and all we have to rely upon is the evidence of the three Croat 'witnesses'. When I visited Bleiburg in 1989, and stood on the castle hill, I could not somehow imagine a massacre taking place under the very noses of Brigadier Scott and his staff officers without it being reported.

However, according to Anthony Cowgill, who has carried out a recent investigation of the subject, considerable slaughter did take place against the tail of the Croat column as Tito's men cut it off inside Yugoslavia (see Tito's signal of 13 May to his First Army. 'You must move your forces most urgently from the Celje area ...in order to concentrate for an attack aimed at the annihilation of this column') according to Yugoslav sources; and also against the head of the column which had been turned round at Bleiburg and had reached Poljana inside Yugoslavia. Here there were reports that the column had been machine-gunned. But at Bleiburg itself Tito's men killed some Croat wounded, and some trying to escape into the woods. No more than 30 to 50 being buried locally.[14]

We must now turn to Brigadier T P D Scott's own account written shortly after the event in the Regimental Gazette of the Royal Irish Fusiliers, under the heading 'Balkan Troubles'.[15]

He writes:

'Early in the morning of the 14th, reports were received from 17th Field Regiment of fighting between the Croats and the Yugoslav Tito troops. The Croats apparently had been fighting on the wrong side. In the evening, a Croat Liaison Officer appeared at the 17th Field [at Bleiburg] offering to surrender to the British and lay down their arms after passing through the British outpost. The Liaison Officer arrived at my Headquarters to tell his story about 9 pm. He said there were two groups of Croats, each of about 100,000 men under arms, and that they were at present attempting to get past the Bulgarian and Yugoslav outposts and surrender themselves to us. Their main object, apparently, was to escape from the Tito régime, and they were not in the least particular about what country they were finally going to so long as it was not Yugoslavia. Further questions revealed that there were half a million civilians, including women and children trailing along behind, and the remnants of a couple of German Divisions – quite a tidy little party it seemed!

The Croat Liaison Officer said that their relations with the Bulgarians were pretty good. They had made an agreement with them that they should be allowed to pass through their outposts south of Lavamund and turn west to Bleiburg.

This manoeuvre had started quite satisfactorily until the Yugoslavs came along, drove back the Bulgarians and then opened fire on the Croats. The Croats lost two or three of their rather doubtful tanks to the Yugoslavia bazooka men, and had some civilians killed by shell-fire, but they succeeded in getting the Yugoslavs back from these crossroads and continued their advance towards Bleiburg and the 17th Field Regiment. The remainder of the Croats were still coming up from the south. If the Yugoslavs had not turned up, it is quite possible that the Bulgarians might have accepted the surrender of the Croats, but that would not suit the Yugoslavs at all. Apparently Yugoslavs and Bulgarians cannot stand the sight of each other. It is awfully hard to know who likes who in this part of Europe. Probably the best assumption to make is that anybody will cut the other fellow's throat for twopence.

On referring this nice little problem of the Croats to higher authority, I was told that on no account could we allow them to surrender to us; they had fought against the Yugoslavs in aid of Germany and Yugoslav prisoners they must become.'

It was now 15 May. Bleiburg Day. It seemed that an 'irresistible force', the Croat column of at least 800,000, was about to meet an 'immovable object' the 17 Field Regiment of about 150 men. Scott continues the tale:

'I reached Bleiburg at 1230 and had a drive around the area. A desultory clatter of musketry seemed to be going on in various directions, but I think it was only the "heartening" type, so dear to the Yugoslavs, and, fortunately, quite harmless as a rule. I could not see anything except the Yugoslavs, and so withdrew to Bleiburg Castle and sent for the opposing commanders with whom I knew Rupert Lecky, commanding the 17th Field Regiment, was in touch. Within half an hour he had rounded up both Generals and turned up at the castle, not altogether sorry to pass the baby.

Our total resources at Bleiburg at that time was Paul Lunn-Rockliffe's battery, a troop or two of 46th Reconnaissance Regiment, a couple of armoured cars of 27th Lancers, and two or three tanks. The battery of guns was deployed in the most open place that could be found, in case anyone should overlook this big display of force, and another battery was moved south of the River Drava to support them – just in case.

The head boy of the Yugoslavs was a Commissar, a most determined young man in the early twenties, who, I gathered, ranked as a Major-General. He informed me, with some emphasis, that the Yugoslav Army was ready to fight, and that he had issued orders for the battle to start in half an hour's time.

His intention was to defeat the Croat Army in the field in battle.

Under no circumstances could he allow any delay in achieving this estimable object.

He did not request any military assistance, as he said that the very large Yugoslav forces which were now deployed in the hills round about were quite adequate to deal with the situation. Moreover, he said, fresh troops were arriving every minute.

It certainly looked as if we were well situated for a front row in the stalls for the ensuing conflict. I had noticed, with relief, that the walls of the castle were exceedingly thick, and the approaches to it extremely difficult!

I suggested to this firebrand that the elimination of the Croatian Army, which no doubt was highly desirable, would be more satisfactorily achieved if the Croats laid down their arms than if it became necessary to attack a force of such large dimensions. They agreed that this was so, but reiterated their desire to start the battle in half an hour.

I did not think it was very likely that the battle would start while he was still with me, and I had taken adequate steps to ensure that he did not leave until I was ready!'

The Tito emissaries then withdrew and Scott sent for the Croatian party.

'The Croats were a much more orthodox looking outfit. There were about ten of them all told, headed by a General and a very nasty looking Commissar. The Yugoslav couple had had an American soldier of Yugoslav extraction as an interpreter. This fellow had apparently been living with them for the last ten months. I kept the American to do interpreter with the Croats so that he could explain what had been said to the Yugoslavs who would then know that there had not been any funny stuff going on behind their backs.

The Croatian deputation was absolutely adamant that both the Army and the civilians with them would rather die where they were, fighting to the last man, than surrender to "any Bolshevists". They pointed out that this movement was an emigration of the entire Croat nation, as they had decided it was impossible for them to live under Bolshevist influence. They requested, therefore, that their plea should be referred to Field-Marshal Alexander as a political matter. I asked them where they were emigrating to, but their destination did not seem to be a matter that any of them had considered. I asked them how they proposed to feed such a vast multitude in a Europe that was already entirely disorganised and extremely hungry.'

Scott told them that an emigration such as this was quite out of the question at the moment. They could not possibly be fed whatever part of Europe they went to. Such an emigration could only take place after careful preparation, otherwise the whole party would undoubtedly starve.

'They suggested that they might go to America or Africa, and I told them that the ways and means for such a movement were completely non-existent at present, and that if they moved anywhere they would be bound to starve. Starving, they insisted was an infinitely preferable course to surrendering to Tito.

The Yugoslav Commander, in the meantime, was sending me messages saying that he could not wait any longer and that the battle must start.

I was getting a little tired of the Croatian Commissar, who took the floor whenever he got the chance, and started delivering himself of political orations.

Quite concisely I gave them the alternatives and five minutes to take their choice.

The alternatives were these. First: That they would surrender to the Yugoslavs. That I would use my influence, though unofficially, to try and ensure that they would be treatly [treated] correctly. Secondly: That they stayed where they were and were attacked by the Yugoslavs. Third: That they endeavoured to advance into the British lines, when they would not only be attacked by the Yugoslavs, but by all the weight of British and American Air Forces, land forces, and everything else that I could get my hands on, in which case they would unquestionably be annihilated.

The chances of survival, I pointed out, were quite easy to determine, and they were in direct relation to the order of the courses as I had given them.'

Brigadier Scott was evidently a good man in a tight corner. He had a major battle brewing up, and once it had started, with his few men, he would be powerless to stop it. So let us see how he extricated himself, and all concerned, from this perilous predicament.

'To put it at its lowest level, it would be difficult for the Yugoslavs to murder such a large number, and it was anyway unlikely that they would want to. Therefore it seemed pretty obvious that a high proportion of the Croat nation would survive if they followed this obviously sensible first course. If they took either of the other alternatives they would be bound to die, so what? After five minutes they sensibly decided on the first course.

The Yugoslavs were brought back into the room, and I told the interpreter to explain the gist of the conversation and what the outcome had been.

An agreement was then made in my presence and signed by the two armies.

The Yugoslavs demanded that the Croats should signify their surrender within one hour, otherwise the battle would start.

I must say this seemed to me rather short notice if the Croats were to put over the surrender business to their unwilling thousands.

I recommended that a slightly longer period should be allowed.

The Yugoslav Commander, however, who evidently knew his countrymen better than I did, said it was quite long enough, and stuck to one hour as being the limit.

Needless to say the Croats complained bitterly.'

It was quite obvious, however, that the Yugoslavs meant business. Scott told the Croats, therefore, that they were already over a week late in surrendering in accordance with the general terms of surrender, and that they were extremely lucky to be treated as prisoners of war at all, and that if they did not hang out their flags within one hour he would call upon all the resources he had to enforce their surrender to the Yugoslavs.

'Off they went. Their time was short. They had to get some white flags out by half-past four.

The terms of surrender were fair enough – the Croatian Army was to be treated as prisoners of war with the exception of political criminals, who would be tried by Allied courts, while the civil population were to be fed and returned to Croatia by the shortest route.

With five minutes to spare, the Croatian Army signified their surrender, and the handing in of arms commenced forthwith.

As far as I was able to see, during the next 24 hours, all the arrangements in connection with the surrender and evacuation were carried out by the Yugoslavs speedily and efficiently.'

This was the authentic story of events at Bleiburg. What happened later when the Croat columns were marched into Yugoslavia was outside the ken of Brigadier Scott; and outside the ken of most of us. It is only now that the true story is beginning to emerge from a more open attitude in Yugoslavia. Scott summed up the Bleiburg incident as follows:

'It is when you are in a complete mix up like this, where anything can go seriously wrong at any moment, that the British soldier really reaches his peak. By some unerring instinct he always seems to do the right thing. The chaps had supreme confidence in themselves, and it never occurred to them that any of these skallywags, who would cut each other's throats without a moment's hesitation, would dare to interfere with them. In this belief they were absolutely correct, and as long as a British soldier was knocking about the chances of trouble were at once reduced in a very great degree. The tremendous prestige of the British Army and all its representatives can only really be grasped when one sees its effect at first hand like this.'[16]

These powerful messages that are now coming through from the men-on-the-ground concerning the behaviour and presence of British troops, are in strong contrast to the tarnished image which later historians would have us accept.

XXIII

The Missing Signal

During the next few days, news began trickling back to the Slovenes and Chetniks, still in Viktring camp, that the real destination was Yugoslavia and not Italy. But even though it was an open camp there was surprisingly little attempt to escape into the woods and mountains. Those few who had escaped from the train spoke of the sound of machine gun fire clearly being heard once the passengers had been disembarked. A few days later, a few straggled back to tell how they had been marched across a railway bridge and machine gunned by Tito guards as they crossed.

On 7 June, Alexander received a communication from a Dr Mika Krek in Rome, leader of the anti-Tito *émigrés*. Dr Krek was a former deputy prime minister in the Royal Yugoslav Government, but was now no longer recognised by the Foreign Office, and was in fact *'persona non grata'* in British diplomatic circles in Rome. Krek reported that:

> 'GOC 6 Armoured division handed over between May 27–31 11,000 Slovene military to Tito partisans and that the officers and several hundreds of men were massacred immediately after returning to Yugoslavia.'[1]

On 10 June a staff officer at AFHQ signalled 8 Army to investigate the report from Dr Krek and report back.[2]

On 6 July 8th Army sent the report compiled by 5 Corps back to AFHQ, with the following comment:

> 'evacuation and return of Yugoslav surrendered enemy personnel was carried out in accordance with orders issued by AFHQ which were based on military situation at the time prevailing which made the clearance of Austria imperative.'[3]

General Morgan, Chief of Staff at AFHQ then replied to Dr Krek:

> 'In reply to your letter of 7 June 1945, addressed to the Supreme Allied Commander, I am instructed to inform you that the Yugoslav nationals, who were repatriated during the latter part of May from Austria to Yugoslavia, had borne

arms for the Germans against the Allied Yugoslav tps of Marshal Tito. They were therefore treated as surrendered enemy military personnel. As such, in view of the situation that existed at that time in Austria, they were handed over to the Yugoslav Military Forces, in the course of the military operations which were then being conducted in parts of that country by both British and Yugoslav forces. This hand-over was carried out on the instructions of this Headquarters.'

In plain language that meant that Alexander took full responsibility for what had happened.

On 10 June Krek writes a similar letter to Sir George Rendel (British Ambassador in Rome),

'In the period May 22 to May 31, the British Military Authorities in Carinthia delivered 11,100 men of the Slovene Home Guard to Tito Partisan Military Authorities in Yugoslavia. Some of the men were shot immediately after returning on the Yugoslav territory, especially all the officers.'

The letter then goes on to give eye-witness accounts of the terrible slaughter that had taken place, amongst Croatians as well as Slovenes. In forwarding this letter to the Foreign Office, Sir George pointed out that this story had been told before, but as Dr Krek was one of the last of the 'old dispensation, his appeal deserves at least our serious attention'.

The Foreign Office minute accepted that Slovene Domobranci were delivered across the frontier to Tito's troops, but this was contrary to instructions and was stopped as soon as the news was received.

'Whatever Dr. Krek's past record, he is now the leading figure in the *émigré* opposition to the Yugoslav Govt. It is not a reputable group, Krek himself takes every opportunity to make trouble not only for the Yugoslav Govt but also for the Allied Commission and AFHQ'.

The minute ends 'I think it would be best that Sir G. Rendel should return no reply to this letter.'[4]

The matter comes to the surface again in September when a Conservative Member of Parliament, Major Guy Lloyd DSO, writes to Philip Noel Baker MP, Minister at the Foreign Office (now under a Labour government). Lloyd has seen Krek's letter and writes:

'Stories of such terrible atrocities and massacre of political opponents are so prevalent nowadays, that I agree they must be carefully authenticated, but this one is so terrible, and involves so many, I really feel it is impossible to ignore without a protest.'

The Foreign Office were inclined to put the blame on 'the military'. John Colville,[5] who had been Churchill's Private Secretary and who was now serving in the Southern Department, minuted that no progress had been made in securing further information on this unpleasant subject as all the people who had been dealing with the subject at the War Office had now been demobilised, 'I think we can do no more than admit that a serious blunder did take place and that the story does not reflect well on the officers concerned', he added on 5 November.

But Colville was at Churchill's side when all these events were taking place and was well aware of the difficulty of getting any decision from Churchill after VE Day.

Here is an interesting cameo from Colville's diary covering 14–21 May, during the time of Macmillan's visit. He complains in his diary of his inability to get Churchill to deal with his daily business,

> '*May 14*. The PM looked tired and has to fight for energy to deal with the problems confronting him ... the settlement of Europe, the last round of war in the East, an election on the way and the dark cloud of Russian imponderability. In Venezia Guilia we stand on the brink of an armed clash with Tito, secure of Russian support, who wishes to seize Trieste, Pola, etc. from Italy without awaiting the Peace Conference. The Americans seem willing to stand four square with us and Truman shows great virility; but Alexander has alarmed them – and incensed the PM – by casting doubts on the attitude of the Anglo-American troops, should there come to be an armed clash with the Yugoslavs. ... At 2.30 the PM went to bed, leaving almost untouched the voluminous weight of paper which awaits his decision.'[6]

Saturday 19 May, Colville notes in his diary,

> 'did my best to put the great array of papers in the box, most of which have been unlooked at for many days, in some order ... Harold Macmillan summoned from Italy because of the Venezia Guilia crisis ....'

Sunday, 20 May

> 'Prof and I devoted great energies to eradicating many of the PM's papers and we did continue to get some of the remainder dealt with.'[7]

Monday, 21 May

> 'Just as the Prof and I had all but reached our goal of getting "the box" dealt with, Attlee rang up ...'.

It is inconceivable, even given the chaotic situation in Downing Street during those days that Churchill and his private secretary did not see Alexander's NAF 975 ('require direction urgently regarding final disposal ...') to the Chiefs of Staff which was under discussion at a Cabinet Committee (on 18 May), and was then allowed to pursue its leisurely way through Foreign Office, War Office, Combined Chiefs of Staff in Washington, before the answer found its way back to Alexander on 20 June, too late to be of any effective use.

The first published narrative account of the sequence of events concerning the repatriation of the dissident Yugoslavs has come from the hand of Nikolai Tolstoy. This alleges that the Commander of 5 Corps, Charles Keightley, and his Chief of Staff, Toby Low, deliberately disregarded orders from above, in that they knowingly ignored an important signal from AFHQ ordering all Chetniks and dissident Yugoslavs to be evacuated to Italy and not to Yugoslavia. This message which, for the sake of convenience I will call the 'DISTONE signal', formed the central point of the author's argument concerning the Yugoslavs.[8] But there is, as has now been shown, a fundamental misunderstanding in this premise. For greater clarity I will repeat the signal No. FX77268 sent on 17 May at 1924 hours.

> 'AFHQ to 15 Army Group, Eighth Army, Distone.
> Copy Macmis.
> 1. Chetnik and dissident Yugoslavs infiltrating into areas occupied by Allied Tps should be treated as disarmed enemy troops and evacuated to British concentration area in Distone. Total numbers incl 11,000 already in Distone believed about 35,000. Eighth Army will keep Distone informed of approximate numbers being thus evacuated.
> 2. Question of final disposal is being taken up by AFHQ.'[9]

Macmis, is of course, Brigadier Maclean's British Military Mission to Marshal Tito. Distone as we have seen is not a hill-town in Italy but District One, an army administration area in North-East Italy.

The signal actually refers to GO258 of 16th. which came from Macmis to AFHQ and concerned the infiltration of Chetniks and Ustachi troops into British occupied areas east of the Isonzo River in Italy. There are no records of copies sent to 5 Corps in Austria for whom it was not intended, as it concerned only Yugoslav dissidents in Italy. It has been alleged that it therefore cancelled out the Robertson signal No. FX75383 of 14 May which said that all Yugoslavs who were serving in German Forces must be handed over to local Yugoslav forces.

But, as Gray told the jury in the recent Court case, 'the Distone order was a request or a directive from Rear Macmis. It applied to Chetniks infiltrating into an area which had nothing what ever to do with 5 Corps, and that is why the Distone order was not even sent to 5 Corps'.[10]

Could the Yugoslav dissidents have been saved? I rather doubt it. Although all directly concerned had forebodings concerning their eventual fate, and believed that they were going to receive pretty brutal treatment when they reached the other side. No one in fact 'knew' that massacres were going to take place until the fugitives came back with their harrowing tales. The onus must rest squarely upon Tito. Were the stories exaggerated? To a certain extent it was natural that these very frightened men should embellish the evidence. They wanted to discredit Tito's communists as much as possible. But we must accept substantially the truth of the accounts which they gave, which may be borne by the discovery of further mass graves.

The critics' misunderstanding of some of the messages which passed, have led them to erect an extraordinary edifice of imagined events, where relationships between the various headquarters and individual staff officers seem to be governed by secret motives, deviousness and deceit. This situation is totally unreal to me, having served at 8th Army headquarters and known the high morale and mutual trust which existed amongst all ranks. It is not a picture which accords with the way that people behaved in those days, and I do not believe that it has the slightest relevance to the case.

So on whom do we pin the blame, if blame there must be? For do not let us forget that only a few days before we were cheerfully killing 'enemy personnel' in large numbers. The pages of the calendar had flicked over but our attitudes were still geared to war, the war was not yet over!

As we have seen in the previous chapter, national policy had been overridden in the case of the Yugoslavs in Viktring camp, in favour of operational needs. It would be a foolhardy person who made a judgement at this distance in time between the situation as seen by the man-on-the-spot, and that envisaged by the policy-makers in Whitehall or Washington. It would seem an easy matter pinning the blame on someone. But as committees of enquiry into great events so frequently find, a combination of a thousand different circumstances contributed to final tragedy.

XXIV

Message from Stalin

The Prime Minister had not expected, nor had he solicited, a reply from Marshal Stalin to his message reporting Marshal Tito's incursion into Austria and Venezia Guilia.

President Truman's message, sent in parallel, had however ended 'I hope that we can count on your influence', which had elicited a reply from Stalin, not altogether helpful, as was to be expected.

Stalin intended that Churchill should see this reply, and sent him a copy on 23 May. The message ran:

> *Personal and secret from Premier J V Stalin to President Truman*
> I think you are quite right when you say that this question is one of principle, and that no action of any kind should be permitted with regard to the territory of Istria-Trieste which would not fully take into account the lawful claims of Yugoslavia and the contribution made by the Yugoslav Armed Forces to the common cause of the Allies in the struggle against Hitlerite Germany.
>
> It goes without saying that the future of this territory, the majority of whose population is Yugoslav, should be decided by peaceful settlement. However the subject under discussion at present is the temporary military occupation of this territory. In this, in my opinion, it is necessary to take account of the fact that it is precisely the Allied Yugoslav forces which expelled the German invaders from the territory of Istria-Trieste, thus rendering important service to the common cause of the Allies. In view of this fact alone it would be unjust and an undeserved insult to the Yugoslav Army and people to refuse to Yugoslavia the right to the occupation of a territory conquered from the enemy, when the Yugoslav people has made so many sacrifices in the struggle for the national rights of Yugoslavia and for the common cause of the United Nations.'

Stalin concludes his message with the suggestion that a line of demarcation should be defined between Field Marshal Alexander and Marshal Tito, (a tactic that had already been tried and failed). But he is adamant on the question of the Yugoslav Administration remaining in place.

> 'Since the Yugoslav inhabitants form a majority on this territory, and since in the period of German occupation a local Yugoslav Administration began

to be formed here, which now enjoys the confidence of the local population ...'.

With these words Stalin loftily dismisses the brutal treatment of
the Italian population by Tito's men. He also ignores the events in
Austria and the attempt by Tito to take over Carinthia. But the message is in polite, almost courteous terms, which he can afford to use
so long as his client Tito is doing the dirty work.[1]

Since the last Cabinet Meeting, on 18 May, which considered Alexander's NAF 975, there has been quite a lot of coming and going
between the Foreign Office, War Office and Cabinet Offices on what
advice to give the War Cabinet.

On 26 May G L McDermott (for D F Howard) signs a letter to
Lieutenant Colonel C R Price who is Secretary to the Chief's of Staff
Committee. It summarises the Foreign Office view on disposal of
the various categories of surrendered enemy.

'Our views on the three categories whose presence in Southern Austria is an
embarrassment to Field Marshal Alexander are as follows,
(a) *Cossacks*. We agree with the JSM that the Cossacks are covered by the
Yalta agreement on the reciprocal repatriation of Soviet citizens and accordingly
consider it essential that all of them who are Soviet citizens should be handed
over to the Soviet authorities in pursuance of our general policy. If we did
not do so in the case of these particular people, it would be a breach of the
agreement and might look like a change of policy in this matter to which the
Soviet Government attach great importance and would be assumed by the Russians to indicate hostile intentions towards them. It might also have very unfortunate reactions upon the Russian treatment of our prisoners of war uncovered
by them. We suggest that Field Marshal Alexander should make arrangements
with Marshal Tolbukhin for the handing over of the Cossacks across the temporary occupational demarcation line.
(b) *Cetniks*. We agree with the JSM that the Cetniks in Southern Austria should
be dealt with in the same way as the Cetniks in Venezia Giulia; that is to say
that they should not be handed over to Tito's forces or returned to Yugoslavia
but should be disarmed and interned, pending a final decision on their disposal
by the British and United States Governments. We realise that it may be of
some embarrassment to 15 Army Group to arrange for the removal of the large
numbers of these Cetniks to Italy; but we could not in present circumstances
agree to the Cetnik troops being handed over to Tito. (It is not of course possible
at this stage to give any ruling on the final disposal of the Cetniks.)
(c) *Croats*. The Croat troops are, in our opinion, in rather a different position
from the Cetniks. They are the armed forces of the Croat puppet state set up
by the Germans and, although we never recognised the establishment of the
Croat State, the Croat troops are in effect the regular forces of a quisling government operating under German direction. There would be less justification than
in the case of the Cetniks for regarding them as irregular forces who have been
taking part in a Yugoslav civil war. We should therefore be in favour of handling
the Croat troops in Southern Austria over to Tito's forces. Such a move would
certainly please Tito and would show him that, in some matters at any rate,
we are willing to treat him as a regular and responsible Ally. We realise, however,

that the United States Government might well not be willing to agree to this rather drastic course, which, as Field Marshal Alexander points out, might be fatal to the health of the Croat troops. If the United States Government do not like our recommendation, we are willing to agree that the Croats be treated in the same way as the Cetniks.'[2]

But military necessity had far out-stripped these more leisurely per-ambulations. The process of 'clearing the decks' was well under way. I do not think that people in London had any conception of the conditions on the ground, which is certainly reflected in this letter.

On 29 May a 'hastener' from Lord Halifax in Washington to the Foreign Office asked 'May I expect your views soon?' But the War Cabinet Chiefs of Staff Committee were not to consider Alexander's desperate need for a decision until their meeting on 29 May. Twelve days after Alexander's request, they approved the Foreign Office letter above, recommending the line that should be taken, but Brooke pointed out that the Americans might possibly object to a policy of handing over all Croats to Tito, in spite of the fact that some 900 had already been transferred. This was duly transmitted to Washington for the approval of the Combined Chiefs of Staff.[3]

On 26 May, the Yugoslav *Chargé d'Affairs* in London had presented an *aide memoire* (diplomatic euphemism for a blunt demand) to the Foreign Office saying that Field Marshal Alexander's advances between Gorizia and Trieste should be stopped. Sir Orme Sargent, Permanent Head, responded that it had been made abundantly clear by the Field Marshal that he required the territory for his lines of communication with Austria, and in any case it was on Tito's initiative that the talks broke down. An acrimonious interview followed, which ended, surprisingly, with the envoy softening his line. The Foreign Office now turned their diplomatic weapons onto 'the military', caus-ing a *démarche* to be made to 'the competent authorities' in order to stop the further movement of allied units eastwards of the River Soca.[4]

But Churchill is playing a different tune. For he demands of Alex-ander,

'I am sorry about your reluctance to include Pola in scope of our demands upon Tito or of your possible offensive. We do not seem to be looking at the situation from the same angle.'

He continues:

'I regard it as the first importance not to back down before Tito's encroachments or to give the impression to the BALKANS or to RUSSIA that we are unable in the last resort to use force. I am sure that if we begin giving way at this juncture there is no limit to which we shall not be pushed.'[5]

Churchill reminds Alexander that there is heavy support from the United States that the demand for POLA must be maintained, 'President Truman evidently attaches great importance to POLA and if it were omitted the US might lose interest in main operations which you have now almost prepared'.[6]

Churchill concludes:

> 'If it comes to fighting you would not of course be obligated to launching an attack on POLA at the same time as the rest of the operation, desirable though this may be. On the contrary, you would carry out your operations as military needs and resources required. I hope you will make every preparation to attack POLA at the earliest moment. I understood you had an amphibious operation in mind.'[7]

Churchill hopes that he has made his views clear. He evidently sweeps aside the withdrawal of Tito from Carinthia, which had taken place ten days previously, as being only a tactical ploy, whilst Tito maintained his unauthorised occupation of Italian territory, including a very important port. Alexander replies that he is at that moment discussing such a plan with Generals McCreery and Harding. As we have already seen from Brooke's private letter to Alexander, 'the military' only considered this to be Churchill's sabre-rattling. But there was a deeper significance, in that unless we showed willing to recover all of Italy's former territory which had been removed from them by force, unpredictable consequences might flow affecting the stability and political control of Italy, which we had just liberated.

XXV

Operation of War, and Stalin's Revenge

The repatriation of the Cossacks, a generic term which included men from many different Soviet Republics and ethnic groups, began on 28 May 1945.

The following message was issued by Brigadier Geoffrey Musson, whose 36 Infantry Brigade bore the brunt of this unpleasant task. It was to be the basis of a talk by unit commanders to their men. Musson explained that under an agreement made by the Allied governments all Allied nationals were to be returned to their country. This meant that the Cossacks and Caucasians now in the Brigade area would be returned to Russia.

'Some of them will be willing to return – a considerable number of the Caucasians have actually applied to do so – but on the whole it will be unpopular.

In order to save trouble within unit areas the officers are being separated from the others today. Men, women and children will be moved as fast as available trains and MT will allow. We have as yet no detailed instructions about their horses and other animals. Carts cannot be taken on the trains so they must be left behind.

This will be an extremely difficult task. We do not speak their language and even if they willingly comply with our instructions it is a tremendous undertaking.

Particularly as there are so many women and children, some of you will feel sympathetic towards these people, but you must remember that they took up arms for the Germans, thus releasing more troops to fight against us in Italy and on the other fronts.

There is no doubt that they sided with the Germans because they expected to regain power in RUSSIA. When they saw that this was not possible they tried to excuse themselves in our eyes. The Russians have said that they intend to put people to work on the land and to educate them as decent Soviet citizens. There is no indication whatsoever that there will be a massacre of these people – in fact the Russians need more people for their country.

Remember what I said in my message yesterday – you have a very big task and a very unpleasant one. Let us carry it out firmly and without bloodshed, but if it is necessary to resort to force, do so promptly and without fear. I will support you in any reasonable action you take.

Above all, try to avoid casualties to yourselves, your officers and your comrades. This will be achieved if you are always on your guard.'[1]

On the previous day, 26 May, Musson had issued orders about the use of fire arms whilst disarming the enemy personnel, which included the following points.

> 'After 1400 hrs any surrendered tps found in possession of arms or ammunition will be arrested immediately and will be liable to the death penalty. If it is necessary to open fire you will do so and you must regard this duty as an operation of war.'

Anyone attempting to escape was to be ordered to halt. If they failed to do so troops should open fire, aiming at the legs if this was sufficient to stop them; if not it was shoot to kill.

> 'If you are approached by an uncontrollable crowd you must shoot to kill the apparent leader. You must *not* fire overhead or into the air.'[2]

These orders were strictly in accordance with the well-tried practice of the British Army in controlling a riot situation. The logic being that once the 'military' were called in they must be expected to use their weapons in the last resort, and not fire indiscriminately into the air which might injure an innocent person some distance away. It was clear from these orders that the view at that time was that although these people may have appeared perfectly peaceful in their camps surrounded by their domestic animals and camp followers, these were the same people which had looted, raped and murdered their way through Italy and Yugoslavia and into Austria. They were held in dread by the civilian population.

I shall not attempt to give a full account of the repatriation of the Cossacks and Caucasians by 36 Infantry Brigade. The story has been told in graphic detail elsewhere. I shall restrict myself to an outline of the event as recounted in the official archives. The main source is a 'post-mortem' report compiled by the Brigade Major on 3 July after the event was over.[3]

The force to be repatriated consisted mainly of two groups. The largest was Domanov's Cossacks consisting of some 22,000 men, women and children. It will be remembered that Domanov was a Red Army renegade who had led his men against the Italian Partisans. They were joined by General Shkuro's Reserve Regiment numbering some 1,400 persons. General Andrei Shkuro was a celebrated Cossack commander from the Russian Civil War, but had not taken part in any action in this one. Likewise, General Peter Krasnov was a civil war Cossack commander who, since 1920, had lived in various European countries latterly in Berlin maintaining close contact with the Nazis. (see Appendix E).

So the Cossack forces then located in the Leinz area numbered some 24,000, and were reasonably well disciplined.

The second main group were the Causacians in a much looser organisation of clans or tribes, numbering some 4,800 persons. They had been recruited by the Germans into national legions and encouraged to liberate their country from 'the Bolsheviks'. Formerly under German command, they were now led by Sultan Kelitsch-Ghirei.

As the Report explains, included in these figures were an unknown quantity of displaced persons of nationalities other than Soviet, and of Soviet ex-prisoners of war who had never borne arms against the Allies. 'Lack of documents and the speed and secrecy with which the evacuations had to be carried out made a complete individual check impossible', said the author of the report. Steps were taken, however, at the time of the evacuations, to segregate persons who were obviously in exempt categories. Some 2,200 ex-PW and displaced persons of nationalities other than Soviet were discovered and sent to the appropriate collecting centres.[4]

The Report continues:

> 'The vast majority of the Cossacks and Caucasians were bitterly opposed to
> return to the Soviet Union. Even before it was known that they were to be
> so returned, they made frequent petitions, in interview and in writing, that
> some other course should be adopted with them. In view of the known feelings
> of the Cossacks and Caucasians in the matter, it was considered essential that
> the fact that they were to be sent to the USSR should be kept from them for
> as long as possible.'[5]

It was planned to separate the officers from the other ranks in order to avoid an insurrection, and unnecessary bloodshed to both sides. And in order to achieve this in the most convenient manner, the officers were told they were to attend a conference on 28 May. It is true that they were lured away under false pretences. But it is also a fact that if some deception plan had not been adopted, this mass evacuation would have merely been an abortive fiasco and a bloody one at that. We would have signally failed to honour our obligations under the Yalta agreement, with all the imponderable consequences that would have flowed from that failure, including the reciprocal repatriation of our own men over-run by the Soviets. Of course, British temper and innate sense of fair play was evidently being tested to the limit. It was an impossible position for those directly involved. Not because of any certainty that these men were going to their deaths, but because of the piteous behaviour of the repatriates who believed that they were. So very hard decisions had to be taken, as can be read in every line of the Brigade Commander's directive. It was proving as hard to break out of war as it was to 'break into it', in the first place. But this, in our heart of hearts, we all knew, all those of us who had taken part in the conflict. So the answer was to obey orders and make the best of it.

Many of the Cossacks refused to be moved when they were told the news, many forming squares and linking arms and legs in an immovable phalanx. Rifle butts, pick helves and bayonets had to be freely used by British troops in order to force them into their transport. Both at the camp at Spittal and on the train en route for the handover place at Judenburg on the Soviet borderline, there were suicides and attempted suicides. Many bared their chests and said they would rather be shot by the British than fall into the hands of the Soviets. All this is clear from the report.

Between 29 May and 15 June some 22,934 Cossacks and Caucasians were repatriated by 36 Infantry Brigade which came under Major General Arbuthnott's 78 Division. Of this number, 1,683 were officers. It is estimated that 2,806 were not accounted for. These had either escaped or were not there in the first place, (probably because the ration strength had been exaggerated). Other divisions were also involved in the repatriation of Cossacks. Major General Weir's 46 Division responsible for the evacuation of 15 Cossack Cavalry Corps, and Major General Murray's 6 Armoured Division, under which was 1 Guards Brigade. Murray's division was responsible for a similar group. All these officers have since come under attack by certain historians for the way in which they handled the repatriations. The criticisms actually amount to the claim that they should have refused to obey an order from their superior commander. Some did protest to 5 Corps Commander more strongly than others, at the onerous responsibility placed upon them and their troops. But all knew that they could not question political decisions which went back to the very highest levels. (If Montgomery had been faced with divisional commanders who complained about his orders, they would have received a very short shrift!)

British responsibility ended at Judenburg at the point of handover. What happened thereafter?

There is little authentic evidence to show that, once the Cossacks were in the hands of the Soviets on the far side of the bridge at Judenburg, they were promptly shot in a disused steel mill. The only evidence from a British source, as to their reception on the other side, is from Lieutenant D Harding of 1 Kensingtons, who wrote this report about the handover:

> 'Our party arrived at the Russian barrier met by Russian Colonel and then by two Russian Generals who ordered prisoners to be paraded. By this time the prisoners evidently felt that Nemesis was overtaking them which could be seen by the expression on their faces. On being paraded, the Generals, surrounded by all and sundry, spoke to one or two individuals. One General then made a grand speech in which he told them that they had been naughty boys but providing they did as was bid of them and worked as every other member of the Russian community, no serious harm would befall them. At this point one could see the immense relief written on the faces of the prisoners as they were led away to an enclosure. The Russian colonel satisfied that all was in order signed a receipt.'[6]

The only firm evidence which we have about executions was the notices which appeared in *Pravda*, on 17 January 1947, that the leaders of the Cossacks, Generals P N Krasnov and S N Krasnov, Lieutenant General Shkuro and Major General Sultan-Ghirey, had been executed.

At the time of the Krushchev era however, some of the *émigré* officers were reprieved and were allowed to leave the Soviet Union.

The 36 Brigade War Diary sums up the situation as follows:

> 'The last few days of the month were fully occupied in an event which we all looked upon as unpleasant but inevitable. The Cossack and Caucasian forces had fought against our ally the Soviet Union, and were thus regarded by the latter as traitors to their country. It was our duty to return them to the Soviets where the fate that awaited them could only be guessed at. A full account of the disarming and evacuation of these unfortunate peoples, the last dying echo of the Revolution, is given in the eye-witness accounts [contained in the Appendices].'[8]

Welsh Guards under General Murray's 6 Armoured Division give a parallel account. General Murray, of all the Divisional Commanders, had raised the strongest objections with Corps Commander General Keightley at the task they were ordered to undertake. Lieutenant Colonel Rose-Price commanding 3rd Battalion Welsh Guards referred to the deception plan, as 'an act of unparalleled duplicity' in his official War Diary. Nevertheless he and his men carried it out.

Extracts from the Battalion War Diary tell the story:

> '*27 May*. Op. Cossack starts, the gist of which is:
> 1. To concentrate and guard Cossack and German Offrs and OR's and transmit them to nearby station for further onward transmission to Russians.
> 2. To guard up to 6,000 horses.
> 3. To guard grooms looking after them.
> Quiet afternoon for remainder of Bn.
>
> After Gurk and Weitensfield ... all was activity. Orders were given out –

3 Coy to guard Cossack offrs and OR's cages, Sp. Coy – German offrs cage and 4 Coy Cossacks groom's cage and horse lines. As an additional embarrassment, news received that one German General and six other offrs had escaped, fortunately not from our charge.

28 May. Cossack avalanche moves into the various cages throughout the day and comes under guard. Extraordinary sight of a coln consisting of about 3,600 horses and wagonettes being driven along by squat Cossacks singing and jingling along in a flurry of dust.

GOC [General Murray] held conference Tac Bn HQ and outlined the actions for the removal and disposal of Cossacks for the following day. Coys had a good time riding and poaching trout from an excellent nearby stream. Div Cmd held a large supper party.

29 May. WEITENSFIELD. Rather trying day. Half the Cossack offrs, when they were informed that they were to embuss, refused to as they had been tactlessly informed that they were going to RUSSIA. Thinking that their fate would be a desperate one, they demanded to be shot or given firearms in lieu. By tactful negotiations and timely display of a Wasp flame-thrower, they were induced to get into TCV's. Just as the coln was moving off, a timely reprieve came from 5 Corps saying that they were found to be White Russians and were to be debussed and put back in their original cages again. This caused widespread rejoicing as no-one relished the idea of sending them to an uncertain fate in RUSSIA.

30 May. Overcast ... all Cossack OR's disposed in three trains. This was completed without incident by 1500 hrs.'[9]

Headquarters 5 Corps gave the total number of 'Cossacks' handed over to the Soviet Forces during the first five days of June as 24,328 persons (plus 5,900 horses) not including stragglers and sick, who were moved later.[10]

Thus ends the traumatic story of the repatriation of the Cossacks from Austria. The only good thing to say about it is that, once the decision had been taken, and responsibility for this must rest with Alexander's AFHQ and political masters back home, then it was directed with a sure hand by General Keightley. He was impervious to the reluctance of some of his divisional commanders. There was no uncertainty, no U-turns (with the exception of the message reprieving some of the White Russians). If there had been any shilly-shallying, it would have put our troops in an impossible position, have ended in the collapse of morale, and a bloody mess.[11]

XXVI

Alexander Visits 5 Corps

Before the events recorded in the previous chapter were barely completed, General Alexander, who was on a leave in Austria, visited 5 Corps Headquarters.

Alexander arrived early on 4 June at Klagenfurt. 5 Corps had had a tough time during the three short weeks since their arrival in Austria and since the so-called ending of hostilities. No doubt he wished to hear with his own ears an account of their operations. He would also have been interested to hear first hand accounts of the withdrawal of Tito's Yugoslavs, and about the repatriations. The mass movement of those people had been very much his concern. His Headquarters had issued the original directives, and he was already beginning to hear reports of the difficulties of loading, and of the Yugoslav and Soviet armies on the other side. However, he was not unduly concerned about what he had expected to be a very tricky operation. Whilst visiting the camp at Viktring he had some conversation with the camp staff and Slovenes and Chetniks still awaiting transfer, and they would not have minced their words in describing the 'horrors' to be expected on crossing the border. He was accompanied there by McCreery, 8th Army Commander, and Keightley, 5 Corps Commander. He is known to have visited Gerald Verney's 1 Guards Brigade, Pat Scott's 38 (Irish) Brigade and Arbuthnott's 78 Division, so he should have been properly 'in the picture' by the time he left on 6 June. Already, in advance of his arrival, a new instruction had come from 8th Army, and on 4 June 1 Guards Brigade had issued an order which stopped the further repatriation of Yugoslavs from Viktring camp.

Although Alexander was perturbed by the reports of the repatriations which he began to receive, and is reported to have shown much sympathy with the plight of the Cossacks, it is difficult to tell at this distance in time whether it came as a complete surprise. For the stories he would be hearing would have been about the resistance that was put up, rather than the reception which they received on the other side.

But one must be mildly surprised that, in view of Alexander's very close connections with the White Russians alongside whom he fought against the Bolsheviks, that he did not take an interest at a slightly earlier stage. When Macmillan came back from his meeting at Klagenfurt (and discounting completely the conspiratorial theory), he must have told his very close friend Alexander about his trip, and about the Cossacks, amongst whom there were reported to be some Whites. For even as a curiosity, this would have interested Alexander with his own past experience (marked by the Tsarist Order of St. Anne which he wore amongst his medal ribbons). However if he did, it was subsumed in the far greater problem of mass evacuation which was the operational necessity then on his mind.

Let us pass then from speculation, to Alexander's return to Caserta, following his visit to 5 Corps. One of the first things that happened was that a Liaison Officer was sent to Headquarters 5 Corps from AFHQ to report further on the repatriations. Presumably this was on Alexander's own initiative, if he followed the Montgomery practice in the use of LO's.

The following is an extract from his report:

LO Report on visit to HQ 5 Corps. 7–8 June 1945.
 'Handover of Cossacks
 There were no details of any incidents during the handover available at Corps. However it is known that incidents did occur, and Corps are obtaining details of these. Reports should be ready in a few days. 78 DIV experienced difficulties – their first estimate of 28,000 was eventually found to be only 22,000, the discrepancy being explained by over-indenting for rations. Some ORs also demonstrated on entrainment.
 Liaisons with Russians
 There are no wrls or tele comns with the Russian forces, liaison being by LOs from both sides and by a Lt.Col from both forces at the joint post at JUDENBURG Sta. Relations are very cordial, but difficulty is experienced in making arrangements as all decisions have to be referred to Marshal TOLBUK-HIN, although there are quite senior offrs on the spot.
 Handover of YUGOSLAVS to TITO'S Forces.
 As with the handover of the Cossacks, this operation was much less difficult than had been anticipated.
 From the Cage at VIKTRING D.2077 the Jugs were taken in TCVs to MARIA ELEND D. 0670 or BLEIBURG D.6178 stations. Escorts and guards at the stations were found by 1 GDS BDE. At the stations JUGs were searched for arms, org into their own units (coys and bns) as far as possible, and entrained.

Care was taken to segregate USTACHI from CHETNIKS, and to provide seats for offrs, women and children.

On completion of entrainment, Tito's guard appeared and took over, a signature being obtained from the JUG guard comd.

As far as is known, there were no incidents whilst the personnel were in British hands, but JUG LO reported 3 suicides and 2 wounded, all believed to have taken place on the train.

Conduct of JUG guards seen by 5 CORPS LO at MARIA ELEND was exemplary.'[1]

There are few explicit details in the LO's Report, presumably eye witness accounts would not have trickled back to Corps Headquarters by the time this was written. In any case what we would call 'horrors' were now everyday occurrences in time of war, and were reported in the form of routine 'casualties' or plain 'suicides'. On the whole, the report states the Russian guards were friendly and co-operative and the conduct of the Yugoslav guards was described as 'exemplary'. Mention is made that incidents did occur, of which no details were then available, and of which Corps was obtaining details. The tenor of the report was that the repatriation operations had gone very smoothly, with the exception of these few incidents.

This is confirmed in a series of Sitreps issued by 36 Infantry Brigade from 1–7 June. Being in message form they are necessarily abbreviated. The Sitrep narrates in its prosaic way:

'*1 June.*
6RWK. Considerable difficulty encountered in loading COSSACKS onto train departing OBERDRAUBURG ... COSSACKS sat on ground with linked arms and legs ... considerable force had to be used to break up groups ... some tried to escape resulting in two killed first camp three killed three wounded second camp.

8 A & SH. Similar difficulties to above in loading from PEGGETZ area. Situation aggravated by greater number women children and presence of priests who conducted services and appeared to incite others to non-co-operation. Again force had to be used resulting in three killed.

2 June
6 RWK. Entrainment COSSACKS at [undecipherable] completed with little difficulty. One block of about 20 trying sit down methods of yesterday had to be broken up by force. 1 COSSACK Regt offered services for fight against JAPAN.

3 June
2 LF. COSSACKS and CAUCASIANS evac by train 31 May 1 and 2 June handed over JUDENDORF without incident.

4 June
6 RWK. COSSACKS evac by train without incident from DOLSACH 1189 men 454 women 245 children total 1888 2 INNISKS patrol to hills SOUTH of LAVANT-LIENZ discovered number COSSACKS who immediately fled into trees and undergrowth 16 surrendered after own troops opened fire.

7 June

Evacuation of COSSACKS and CAUCASIANS less stragglers ... completed.'[2]

It is understandable that such reports did not set the alarm bells ringing particularly as no news of shootings on the other side had yet been confirmed. Colin Mitchell who was then a Lieutenant serving with the 8 Argyll and Sutherland Highlanders described it as follows:

'Around the end of May we were told that the entire Cossack and Caucasian Divisions were to be handed over to the Russians. We thought this was sad but not our affair. When they were concentrated for onward routing there was "resistance", but not much when it was apparent that we meant it . . . .

Those involved in the actual handling just thought of it as part of their duty, certainly at the time, I remember one friend being particularly bitter about a trainload of Cossacks, for which he was OC Escort, being unloaded and the officers immediately separated from the OR and families, and marched off to be shot. Whether he actually witnessed the shooting I cannot recall.

On the whole my sympathies were not over-extended. These people had a tough record as L of C anti-Partisan troops. But because they were so primitive, accompanied by their household goods and families, it was difficult to equate them with the Germans we had been fighting some weeks earlier (in today's climate of Human Rights etc. it is probably difficult for people to regard our view as anything other than callous). But we, as you know so well from your own experience, were simply glad to be alive and the war over.'[3]

Was Alexander ignorant of what was going on? I hardly think so because it was his own headquarters which had issued the executive instructions 'to clear the decks', and for the repatriations to begin. To say that Alexander knew nothing about it, and it was all a conspiracy between Macmillan and Keightley of 5 Corps, is straining credulity too far. As to Alexander's own reactions, it is said that he was upset by the reports which he heard. But one can only take a leaf out of Montgomery's book when facing similar circumstances in Germany. There was no doubt in his mind what had to be done. The millions had to be returned to their own countries (whatever the conditions there), so that other millions might survive.

Having spoken to several of Alexander's surviving personal staff and others close enough to know his mind, my firm impression is that Alexander was not over-distracted by the repatriation reports, this was 'war' or the unfortunate consequences of war, and we had to get on with it. As to his former comrades of the White armies in 1918, one or two of whom fell victims to his repatriation policy, that was another 'war' with other friends, and other enemies.

Churchill was also not unaware of the situation. On 20 May 1945, before the repatriations had taken place, he asked General Ismay (his link with the Chiefs of Staff Committee),

'Could I have a further report on the 45,000 Cossacks of whom General Eisenhower speaks in his telegram. How did they come into their present plight? Did they fight against us?'

Churchill adds in a footnote to this record, that he was told that, 'The Germans recruited a cavalry corps of 45,000 Cossacks, and used them against the Partisans in Yugoslavia.'[4]

Donnison, the official military historian enlarges on this saying 'These had fought with ferocity if not savagery, for the Germans, and had now fallen into the hands of the Allies ... Unfortunately, the provisions of the Yalta agreement regarding the repatriation of Soviet nationals left the Allies with no choice.'[5]

War, or 'peace' as we must now call it, cannot simply be one long drawn out crisis, as historians would have us suppose. We would not be human nor would life be bearable without the occasional hilarious episode, as this account by Brigadier Pat Scott of 38 Irish Brigade shows.[6]

On the 5th June, Field-Marshal Alexander visited Brigade Headquarters with Generals McCreery, Keightley and Arbuthnott – in fact for a short time the whole chain of command was represented at our modest Headquarters, for the COs were also present. We were scheduled to entertain the company to tea.

We started the ball rolling with the drums and pipes of the Brigade playing "Retreat". After watching this for a short while, everyone retired to tables under the trees where we had a good old-fashioned blow-out of sticky cakes and strawberries and cream, while the pipes and drums continued their melodies from a nearby field. After tea, the Field-Marshal went over to see the musicians at closer quarters and I introduced him to the Drum Majors and Pipe Majors of the three Battalions. Up till now everything had gone according to schedule, but a heavy storm was blowing up – as it did most afternoons – and as I knew the Field-Marshal's time was up I made signs for his car to appear. He seemed interested in our house – I had told him that it was a Hitler Youth School – and instead of driving off he said he would like to have a look round. I led into the house, and the first room I went into was Paddy Bowen Colthurst's bedroom. A scene of utter confusion greeted us! It looked rather like a cross between a Quartermaster's store with a mad storeman and a broken down junk shop. Muskets of all shapes and sizes lay about. Doubtful looking fishing rods, large packing cases of I know not what, bottles of half-eaten cherries and a great assortment of drink that might be added to them on suitable occasions, pieces of raw leather which stank to high heaven and a few old dog bones – the dog had been using most parts of the room as a bed too at one time or another! Everyone stood spell-bound, not knowing quite what to look at first. In the hushed silence that ensued the Army Commander was heard to remark, "Yes, the Germans did leave a lot behind them, didn't they?".[7]

So ended Alexander's visit to 5 Corps. The dust of war had now begun to settle over Austria. The troops began to enjoy a brief 'golden age', of riding, of fishing in the streams; of boating and swimming in the numerous lakes of this beautiful province. 'Fratting' was still taboo, but they got round it by describing their girl-friends as 'slave-labour', a category exempt under the rules. It was a brief respite, for soon they would either be on a draft for the Far East war, or struggling to cope with demobilisation in their strange and shattered homeland.

PART SIX

THE AFTERMATH

XXVII

Summer Solstice

On 26 July 1945 the results of the British General Election were announced. Against every forecast, Churchill, Britain's war leader, was swept from power in a landslide Socialist victory. The unimpressive Clement Attlee stepped into No 10 Downing Street. According to Jock Colville, who inherited a new master, 'there was world stupefaction, not least at Potsdam, where Stalin supposed that Churchill would have "fixed" the results'.[1] A senior Labour figure, Dr Dalton, admitted that during the war, whilst the Tories had left their constituencies untended, their agents mostly being away fighting, he and Herbert Morrison had spent much time and effort ensuring that the Labour electoral machinery was in good order![2] So it was not simply that the Forces vote had 'gone Labour', in part due to the assiduous socialist propaganda disseminated through the Army Bureau of Current Affairs.[3] Be that as it may, we will now be watchful as to what effect change of government had on the repatriation policy and upon relations with the Soviet Union and Yugoslavia.

Meanwhile British occupation of Carinthia was not entirely without trouble. On 7 June, Belgrade was reporting to the Foreign Office that Tito had made a speech on 1 June at Celje in Slovenia containing the following words:

> 'Carinthia [sic] has been liberated by us but international circumstances were such as to compel us to make a temporary withdrawal from it. Carinthia is ours and we shall fight for it.'

'What are we doing about this?' was scribbled on the Foreign Office memo, presumably by one of the incoming ministers. 'We were preparing to ignore it' was the official's reply. 'It will of course be a different matter if the Yugoslavs start seriously infiltrating'. Another minister adds:

'I fear the Russians have decided to give us a bad time over Carinthia. I don't think protests will cure this, and certainly I see no point in protesting to Moscow now about the *Pravda* article.'

The *Pravda* article, which was dated 2 June, accused the British occupation forces of allowing complete freedom to Fascist outcasts, the SS, 'Butcher Rupink', etc. etc. Many SS men, the paper claimed, Nedic supporters and White Guards had been taken on by British Military Administration as Police and were carrying on terror and atrocities against the Slovene minority. These had intensified since the Yugoslavs withdrew.[4] No doubt Tito had a bad conscience about the Croat and other massacres and was now making a completely unfounded accusation against us.

On 22 July, 8th Army Commander McCreery's Military Assistant produced for him some up-to-date figures on surrendered personnel and DPs in Austria. At that date and since the 3 May, a total of 50,533 Russians, including Cossacks and Caucasians, had been repatriated (with 3,927 being still unwilling to go). 29,730 Yugoslavs including Croats, Serbs and Slovenes had been repatriated (with 1,023 unwilling to go). A very small figure of 16,379 allied PoW had been repatriated to us in return.[5]

At a meeting on 2 July at SHAEF, (Displaced Persons Branch), Brigadier Salisbury-Jones (in the chair), gave some interesting facts on Eisenhower's repatriation programme. He said that there were three reasons why SHAEF should continue to press ahead with the repatriations.

1. Consideration for the people themselves.
2. Convenience – they are more easily looked after in their own country.
3. Our repatriation record in the past.

In this connection he stressed the fact that the armies (under General Eisenhower) deserve credit for the repatriation of 3 million people within two months of the end of war.[6]

The SHAEF people were taking an understandable pride in this record as an humanitarian exercise aimed at providing basic food and shelter for those persons in their homelands, which was not obtainable in stricken Germany. Unfortunately, impending military operations in Austria and the haste with which the evacuation had had to take place, had made the AFHQ operation appear so different. For there was little difference in the treatment that could be expected on return home from either theatre, except for those Russians who had joined the enemy.

A very interesting visit to Carinthia was made 6–8 June by W H B Mack (Foreign Office representative at AFHQ Caserta, who was destined for the Allied Commission in Vienna). His report to the Foreign Office is too long to include *in toto*, but a few excerpts will give us the feel of things. Referring to the unauthorised occupation of Carinthia by Tito's men, Mack observes:

'They looted at will, removed Austrians as they chose and in general behaved in a manner which was more than embarrassing for the British Commander. The successful handling of this situation reflects the greatest credit on General Keightley and all concerned. There is, however, a strong feeling among the local British military authorities that publicity should be given to the work which they have done.'

and he adds significantly,

'It was also considered locally that some publicity should be given to the Yugoslav atrocities. On this point I advised that nothing should be given out by Corps headquarters. At the time that I was there, Tito's reply about Venezia Giulia [the ultimatum] had not yet been received. I informed the Corps Commander that only London and AFHQ could judge what could be given to the press and that it was essential that nothing should be given out in Klagenfurt which would hamper the negotiations with Tito which were then proceeding.'

However Mack advised 5 Corps that a full dossier on Yugoslav atrocities should be prepared as soon as possible for use if required. Remnants of the German forces, mostly SS, were still being rounded up in the hills. They were usually given away by the local inhabitants. The general security situation in Carinthia was very satisfactory.

'For example General Floyd [Chief of Staff Eighth Army] and I drove in a jeep without an escort for more than an hour over some of the wildest country between the valleys of the Drau and Gail.'

The non-fraternisation policy was however causing some problems. The Army commander felt that the Austrians should realise that they had fought against us. The Austrians themselves however were plainly puzzled. At the present moment the French were fraternising wholeheartedly in Voralberg, and making themselves very popular. The American forces from SHAEF had been treating the Austrians in Salzburg and Upper Austria in the same way as the Germans (one American commanding officer remarked 'I hate them all'). However a reconnaissance party of six hundred Americans at Lienz in Western Carinthia were causing a lot of embarrassment by fraternising freely. No doubt to the envy of the British troops! Mack then gives a welcome pat on the back to the hard-pressed British soldier:

'It is impossible to speak too highly of the British soldier in Carinthia. He walks about completely unconcerned, treats everything with great good humour, observes the non-fraternisation order without question and in fact looks what he is, namely the real *"Herrenvolk"* of Europe. He shows every sign of being happy and contented and making the most of one of Europe's playing grounds.'[7]

In mid-June a misunderstanding arose between the American and British Zones. It had been agreed with Third US Army that approximately 10,000 Yugoslavs could be repatriated across the British zone of Austria into Yugoslavia. The first train of approximately 2,000 arrived at Mallnitz on the evening of 19 June. Apart from one shooting incident reported, the evacuation was completed without incident.

The second train of 2,700 arrived the morning of 22 June. Two Yugoslav liaison officers from SHAEF, surprisingly 'protested' that no coercion should be used, but on our part no undue encouragement to stay behind was given. Of this party, 13 refused to be repatriated, maintaining that the Americans had promised that once in the British Zone they would be given the choice of either to go or to stay. They demanded they should be allowed to address their people on the next train, which was refused. After that, eight of this party decided that, after all, they would return to Jugoslavia. 5 Corps now gave instructions to 78 Division, responsible for this operation, to accept no unwilling personnel, from the Americans. But this proved impossible because it now appeared that trains arriving in Mallnitz, the interzonal exchange point, had no US escorts! In any case 13 (US) Corps refused to accept their return, giving as their reason 'we have no authority'. It was almost impossible to stop trains at Mallnitz owing to the very large scale move of DPs through this point.

The third consignment of 2,300 arrived on 23 June. Of these 850 officers (including one former army commander, General Brasichia, and five divisional commanders), and 74 other ranks refused to go on from Mallnitz. Most of these were Serbian (royalist) officers captured by the Germans in 1941. No wonder they refused to go on! An incident appeared imminent when rival factions, royalists and Titoists started demonstrating against each other. In the laconic phrase of the report, 'incident was controlled without difficulty by intervention of Brit.Offr.' 13 (US) Corps still maintained that they had no authority to receive back the 900 unwilling people. However all was soon arranged amicably by the arrival of an American Officer who came with a handsome apology and the 900 men returned to the US Zone. Even after this fracas a further train arrived and was evacuated to Rosenbach without difficulty which seems to show that not all Yugoslavs were unwilling to return to Tito's Yugoslavia.[8]

Now 8th Army sends a worried note to 5 Corps:

'Reports have reached this HQ to the effect that in the course of evacuation to Russia of Soviets and displaced personnel, considerable hardship has occurred in a number of cases. This was due to the fact that men, women and children have been included in the parties who are not Soviet nationals as defined in AFHQ letter CR/3491/91-BR of 6 Mar 45, contents of which were notified to you in this HQ letter M6451A of 13 Mar 45.'

(We are familiar with these letters which are referred to in Chapter XX).

The letter goes on:

'In certain cases this has resulted in families being broken up; in other cases, women and children were made to travel with their menfolk when it would have been advisable to have allowed them to remain.

The Army Commander [McCreery] fully realises the magnitude of the problem and considers that your HQ handled it with great skill and competence in view of the great difficulties involved such as language, numbers to be dealt with, the cases of hardship or irregular repatriation were chiefly due to the impossibility of accurately classifying the inmates of the camps before repatriation commenced.'[9]

Note this passage for it 'gives the lie' to those critics who accuse 5 Corps of countermanding the written instructions already given about screening, by verbal means of which of course there is no record left. 8th Army is already saying that it realises that proper screening was impossible under the circumstances, thereby exonerating Commander and Staff at 5 Corps for any negligence in this respect.

It is surprising to me that anyone could have imagined that screening was likely under Alexander's 'clear the decks' policy or 'an operation of war' as Musson put it. Russian and Yugoslav trained interpreters or interrogators did not grow on trees! Most interrogators were trained in German, as the Russians and Yugoslavs were our allies for whom there was no interrogation priority. Now that things had quietened down McCreery gave a fresh directive to 5 Corps. The effect of this would be to slow up the repatriation process, which as we will see, would greatly exacerbate relations between British and the Soviet Union at a time when the government was deeply anxious not to offend their ally.

The words of the final paragraph ran as follows:

'In view of certain representations which have been made about the hardships which repatriation has caused, the Army Commander wishes to ensure that no repatriation takes place in future of any one without full classification by the Displaced Person Branch of AMG. ... This is particularly necessary where displaced personnel may still be mixed up with surrendered personnel and is to ensure that no men, women or children are repatriated to the Soviet who are not Soviet citizens. On no account is any force to be used in connection with any repatriation scheme.'[10]

In the 8th Army letter to 5 Corps of 13 June, referred to above, the words 'Reports have reached this HQ', probably refer to reports made by British Red Cross field officers to their HQ in London. These reports caused Miss Warner from that Office to approach the Foreign Office on 13 July to try and verify the facts. The Red Cross reports referred to 'pathetic and agonising scenes in some of the Assembly Camps' when some of the refugees were told that they were returning to their own countries. In particular, the report singled out the camp guarded by the 8 Argyll and Sutherland Highlanders, where, it was alleged, after a conversation with the adjutant, that there was no registration system for the camp inmates, no Russian interpreters, no proper screening etc. etc. This report has recently come to light in the private papers of the official concerned. Having seen this report, I decided to check with a member of the regiment concerned, who was out there at that time. I received a letter in reply from Colin Mitchell, (then Battalion Intelligence Officer), from which I quote.[11]

> 'Ernest Macmillan, the Adjutant of the 8 Argyll's was a temporary officer [wartime commission], an artist by profession, utterly charming, cultured and intelligent. He knew the form over the Cossacks better than anyone, had a far broader view than the company commanders and was very much in the mind of Alex Malcolm, who commanded .... It was the misfortune of the Cossacks to be on the losing side, just as you and I – both wounded that year – lived to be on the winning side!'

As regards the interpreters:

> 'Interpreters were always in short supply. I had the best two in the "I" Section and after I left the battalion the best one ... turned out to be in the SS – which gives some idea of the shambles existing in these first few weeks after VE Day (you probably saw the same sort of problem in BAOR). . . . Any attempt "to register the camp inmates" is a ludicrous suggestion to anyone who was dealing with the problems on a day-to-day basis on the ground.'[12]

However when General Keightley returned on leave to the United Kingdom, so concerned was he with these reports and the implied threat that Red Cross workers might be withdrawn, that he arranged to meet Lady Falmouth, Head of the British Red Cross Relief Department, whilst in London, on 18 July. At the meeting the whole question was thrashed out. Lady Falmouth's record of the conversation is given in these excerpts.[13]

> 'I asked him what the position was of all the displaced Russians and Yugoslavs, and he told me there were two incidents which gave rise to the story. In the first incident, several thousand Cossacks were taken prisoner, but had been for the last three and a half years fighting in the German ranks; they were dressed in German uniform and were taken prisoners of war. With them were

some 1,500 or so Russian men, wives and families; they were an armed body moving around in regiments.'

Lady Falmouth tells us that the General told her that it had been decided, in accordance with current policy, that these people had to be returned to Russia. They were interviewed and agreed to go. The men went willingly, but the women protested at first under the instigation of their priest, but subsequently followed him into the train.

'A British officer accompanied them into Russian territory ... there was no evidence at all that they had been shot.'

Keightley then tells her,

'In the case of the Yugoslavs, there were a considerable number of Yugoslav Displaced Persons (not soldiers), they were asked if they were prepared to return to Yugoslavia and expressed themselves quite willing, in fact volunteered ... after they got into Yugoslavia six of them dribbled back and said that the moment they crossed a bridge, they were all machine-gunned. On this information being received, no further evacuations to Yugoslavia were made ... General Keightley gave me a categorical assurance that there were no unwilling people being sent back.'

Some confusion arose in many people's minds at the time, as to the difference between DP's and 'camp-followers'. Camp-followers were considered to be part and parcel of the contingent to which their menfolk belonged, but were usually given the option as to their return. Almost invariably they chose to follow their menfolk. But one can see from the account of this interview that exactly what happened in this troubled period was still far from clear.

XXVIII

Winter of Discontent

Several more chapters could be written concerning the aftermath of the Second World War in Austria and Germany. But I will confine myself to this one, trying to draw out any matters that have a direct bearing on the earlier happenings in the spring and summer of 1945. One the whole it will be found that subsequent policy bears out the decisions that had been taken in the heat of action, and in many respects a more uncompromising line over repatriations was taken thereafter. Whereas the soldiers had been exposed to the practical difficulties on the ground, of rounding up; of screening people without any papers; of resisting the importunate demands of the Soviets, and of the physical difficulties of moving people unwilling to go, that is to say that the soldiers were taking the brunt of policy laid down on high, the Foreign Office chose to ignore those difficulties and insisted on adherence to the letter of the law. The Foreign Office was itself subject to various pressures.

First, the incoming government in Britain was a Socialist one which, at that stage, wished to maintain close fraternal links with the Soviet Union.

Second, the Yalta agreement, which provided for no other policy but repatriation for Soviet citizens, however willing or unwilling they might be, was still the determining factor. The Cold War, which of course in time changed British policy towards the Soviet Union, had not yet altered perceptions.

Third and most immediate, was the forthcoming meeting of foreign ministers due to take place in Moscow at the end of December. There was a belated realisation on the part of the Foreign Office that the British Foreign Secretary, Ernest Bevin, might well appear at the negotiating table empty-handed. By not making haste to send back the remaining Soviet citizens, Foreign Office officials feared that he would be put in a very weak position over other vital issues. Such as, for example, Allied access to Berlin. As it turned out, the Soviets were to make most serious accusations against the Western Allies, from the very start of the Moscow Conference, on the issue of the repatriation of 'Soviet citizens'.

To our eyes today, accustomed to a high profile on 'human rights', the attitude of the British Government anxious to honour the most outrageous demands of the Soviets may appear craven. But I am once again forced to resume the mantle of my other self and step back in time and taste once again the bitter medicine. In Britain we had a country exhausted after six years of war, much of it a single-handed effort: a total dislocation of the means of livelihood, industry and commerce: widespread destruction in the United Kingdom's towns and cities; a chronic lack of manpower and the continuation of wartime rationing. A massive programme of Socialist legislation was shattering the fragile framework still surviving. And brooding over it all, the Soviet military leviathan, virtually intact and poised for any opportunist action.

It was not a strong or enviable position for the negotiating table, even though some of the wounds were self-inflicted!

And satiated as the reader must be with human beings being treated like so many of Gogol's 'dead souls', we must take note of the harsh facts of continuing British policy.

On 6 December, the Foreign Office writes to the War Office that their attention has been drawn to a conference held in Berlin on 29 October last, at which it was stated that 'the Commander-in-Chief [Montgomery] was not prepared to use force for the repatriation of Soviet nationals; no publicity will be given to this decision'.

The Foreign Office letter continued:

> 'We are both mystified and alarmed by this statement, which is of course quite contradictory to His Majesty's Government policy as recently confirmed by our Secretary of State [Mr. Bevin]. ... Furthermore, when this specific issue was raised in a telegram from Berlin (ARGUS 95) on which you asked for our views ... we made it quite clear that our policy in respect the use of force had not changed, and that we should abide by this policy in all British zones, whatever the Americans might do in theirs ... Yet at a meeting held in Berlin 13 days later, the contrary policy was laid down, apparently by the authority of the Commander-in-Chief.'

The letter admitted at the end that a Foreign Office representative had been present at the meeting. He evidently had failed to report the misdemeanour.[1]

The situation in Austria now comes under scrutiny. Our diplomatic mission in Vienna had already been asked to report the progress of continued repatriation by BTA (British Troops Austria), and had come up with the figures of 58,000 undisputed Soviet nationals (surrendered personnel) already repatriated and 5,000 displaced persons. As the former were repatriated as military units, they may have included a proportion of men of Russian origin who were not necessarily undisputed Soviet nationals, the telegram admits. But it is the next bit which incurs 'the Office's' ire.

That undisputed Soviet nationals

'Unrepatriated from the British Zone number 416. Some 1,100 believed to be at large and unwilling to return. In addition there are in camps in British Zone 1425 White Russians, 1,353 Ukrainians and 380 Russians who fought for the enemy. It can be assumed', the telegram concluded, 'that they do not wish to return, as they have had ample opportunity of doing so.'[2]

The reply comes back from the Foreign Office the same day.

'Your telegram 234.
1. We are dissatisfied with the situation revealed by your telegram under reference. Under Yalta Agreement, which it is the obligation of the British Military Authority to carry out, HMG are obliged to repatriate all Soviet citizens to the USSR.'

Then the rules governing Soviet citizenship are spelt out under subheadings a), b) and c).

'In view of (c) above we are disturbed to see from your para 2 (group indecipherable) believed to be from 1,500 Soviet citizens in British Zone of Austria. Why is this, and why has no progress been made since September . . .?'

The hectoring tone of this message reflects the nervousness with which the approach of the Moscow Conference was greeted by the Foreign Office.

At about the same time, another problem was on the minds of the British Foreign Service, as it had now become, (the title 'Diplomatic' having been dropped by the new government). There was a difference of opinion between the British Government and Americans on 'the use of force'. Although Eisenhower had earlier adopted the use of force in the zone occupied by SHAEF, there had been a change of policy at the end of October. Eisenhower was being reported in the press as having abrogated that 'para' of the Yalta agreement relating to the use of force.[3]

So, on 11 December, a junior official in the Foreign Office drafted this letter to the War Office. On this occasion he was referring to a 'return' of numbers from General Headquarters, Central Mediterranean Forces.

'This reply seems to us both incomprehensible and self-contradictory' runs the letter. And then after disputing the arithmetic of the repatriation figures, it continues, significantly:

> 'In view of the forthcoming talks in Moscow, it is absolutely essential that we should induce the Americans to make up their minds on this question of the use of force in the repatriation of Soviet citizens held in Italy. We cannot, however, press them for as long as we ourselves do not know the dimension of the problem or even whether there still *is* a problem.'

The letter concludes, 'I have serious misgivings that we may seen [sic] badly caught out in this matter, perhaps during the discussions in Moscow, unless we can very rapidly bring it to a head in Washington.'[4]

The recriminations continue. Our man in Vienna, Mr Mack, replies briefly to the Foreign Office on 16 December 'I have informed Military Authorities of your views', then goes on to explain that as a result of explicit instructions from AFHQ dated August 31, there had been no forcible repatriation since the Cossack Corps was handed over to Russia in the early days of British occupation, although the Commander-in-Chief [Alexander] had ordered all means short of force to be used. He then goes on to explain the difficulties of 'screening'. That those people were mostly without identity documents and many of them had an interest in concealing their original place of domicile. Information could only be obtained by detailed interrogation and even then accuracy could not be guaranteed.[5]

The British Commander-in-Chief, McCreery, backs this up with a similar message, also pointing out that he has not enough British troops in any case to round up all those on the loose, or even erect wire around the camps; and any hint of forced repatriation would only encourage those in camps to break out, and become bandits in preference to dying of starvation whilst at large. He also points out that whilst the necessity for complete discharge of our commitments under the Yalta agreement is fully understood, 'the Soviet element here [Vienna] has at no time complained that we were failing to repatriate Soviet citizens by force', only about treatment and non-segregation etcetera.[6]

The Foreign Office now re-assuming the full authority of state which they had conceded to 'the military' during the war-time years, will have none of this:

> 'The arguments advanced by General MacCreery [sic] against forcible repatriation seem to us quite unconvincing. Firstly, we cannot accept the statement in paragraph 6 (c) of his signal [McCreery's No 10146. Para 6 (c) had stated

that 'a high percentage of Soviet DP consist of women and children against whom the use of force by British soldiers would be contrary to normal British practice], that the use of force would be "contrary to normal British practice". As far as we are aware, the situation which gave rise to the Yalta agreement is without precedent in British history, and we do not therefore see the relevance of any reference to "normal practice". If General MacCreery [sic] means that the use of force would be incompatible with our traditional policy of not handing over political refugees to the Government to which they are opposed, we must point out that the traditional policy of granting asylum is normally only applied to persons who reach the United Kingdom or British territory and not to persons who have fallen into the hands of British forces in the course of military operations. Secondly, although this is not really within our province, we find it difficult to believe that there are not enough troops in the British zone of Austria for a repatriation operation of this nature, especially if taken by stages. What, do you think?'[7]

This letter from Brimelow (Northern Department, Foreign Office) to Hammer (War Office) then ended with a virtual ultimatum.

'We cannot accept the arguments advanced by General MacCreery as valid grounds for recommending to the Secretary of State that the policy laid down by the War Cabinet and confirmed by him should be modified. As you know, similar arguments were advanced by Allied Force Headquarters in respect of Soviet civilians and Cossacks in Italy, and were taken into account by the Secretary of State when he gave his ruling last August. We have, of course, no desire whatever to press for the admission of Soviet troops into the British zone – this was merely a suggestion – but it must be made clear to the military authorities concerned that, if Soviet troops are not to be invited to discharge these functions, then they must be performed by British troops. We much hope that you will agree to our telegraphing to Vienna on the lines of the attached draft and that you will agree to send similar instructions to General MacCreery. Otherwise, of course, we shall have to inform the Secretary of State in Moscow why the policy laid down by him is not being applied in Austria.

In view of the possibility that this matter may come up at any moment in the current discussions in Moscow, we should like to let our Secretary of State know as soon as possible that he would be safe in saying that urgent measures for the repatriation of these people are now being taken. I shall therefore be grateful if you will treat this subject as most immediate.'[8]

He is saying, putting it into blunt terms. Implement the policy laid down by the War Cabinet, or the Foreign Secretary must inform the Cabinet that you refuse to do so.

I have taken the liberty of including a greater part of this letter because it explains to a lesser or greater degree the meaning of both past events and those to come. Firstly, the unwavering attachment of HMG to the very letter of the Yalta agreement, which agreement, although not specifically mentioning 'the use of force', assumes it. Secondly, the total absorption of the Foreign Office mind by the imminent Moscow conference, and not letting the Foreign Secretary be caught 'with his trousers down'. For after all, Bevin had already stated in trenchant terms that all these people must go back home. The close ideological links between the new Socialist Government in Britain and their Soviet counterparts must on no account be endangered. Laying aside all accusations of 'conspiracy', or the existence of a 'mole' in the Foreign Office, I think this is the simplest explanation of the 'heartlessness' charge levied against that government. But it is for the Labour Party to answer such charges alone, for had they not insisted on prematurely breaking up the wartime coalition against Churchill's wishes, and taking on single-handed the onerous responsibilities for the aftermath of war? It is for politicians to answer for policy, not the civil servants who were simply doing what they were told.

So how did it all end? On 22 December, at the moment the Moscow Conference of Foreign Ministers was meeting, the British Cabinet Offices were informed by the Joint Staff Mission in Washington of a new US War Department directive to United States Forces in Europe. It began

'Over 2,034,000 Soviet citizens have already been repatriated from Western Germany, leaving only approximately 20,000 Soviet citizens in the US Zone in Germany. It is the policy of this Government, pursuant to the agreement with the Soviet Union at Yalta, to facilitate the early repatriation of these persons to the Soviet Union.'

It then laid down the following instruction, of which I give the key extracts:

'1. Persons who were both citizens of and actually within the Soviet Union on 1st September 1939 and who fall into the following classes will be repatriated without regard to their wishes and by force if necessary:
A. Those captured in German uniforms.
B. Those who were members of the Soviet Armed Forces on or after 22nd June 1941 and who were not subsequently discharged therefrom.
C. Those who are charged by the Soviet Union with having voluntarily rendered aid and comfort to the enemy, where the Soviet Union satisfies the United States military authorities of the substantiality of the charge by supplying in each case, with reasonable particularity, the time, place and nature of the offences and the perpetrator thereof. A person's announced resistance to this repatriation or his acceptance of ordinary employment in German industry or agriculture shall not of itself be construed as constituting rendition of aid and comfort to the enemy.'[9]

So was that the end of it? Not quite. McCreery accepted his orders, but pointed out to the Cabinet that 'the use of force' might mean the use of firearms and the need to shoot people to enforce that policy. At this Ministers balked. They had not fully realised the consequences of their actions. In January a hurried meeting of Ministers was called, and there we will leave them, to digest the multifarious problems of 'the aftermath of war'.

XXIX

Repatriation in Reverse – War Criminals Enter Britain

By 1947 the Cold War had spread its icy grip across Europe. An iron stockade (or curtain), had been planted by the Russians and their satellites along their western borders, stretching from the Baltic Sea to the Adriatic. Attlee was still Prime Minister in Britain. Forced repatriations were still taking place, but the Cold War with the Soviet Union had changed a lot of things, including attitudes in government.

At the beginning of 1947, a crisis had developed over the future of the prison camp still holding refugees at Rimini. It contained some 30,000 surrendered enemy personnel, a mixture of Ukrainians, Yugoslavs and Balts. The Allied armies were just about to leave Italy and the future of the camp was now under serious question.

As we have seen the 1 Ukrainian Division, alias *SS Panzer Grenadier Division, Galizien* had been evacuated to Italy by General Keightley along with Rogohzin's *Schutzkorps* in unit 'block screening' in May 1945. They were deemed ineligible for repatriation in view of the fact that they had never been domiciled within the Soviet Union as her borders existed at 1 September 1939. The Balts, from the 'republics' of Latvia, Lithuania, and Estonia had been recruited by the Germans into the Waffen SS or paramilitary police units at an earlier stage of the war. They were absorbed into the Wehrmacht or Waffen SS as 'Germanic Legions' and fought on the Eastern Front.

Unbelievable atrocities and genocide had taken place in the 'republics' of the Baltic States, Byelorussia and the Ukraine during the war years. When the Soviets entered Latvia and Estonia in 1939, in accordance with secret protocols under the Molotov–Ribbentrop Pact, they set about the liquidation and elimination of 'undesirables' by execution and mass deportation; the Jews in Latvia and Estonia are alleged to have collaborated with the Soviets in this work. But when the pendulum swung the other way, with re-occupation by the Germans in 1941, the Latvians and Estonians collaborated equally enthusiastically in exterminating the Jewish population.[1]

The Latvian Red Cross had estimated that during the year of occupation by the Soviet Union, Latvia lost 35,828 people in deportations and executions; when the Russians returned in 1945 the process continued with 140,000 Latvians being deported, 100,000 were lost in subsequent collectivisation.[2]

During the German re-occupation between the months of June and November 1941 alone, the mass murder of Jews took place in all three Baltic States: over 120,000 were killed in Lithuania, about 70,000 in Latvia and virtually all in Estonia. According to the Hetherington-Chalmers Report (CM 744), the Germans encouraged local killing squads and so expert did these squads become that they began to be used on a far wider scale.[3]

Hetherington sums it up thus:

> 'Balts collaborated with the Germans in killing their Jewish fellow-citizens and because of their successes in that task they were also employed to kill Byelorussian Jews. In the Ukraine, the Ukrainian militia helped to kill the Jews and took actions against partisans. As in Byelorussia, raids against villages suspected of harbouring partisans frequently resulted in the destruction of the entire village and the slaughter of all its inhabitants.'[4]

But as one can see from these figures alone, it was not a one-sided affair. The Jews in the Baltic States who sided with the communists could be accused (and are so by the gentile survivors), of sowing the wind, only to reap the whirlwind. And it was some members of the Nazi 'killing squads', absorbed into police or SS units, who eventually ended up at Rimini camp, ineligible for repatriation as they had not lived within the borders of the Soviet Union when war broke out.

By 1947, the government was in a quandary as to what to do about the Rimini camp. If they simply abandoned the responsibility, the Italian government would have no option under their new Treaty with the Soviet Union but to repatriate them to the Soviet Union or Yugoslavia. The Soviet government had already warned Britain that in their view most were eligible for repatriation, particularly as they included numbers of war criminals.

Ernest Bevin, the British Foreign Secretary, then prevailed upon Fitzroy Maclean, who had by then resumed his seat in the House of Commons, to come to his aid, and in view of his undoubted knowledge, to conduct a major screening operation in the camps at Rimini and Eboli in Italy, which also included large numbers of Ukrainians, Balts and Yugoslavs. Screening of the Yugoslavs was carried out without too many political difficulties. As far as the Ukrainians were concerned, it was found impossible to deal with the numbers involved in the time available and Maclean was suspicious that many had served in the SS. As it turned out, screening only took place in the most cursory manner, if at all, and there was no evidence to rely upon except the subject's own word, which was deeply suspect.

Speaking of the Galizien's, Maclean cabled that if they were to come to Britain 'It must be borne in mind that we only have their word for it . . . that they have not committed atrocities or war crimes.'[5]

It was in January 1947 that A W H Wilkinson, Foreign Office Refugee Department, in a minute commenting on the conclusions of a Cabinet discussion, set the tone for an operation which was to shift, over a period of some 5 years, 90,000 former enemy personnel (many of them war criminals) into the United Kingdom. Wilkinson noted on 22 January:

> 'There have been indications recently that other countries, especially Belgium, have become interested in the recruitment of displaced persons, to relieve labour shortages at home. Unless speedy measures are taken by the competent departments of HMG, we may find that other countries will have skimmed the cream of the displaced persons, especially the Balts who are undoubtedly the élite of the refugee problem.'[6]

Meantime a series of reports were coming through from Maclean at Rimini.

On 21 February he cabled the Foreign Office:

> 'In the first place these men [SEP] have in the past two years had ample time in which to disguise their identity and this Commission has no machinery whatever for criminal investigation work . . . Secondly, with one exception, none of the camps are guarded so that at the first sign of danger all those with guilty consciences would clear out.'[7]

On 22 February Maclean signals to the Foreign Office, on the Ukrainians:

> 'Careful screening has shown itself to take much longer than anticipated. A fortnight has been required to screen 200 men. Really careful screening of the whole camp would take many months.'[8]

Sir George Rendel, Supervising Under Secretary of the Refugee Department at the Foreign Office, in a note on 27 February, suggested that as these men (the Ukrainians) were technically our 'prisoners of war', they should be brought over to the UK as such, thus obviating the difficulties of giving them DP status with the stringent screening requirements of the international refugee organisations.[9]

In a note the same day (27 February), to the United States Embassy, he lays the FO dilemma strongly 'on the line':

'If these people remain in Italy as a responsibility of the Italian government, and the Italian government are asked to hand them over under Article 45 [of the Treaty], one of two things will happen. Either the Italians will succeed in rounding up and surrendering these people, in which case there will be an outcry in England and America as soon as the news is known of the fate which awaits them, or alternatively, the Italian Government will be unable or unwilling to surrender them all, in which case a major political dispute is likely to develop between them on the one hand, and the Jugoslavs and Russians on the other. In the second event, we can be pretty sure that the Jugoslavs and Russians will press their rights strongly. Our forces will by then have evacuated Italy, and the Italians will be quite defenceless. The Jugoslavs and Russians will have the Treaty right on their side, and it is quite conceivable that they might even insist on sending a military expedition into Italy to round up these people.'[10]

Maclean, from Rome, now gives his opinion that 'one is unavoidably forced to the conclusion that whatever happens, it will be necessary to move all to North Africa or some other British controlled area.'[11] But it soon becomes clear that the North Africa loophole is closed, as Wilkinson has already made clear in a minute on 20 February, when he notes:

'The project of removing innocent political dissidents to North Africa is meeting with considerable difficulties and if these unfortunate people are to be protected from forcible repatriation it will be necessary to find them a home elsewhere.'[12]

Although Wilkinson has it in mind that the scheme to bring the Ukrainians to the United Kingdom as PoW (technically SEP) might prove a useful precedent for bringing in the Yugoslavs as well,[13] such a policy is not accepted universally in Whitehall. Carew Robinson, Under Secretary at the Home Office, writes:

'The difficulty will not be lessened by the fact that the whole of the men in question have admittedly fought or served on the side of Germany ... and from the Home Office point of view we must urge that every possible expedient be adopted for disposing of them otherwise than by conversion into civilian status in the United Kingdom.'[14]

Brimelow, of the Northern Department is also sceptical about the desirability of admitting all to the United Kingdom.

But Hector McNeil, Foreign Office Minister of State, is already writing to Prime Minister Attlee about the refugee situation in Italy:

'This situation is becoming very critical, and I feel that every possible means should be taken to remove displaced persons from that country, particularly in so far as it may benefit our own labour situation.'[15]

Although virtually no screening had taken place, or on an extremely perfunctory basis, amongst these people, many of whom had served in the SS, it was the intention that recruitment for labour purposes should have priority over security screening. (According to Nuremburg Tribunal rules, membership of SS Units was evidence of war criminality.) But in the case of the Ukrainians, Prime Minister Attlee had already given approval for them to have shipping priority over all other claimants, such as the return of German PoW from the Middle East or the repatriation of Poles then in Britain.[16]

It was in this way that the Waffen SS Galizien division came to Britain and was rapidly absorbed into civilian life.

The All-Party Parliamentary War Crimes Group, in the Summary on their *Report on the Entry of Nazi War Criminals and Collaborators into the UK 1945–50.*[17] had this to say about the Ukrainian Waffen SS let into Britain:

> 'Many members of these forces may at one time have participated in "Actions" conducted by *Einsatz-gruppe* units – the mobile death squads – in Russia and Poland.'

And on the motive:

> 'The Government viewed the presence of the Ukrainians (many of whom were sought by the USSR) in Italy as a political inconvenience.'

And on screening:

> 'The FO concluded that, as time was short, screening need only be cursory, just a tiny cross-section of Ukrainian internees – about 1 in 25 were screened for their wartime activities.'

As for the Soviet Union's extradition requests for alleged war criminals:

> 'The FO chose not to treat them seriously.'

Whatever may be said about the Foreign Office or other departments in Whitehall, it was the government of the day which willingly took upon its own shoulders the onerous responsibilities for the aftermath of war.

It is not my intention to suggest that a new witch-hunt should take place after all these years, rather to point out that those who refuse to face facts and who ignore the basic security of the State are lighting a time-bomb with a very long fuse.

Repatriation of 'wanted-men' was an obligation between allies. This experiment of 'repatriation-in-reverse' created many more problems than it cured, the results of which we are seeing to this very day.

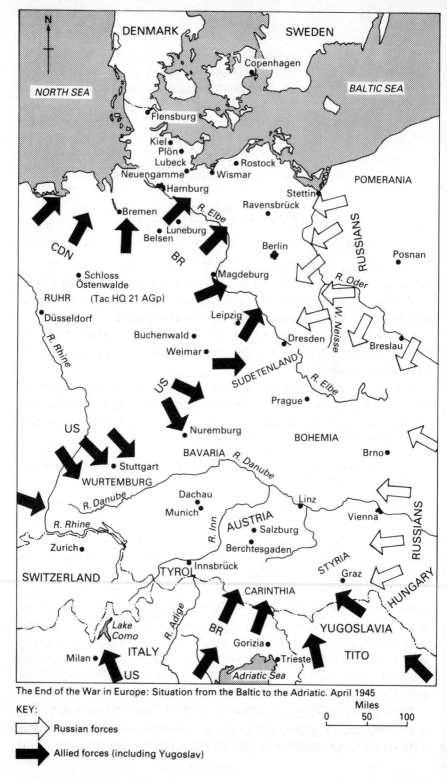

The End of the War in Europe: Situation from the Baltic to the Adriatic. April 1945

KEY:

⟢ Russian forces

➤ Allied forces (including Yugoslav)

6. The End of the War in Europe: Situation from the Baltic to the Adriatic. April 1945.

XXX

How it All Began

I have left this part of the story till the last, because it was outside
the scope of my original enquiry, which was the sequence of events
in Austria. None-the-less, what is to follow gives us our first main
insight into the formulation of the repatriation policy.

It is here that we need to ask the big questions. How did it all
begin? To whom could be ascribed the ultimate responsibility? Where
did the buck stop?

In the summer of 1944, just after the Normandy landings, a government minister, Lord Selborne had written a very agitated memo to
Foreign Secretary Eden, deploring certain decisions taken in the Cabinet (of which he was not a member).

> 'Very unhappy about Cabinet decision to hand back to Russia all Russian sub-
> jects who fall into our hands in Europe.'

In Normandy, much to our surprise, our troops begin to capture
large numbers of Russians clad in German uniform. It was no less
a surprise to our Russian allies, who, of course we informed immediately. In fact the Soviets did not at first accept it, it was out of the
question that Russian soldiers could be found serving in the German
Armed Forces. In an earlier chapter I have recounted how I myself
came across a Cossack unit, probably no more than a squadron,
in possession of some outbuildings near the Commander-in-Chief's
headquarters. Many of these Russians were L of C troops, low-grade
units who had been occupying ground deemed safe by the Germans
from invasion, but their presence certainly came as a surprise to me
and others at the time.

The capture of Russian soldiers on the Western Front (and some
in the Middle East as well) began to concentrate the British War
Cabinet's collective mind on the whole question of the exchange of

prisoners over-run by either side.

Lord Selborne's reaction had been to a Cabinet meeting held on 17 July, at which the principle to hand back captured Russians, if the Soviets asked for them, was agreed upon.[1]

Selborne then addressed a memo to the Prime Minister on 25 July, in which he 'greatly regretted' the Cabinet's decision to send these men back to Russia. 'It will mean certain death for them'. He had heard from his SOE officers, who had interviewed such prisoners, of an instance where a Russian who refused to join a German Labour unit was promptly shot. Selborne had been discussing the matter with his French colleague M. d'Astiev who had an idea that they might be invited to join the French Maquis, and subsequently offered refuge in the French Colonies or Foreign Legion.

Harold Macmillan suggested in a telegram from Caserta on 27 July, that the Soviets (the Sudakov Commission) should have the option of selecting from the prisoners those whom they required for the war effort 'those whom he rejected will remain prisoners of war. Those whom he accepts for future service with the Soviet Forces will be repatriated to Russia' but added a rider about the fate which 'may in reality be in store for them.'[2]

Churchill's reaction to Selborne's note is to suggest to the Foreign Secretary that the matter might be reconsidered. 'I think we dealt rather summarily with this at Cabinet'. The PM felt that even if we were somewhat compromised all 'the apparatus of delay' might be used.[3]

Now the Under Secretary at the War Office, Sir Frederick Bovenschen, writes to his opposite number at the Foreign Office, Sir Orme Sargent, and adds a new twist to our understanding of this affair.

In the Middle East, as Macmillan pointed out, there was to be a separation of those captured Russians in German uniform who were fit for further service and those who were not.

> 'We did not tell the Russians that those who were unwilling to be repatriated are not in fact being handed over. This condition was agreed between the Foreign Office and the War Office – I think at the War Office suggestion – in order to prevent a situation arising in which the Russians maltreated their compatriots who were handed back to them and the Germans found in this a pretext for reprisals on British and American prisoners of war.'[4]

So this was how it started, we were not apparently too worried at that stage about British prisoners in Russian hands, for the Russians were not far enough west in August 1944 to have over-run any camps. But, as Bovenschen makes clear, we were seriously worried that our repatriation of Russians in German uniform might encourage the Germans to take reprisals against our prisoners in their hands! We must remember that there was still a war on, with no clear end in sight, the Crimea Conference at Yalta was still six months off. And again, another unexpected situation at that time was that Soviet nationals (as they probably were) were 'too frightened' to refuse to return. As far as those in the Middle East were concerned the protection given by this 'freedom of choice' was completely illusory. 'The Russian prisoners are afraid, apparently to refuse to go back. It is also clear that some of those who do go back are going to be very roughly treated.'[5] We were then expecting, as a post-script to Bovenschen's letter makes clear, that the numbers of Russians captured might be so great that we would have difficulty in handling them as prisoners of war.

On 2 August, Eden replied to Churchill's memo which had asked him to 'look again'. He tells the PM that he has considered this question more than once recently and has already acted with the Soviet Embassy on the basis of the Cabinet decision taken on 17 July.

> 'From the standpoint of our relations with the Soviet Government there are very strong arguments in favour of allowing the Cabinet decision to stand and of returning to Russia any of the prisoners whom the Soviet Government want, subject always to the proviso, upon which we and the War Office agree, that the men should not be put on trial so long as there is any danger of German reprisals against British or United States prisoners.'

Eden then gives his reasons in detail, of which the following extracts are apposite:

> 'It is important to treat the Soviet Government in this matter as nearly as possible in the same way as the other Allied Governments whose nationals have been captured in German formations. The procedure which I advocate will have this effect. Provided that we protect British and American prisoners from all risk of reprisals, it is no concern of ours what measure any Allied Government, including the Soviet Government, take as regards their own nationals and we should be in an indefensible position if we tried to dictate to the Soviet or any other Allied Government what steps they should or should not take in dealing with their own nationals who may have committed offences against their own law by serving in the German formations.'[6]

Eden points out that we surely do not wish to be permanently saddled with a number of these men and if we do not return them we shall have to decide what to do with them both here and in the Middle East. He also reacts to Selborne's suggestion about them joining the French; that there would be serious trouble with the Soviet

Government if we handed these men over to the French without their permission. And then he reiterates the nub of his objection:

> 'To refuse the Soviet Government's request for the return of their own men would lead to serious trouble with them. We have no right whatever to do this and they would not understand our humanitarian motives. They would know that we were treating them differently from the other Allied Governments on this question and this would arouse their gravest suspicions.
>
> Finally the position of our own prisoners in Germany and Poland who are likely to be released by the Russians in the course of their advance is material to this question. It is most important that they should be well cared for and returned as soon as possible. For this we must rely to a great extent upon Soviet goodwill and if we make difficulty over returning to them their own nationals I feel sure it will react adversely upon their willingness to help in restoring to us as soon as possible our own prisoners whom they release.
>
> For these reasons I am convinced that, if the Soviet Government want these men back for their own forces or war effort, we should agree to send them back from both here and the Middle East, subject to the exigencies of transport and subject to obtaining from the Russians a firm undertaking covering the risk of German reprisals. The men can be used in agricultural or other useful work while arrangements for their repatriation are being made.'[7]

These arguments which the Foreign Secretary deployed were powerful ones. For our prisoners of war in German camps were vulnerable on two counts. One the one hand, from the Germans in the form of reprisals. On the other hand, from the Russians, who having advanced and over-run them, might delay repatriation until we had returned every single man of theirs.

Churchill accepted the weight of the argument as, eventually, did Lord Selborne.

And so it was that this memorandum from Eden to Churchill became British policy on the repatriation of Russian prisoners. It was to be incorporated into the Yalta agreement and was to remain British policy consistently for the next three years, from 1944 to 1947.

But nevertheless, the Minister of War, Sir James Grigg, felt that he needed full Cabinet backing for a policy which it would be his task to carry through. His letter, which I reproduce in full, in Appendix G[8], shows, better than I can, the agonising decisions of those war-time years. Nowadays we would call it a 'Catch 22' situation, each alternative course had grave disadvantages. We simply had to take the lesser of the two evils.

On 4 September 1944, the War Cabinet approved the policy after a short discussion directly arising out of the misgivings expressed by Selborne and Grigg.

The conclusions were threefold:

First that we should agree with the Soviet request to repatriate their prisoners from the United Kingdom.

Second we should instruct the Middle East authorities to send back all Russians, whom the Soviet Authorities wished to have back, irrespective of whether the men wished to return.

Third that shortage of shipping made it impossible for us to accede to their request that we should arrange for their repatriation from the United Kingdom directly.[9]

Even in 1944 the use of force was implicit in the decision of the British War Cabinet.

There was one further important question which came up at this time. Macmillan raised the point from Caserta about handing over to the Russians Soviet prisoners who were originally captured by the United States. His American colleague had queried whether this might be in breach of the Geneva Convention.[10]

The reply from the Foreign Office was as follows:

> 'This is a familiar point, the answer to which seems to be as follows. In spite of the provisions of the Geneva Convention, it is not possible for a soldier who is captured by his own forces while he is serving (for whatever reason) with the enemy forces to claim vis à vis his own government and his own law the protection of the Convention. We should certainly not be prepared to grant such a right to a British subject captured while serving in the German forces. If such a man is captured by an allied force the Allied government is entitled to hand him over unconditionally to this own government without rendering themselves liable for a breach of the Convention.'[11]

The answer therefore to the question which I posed at the beginning of this chapter, as to whose was the ultimate responsibility for the repatriations that took place from the British zones of Germany and of Austria in the period 1945 to 1947 is quite clear from the above. The ultimate responsibility was that of the British War Cabinet of the wartime coalition government which had the universal support of the British people. Those provisions were formulated in agreement with our United States Allies, were incorporated into the Yalta agreement, which was jointly signed by the governments of the British Dominions, Canada, Australia, India, New Zealand and South Africa.

The agreement of Yalta was forged in the heat of war. Its provisions were carried out in that turmoil of the first days of peace.

It would take a brave man to say that, knowing Stalin, we should never have accepted Russia in a 'marriage of convenience' in the first place. That raises even bigger questions which go quite beyond the scope of this book!

The message which I wish to convey to the reader at the end of this book is that one should not be waylaid by individual incidents, however horrific these may seem. Look at the picture in the round. The block under the mason's hammer has no significance on its own, however misshapen it may be; once part of the building, its true significance is revealed.

It is not my intention, therefore, to deliver a series of weighty conclusions. Such clear-cut decisions I do not believe are possible given the passage of time. Anyone who believes that anything in wartime is cut and dried is suffering from a serious delusion. War is a mess. The warrior's aim must be to bring some order out of this confusion, in order to carry out the policies of his government. The historian's aim, often enough, is to bring about some preconceived conclusion. Obviously I have been at pains to answer some of the allegations raised by other authors, which have so distracted opinion on these events and damaged the reputation of British arms in the final stages of the war. Six years is a long time in my or in anyone's life. Time enough to learn the cruel facts of life, and to have the truth seared into one's memory. Many historians will continue to write and argue over these events, many not then born, or old enough to remember. I can only offer this up as a contribution to the record, by someone who was involved in the whole affair, and its aftermath.

It will be in the memory of others reading this book of more recent examples of precisely the same dilemmas, of mass migrations starting which have to be reversed; of prisoners of war unwilling to return to their homes; of starving refugees, the victims of war's aftermath. Only one thing is certain in these affairs, that history has a habit of repeating itself.

Epilogue

The Friuli and Carnia Revisited
Memories of the Cossack Occupation

The reader may be mystified that I set out upon such a wild-goose chase after a lapse of 45 years. But in the event I was well rewarded. For the bitter-sweet recollections of the times of *i Cosacchi* remain vivid in the memory of those who experienced them. To a younger generation, it has now passed into the realm of folklore. But *i Cosacchi* were at once so strange, so uncouth, and so outlandish, that they were not easily forgotten. Only memories of the brutality having softened with the passage of time.

It was thanks to the good offices of Peter Lee (Ex-SOE) and Paola Del Din Carnielli (Ex-Osoppo Partisan leader), that I was able to visit the area. I chose as my companion Christopher Thursby-Pelham,[1] who had advanced through this area with the 8th Army. We were greatly assisted by the services of an interpreter, James Chamberlain,[2] a resident of Udine. We set out in October, 1990 with the object of seeking out Partisan veterans in Carnia and the Pre-Alpi who could give eye-witness accounts of the SS/Cossack campaign against the Partisans.

So let me first describe the scenery against which the drama was played out, as I saw it with my own eyes. Imagine a flat plain stretching from the Adriatic to the Alps. Out of it suddenly rise the most staggering white limestone crags and peaks. Broad valleys separate the mountain mass, these almost entirely occupied by rock-stream moraines of the river system, dominated by the Tagliamento, either in spate or dry and arid, according to season. The Georgians would certainly have recognised this as being not unlike their homeland, the Caucasus. The Cossacks would have looked in vain for any *steppe*, unless they looked towards the Friulian plain. For this unpromising land the

Germans had designated as their new national home of *Cossackia*. The alpine barrier forms the frontier between Italy, and Austria to the west and Yugoslavia to the east. Farther to the west still, the Dolomite massif begins to swallow up the limestone crags of Carnia, whilst to the east is found the only genuine pre-alpine country; devoted to wine-growing on the lower slopes, then rising through chestnut woods to high alpine downlands, offering ideal DZ for Partisan supply.

These stories which I am about to recount are set down as they were told to me, in a disjointed and sometimes repetitive fashion. Usually in circumstances far from ideal, the narrator and interpreter often speaking simultaneously. But even after the passage of time, they give a vivid impression of life in those days.

THE COW WITH SNOW ON ITS BACK

But first to Tolmezzo, a strategic road junction in Carnia, where the barracks was held by Germans. Here we met a man whose home had been occupied by Cossacks.

Dr Romano Marchetti and his wife remember it thus. There had been two drives through Carnia, the first was by the SS and Cossacks combined, the next invasion was of Cossacks and their families. After that, their behaviour began to improve but before then there had been several nasty incidents.

At the village of Imponzo, north of Tolmezzo, the parish priest was killed trying unavailingly to defend some village girls against attack by Cossacks. The wife of the commander of the Osoppo, among others, was raped, and when he tried to defend her he was taken and put in prison. That was Vergendo. At Satrio, also north of Tolmezzo, a man who tried to defend his wife was taken off to prison in Germany where he died. At the village of Forni, west of Ampezzo, the Germans burnt everything in the village.

Dr Marchetti had an adventurous time towards the end of the war when he tried to persuade the Cossacks to surrender. He told them 'the war is over' and then described to us the sequence of events.

'Then they blindfolded me and took me to Villa Santina. They made me wait till the SS Colonel arrived. I thought my last moment had come. Then after interrogation they let me go! How am I still alive?'

But the insignificant events are sometimes those that stick in the memory. The Cossacks who occupied the Marchetti house, had burnt a hole in their living room floor, the very room where we were sitting making a lunch of *prosciutto croudo* and a bottle of the local wine called *Tocai*. Chris Pelham recorded our visit thus:

> 'In the course of the two hours we spent with the Marchettis, we learned a lot about the activities of the Cossacks in Carnia. Their arrival. Their aristocratic officers, a roughness of the simple soldiers, initially brutal but becoming milder with the arrival of their families. Their transport mostly wagonettes (Signora Marchetti had been given a lift in one from Villa Santina to Tolmezzo), and a few Bactrian camels. The Cossacks wore long cloaks and strange hats.'

But the memory most treasured by Romano Marchetti was of the Cossack cow kept in the garden. In summer it was not such a strange sight. But when winter came it remained there, but now 'with snow on its back'. The strangeness of this sight is to be partly explained by the fact that Italian *contadini* invariably, in those days, brought the cows or oxen into the stalls under or by the side of the house. Here the warmth which they generated provided the primitive but effective central heating system. A cow left outside was like having a radiator out in the garden!

THE LADY OF THE GOLDEN STAR

Next, to the mountain village of Villa di Verzegnis. Here at the *Stella D'Oro* we met an old lady, the wife of the former Padrone. The Golden Star Inn had been the headquarters of General Peter Krasnov during the Cossack occupation.

General 'Pyotr' Krasnov was a romantic but controversial figure who had been the Field Ataman of the Don Cossacks in the revolutionary war, later taking part in the Baltic campaign with the White armies. In exile he became a novelist extolling the virtues of the Cossack life. At that time he established close contacts with the Nazis, which eventually led to Himmler's control of the Cossack forces. Claudio Magris has woven a strange mystery story concerning his life in this village and his death. We asked the old lady whether she remembered General Krasnov, and showed her a photograph.[3]

> 'Po Po Po! Yes he was indeed here. Always very smart. *Molto gentile*. Very good mannered. Always on horseback with an escort of many horsemen. Upstairs very comfortable in his room. Before that I had his second-in-command. A man with a *barbe bianco*, right down to his waist. So much hair on his face that you could only just see his eyes,'

and she made two rings with her fingers.

The village of Villa di Verzegnis clings to the wooded hillside of the mountains. It was not ideal Cossack country, for Krasnov's headquarters as it was almost impossible for wagons to leave the road. For horsemen, it was another matter.

MURDER AT IMPONZO

We next made our way to Imponzo. This village lies just off the route of one of the passes through the Carnic Alps, whose church overlooks the village and dominates the valley. The evening sun now cast a theatrical light upon this landmark. There were two old women in the churchyard tending the graves. One turned her lined face towards us.

We asked her:

'Were you living here during the war?'

The old lady replied that she was.

'Was it here that the priest was murdered by the Cossacks?'

'*E vero*. He was battered to death down there in the square. I can show you his grave.'

We walked through the churchyard. The inscription read:

'Joseph Treppo. Born July, 1902. Killed 9 Oct 1944'.

This must have been the beginning of the *Rastrellamento*.

'*Brutti tempi – Brutti tempi*' the old lady murmured, '*l'inverno de quaranta quatra. I Cossachi – i freddo – niente da mangiare*'. (The winter of 1944. The Cossacks – the cold – nothing to eat – the partisans – brutal times).

THE COW WITH NO MILK

We retraced our steps after this sombre encounter and made for our next rendezvous, the village of Interneppo, one of a constellation of villages, Alesso, Oncedis, Braulins, Trasaghis and Peonis, occupied by the Cossacks. Here we met a middle-aged man who had been a boy during the time of the Cossacks. The village of Interneppo had been cleared for the Cossack occupation on 8 October, 1944 (these dates are not forgotten) except for one house, his own. That was far too near the cliffs for the safety of the Cossacks.

Periodically, the Cossacks used to go out on patrol, pushed from behind by the SS. They were frightened of the Partisans. The first wave, accompanied by the SS, was the worst. Then, as we know, the families came and the behaviour was better.

The Cossacks used to go up to the hill and milk a cow belonging to one of the villagers. On one occasion the owner had got there first. The Cossack was disgusted, and ran down the hill arms akimbo crying angrily 'No milk! No milk!' in Russian. This picture apparently made a deep impression upon the boy, and he remembered it to that day. Everything that could be used for firewood was taken. The windows, doors and door frames – everything was sawn up, even the matrimonial bed. And our friend demonstrated how it was cut up in slices!

To return to our own story, it was now towards the end of a long day. It was pitch dark, but our next meeting was at an unlit crossroads, with an occasional lorry thundering by which made conversation almost impossible! There are still rivalries between the various ex-Partisan groups, and we had to be careful not to be seen or overheard.

THE DROMEDARIES OF ONCEDIS

We were now led to another village, Oncedis, to meet a jolly lady who had known the Cossacks well, Antonia Peressini. The reason that she knew them well, was that a whole family had been billeted in their house, and had occupied the kitchen. As a girl of 17, she feigned marriage, and like many other girls in the village, wore a wedding ring for protection. To the Cossacks' question 'Where is your husband' she answered '*Non sapero. Prigonieri di guerra*'. (I do not know. A prisoner of war.)

> 'Each Cossack soldier had the name of his village tattooed on his finger, such as *Don* or *Rostov*. *I Cossachi* believed that the Carnia was now theirs. You could get on all right as long as you accepted that everything belonged to them, every one of your possessions including the contents of the barn, hay, eggs and milk, was theirs. Even in March of 1945, they asked us where the village fields were, and there they went and sowed potatoes! They had camels and big huge dromedaries, at which the village was amazed. They taught us Cossack songs.'

And we left Antonia and her son to the accompaniment of these dirges. Obviously the village girls had got some entertainment out of their uninvited guests.

THE COUNTRY WEDDING

It was now time to hear something of the surrender. The action I am about to describe took place during the closing stages of the war in Italy in a group of three villages south of Udine where the Partisans operated in conjunction with those in the mountains in the area known as '*la bassa friulana*' (the Friuli plain). As the story is rather complicated, I will describe the villages and their part in the story, first. The narrator is a Signor A Mosanghini, who was the commander of about 100 Osoppo Partisans operating in that area, mainly sabotaging German communications.

The first village was Sant Andrat, 15 kilometres south of Udine where the wedding took place. The second, Talmassons, nearby, was the location of the Cossacks' billets. And third, Mortegliano, a little nearer Udine, was the spot where Mosanghini took the Cossacks' surrender. The action took place between 28–30 April, 1945. The Cossack strength was about 600 under the command of a colonel.

Mosanghini tells his tale:

28 April

'On the 28 April, a wedding was in full progress in the village church at Sant Andrat. Suddenly shots are heard. It is the Garibaldi Partisans who are shooting at the Cossacks and they have killed three. After the wedding, which went on in spite of the shots outside, the bridal pair left the church to go to the reception which was ready in a large room nearby. During the reception, the Cossack commander sent a patrol to Talmassons to look for the three missing Cossacks. During the search, the body of one of them was found behind a hedge. The patrol retraced their steps and when they heard the merry-making coming from the reception room, they went in and told the 35 guests, including the bridal pair, to report to the Cossack colonel in Talmassons for questioning. The men were separated from the women with the intention of killing them for being responsible for the shooting. At this point a Town Hall official arrived from Mortegliano to plead for the 35 suspects. The official assured the commander that they had nothing to do with the killing and they were immediately released.'

29 April

In the afternoon, Mosanghini went to the local German detachment commander to demand surrender and the handing over of arms as the Allies were approaching. The commander, helped by a *'maresciallo'* (highest of the non-commissioned officers), who acted as interpreter, did not accept the proposal, which was that all the arms belonging to the group, with the exception of the commander's, were to be shut up on the premises until the arrival of the Allies. In the meantime, the Osoppo-Garibaldi Partisans should engage themselves to safeguard the lives of the unarmed men and provide for food and everything necessary to them. But late that evening, the Wehrmacht was compelled to leave by order of the Todt Organisation commander, who operated in Mortegliano. The Todt commander also ordered the Cossacks to move from Talmassons to Mortegliano where they occupied the rooms evacuated by the Wehrmacht and other places requisitioned at the last moment.

30 April

Early in the morning, Mosanghini went to the Todt commander to demand the surrender of his party. After a long discussion, the claims on both sides became less severe. The Todt commander (Schuster, by name) asked to be given the most powerful and efficient car on the parking place. Mosanghini agreed. Schuster left at about 11.00 am and was thus driven out in style.

Mosanghini continues:

> 'At this point a new incident took place. A boy was told to go and fetch two guns from the hiding place where the Partisans kept all their arms. But while he did so, he was seen through a window by two Cossacks who immediately seized him and took him back to their commander. When I was informed of this, I rushed across and was there just in time to kick the unfortunate boy into the nearby parish priest's house, which probably saved his life. I then tried to explain to the Cossacks that the two guns belonged to the Partisans and introduced myself as their commander. In spite of this, the two Cossacks refused to return the guns. Then I asked to be taken to their Commander. It was thus that I found myself discussing surrender with the Cossack colonel through a Polish interpreter, who worked with the Todt Organisation but was in league with Osoppo. He knew German, Italian and a little Russian.

The conversation with the Cossack commander took place in German. The Cossack commander's name is not known, neither is his rank, but the interpreter addressed him as colonel. Signor Mosanghini informed the commander that the Allies were about to arrive and asked for his surrender.

> 'The colonel took his pistol out of its holster, flicked it up into the air, caught it by the barrel, handed it over to me and said: "Take it and kill me. I will never surrender to a Partisan, because I've always been a soldier". The Osoppo leader took the pistol and put it back into the colonel's holster saying: "As a man I can't accept that, because you are endangering the lives of your men as well as those of the villagers".'

Then the Cossack colonel called all his officers together and asked Mosanghini what he and his Partisans really wanted. On being told 'surrender', they refused. The Partisan leader then showed them his green Osoppo scarf, together with a piece of tricolour flag. The colonel of the Don Cossacks promptly shook hands with him and his 20 officers followed his example. They greatly feared what the Communists would do to them once they were back in Russia. They felt safer with the Osoppo after Mosanghini's statement, as Osoppo Partisans were as anti-communist as they were.

So it was that a lone Partisan leader took the surrender of about 600 Cossacks, and to safeguard their passage against attack by Osoppo or Garibaldi men, he marched at their head towards Udine.

The colonel thanked Mosanghini for his co-operation and said: 'If they attack, we will defend ourselves'. To everybody's relief that did not happen.

The love of the Cossacks for the grand heroic gesture, is here clearly seen where the colonel 'handed Mosanghini his pistol and asks him to shoot!' This kind of incident was repeated many times in Austria.

The interview I have described took place in the apartment of Professor Deganutti, who spoke excellent English, having been a teacher in that language. At her flat in Udine, apart from Signor Mosanghini, were her two sisters. Her third sister, Cecilia, was not present. She had been a Red Cross nurse, working amongst the Partisans. Eventually captured by the German SD, she was taken to the Risiera (a disused rice factory) near Trieste, which was used by the Germans as an extermination camp (the only one in Italy) for both Italian and Yugoslav Partisans. Here it is believed she was burnt alive in the crematorium. This extermination camp came under the command of, and was no doubt established by, the infamous SS Gruppenfuhrer Globocnik, who had set up the notorious extermination camp at Treblinka in Poland. Cecilia was awarded the *Medaglia d'Oro* posthumously.

I asked this very moderate and level-headed group what was the feeling amongst the people – about the Cossack occupation, and received the following replies:

> 'People were not pleased to see them in Montegliano. However, in the few days they were there they did nothing wrong.'
> 'Like barbarians – did bad things.'
> 'A very bad reputation in Carnia.'
> 'At Ovaro – they burnt the village down.'
> 'In Osoppo one day they got drunk and all the women and little girls were violated.'

DEATH OF BARBA LIVIO

But taking the surrender of the Cossacks was not always so successful. Zoffo Romano, after serving as an infantryman in Croatia, where he distinguished himself, entered the Resistance in September 1943 with the Attimis group under the pseudonym of *Livio Ferro*, later known as *Barba Livio* on account of his red beard. [4]

By April, 1944, *Barba* was in command of an Osoppo group in Carnia. After the Armistice, Hitler proclaimed two special operational zones, in the Tirol and the Adriatic Littoral to guard his line of communication. In the middle of June, 1944, Barba Livio had received the Manfred Beckett (Czernin) mission-drop. He was now re-deployed to the East side of the Tagliamento river, where a man named Bolla was the commander of the 1 East Osoppo Division. (He was later killed by the communist Garibaldini Partisans working with Tito's 9 Corps.)

Having tested Barba Livio's capabilities and courage, Bolla entrusted him with the command of the VI Osoppo Brigade (comprising the Val Torre, Tarcento, Prealpi groups). During December, 1944–January, 1945, Barba was with the MacPherson Mission in the Uccea, Selva Carniza, Resia, Chialminis and Cergneu zone, where he and the Osoppo men frequently faced much larger elements of Tito's forces because of problems connected with the frontier.

On 26 April, 1945 the Cossacks in Tarcento (Villa Scoccimarro) indicated that they wished to negotiate a surrender. Barba Livio went to Villa Scoccimarro together with a civilian. The next day he went back to his own headquarters saying that the Cossacks were willing to surrender and to give up their weapons to the Partisans. This would happen on the following day, after Barba Livio had first met a Cossack officer: they had agreed initially to an unconditional surrender of the garrison troops of Cassacco (near Tarcento).

In order to give further details of the terms of the surrender, Barba Livio accepted an invitation to go to the Cossack headquarters at Villa Orter (in Tarcento) together with two Patriots (the Osovani called themselves Patriots, not Partisans): he was wrong to do this, as treachery was planned.

On 30 April, at about 1.00 pm., the wife of the villa's caretaker, who lived in a small house nearby, saw the poor men (the Patriots) pushed out of the villa, their hands bound behind their backs, and being subjected to abuse, beating and torture. They were taken to the place where they were shot: there was more groaning and moaning and then several rifle-shots. Then the dying victims, crying in pain, were taken again into the villa. There was a big explosion and the villa was destroyed.

When the Cossacks left, people went to search for the victims in the cellar of the villa. The sight was appalling: Barba Livio was a shapeless, smashed body, only to be recognised by his red hair. He had several bullet wounds in his body, three in his head and his throat had been cut.

A PRISONER OF THE COSSACKS

My final story is from another Osoppo leader who became a prisoner of the Cossacks. Like my last account, it is typical of war – the unexpected always happens. Giancarlo Chiussi, whose tale it was, spoke quite frankly about his political history. He had started life as a fascist, like all Italians at this time, because otherwise it was impossible to find work. He was in fact expelled from the Fascist Party in July, 1943, then moved to the Action Party (middle-of-the-road socialist), and ended up as an Osoppo Partisan. At the outbreak of the war he was a well-known ski-ing and swimming champion.

Chiussi explained that he was second-in-command to an Osoppo group. His commander's name was 'Walter' (Albino Venier). The Cossacks were violently anti-communist so the Osoppo had a slightly better relationship with them, than the red-neckerchiefed Garibaldini.

In December, 1944, above the 1,200 metre level, all was snow. There was no clothing and no food. The problem of 'wintering' the Partisans in valley centres was a big one. On 27 December, Chiussi and his commander 'Walter' left Mosdell's headquarters (the BLO in that area) whose hideout was near the settlement of Trischamps under Mount Arvenis. They were making their way down to the valley to find work and shelter for their men. On the way to Ovaro, they were caught by the Cossacks. Searched, Chiussi's watch and wallet were taken. Interrogation followed by a Cossack major and an interpreter. The Major told him not to twist his words, as he never answered a direct question, and for this 'Walter' was beaten up. Now, mysteriously, a dish of *polenta* arrives from the parish priest. In the maize porridge is concealed a note saying where a rifle was buried. A risky move by the priest. The interrogator 'tried it on' by saying 'Your friend says that you've got weapons!' The Cossack major put a pistol to his face. 'Don't kill me here', cried Chiussi. 'Take me outside. I'll make less mess!' He added in telling us the tale that it was very important to be polite to Cossack officers. But the Major hit him in the face with his pistol. At this he told the Cossack:

'I am Italian – this is my country – you are the interlopers.'

At this the Cossacks beat up 'Walter' again and he was forced to divulge the secret of the rifle buried above the village of Mione. The Cossacks took them there to look for it. They couldn't find it. So they put them both against a rock and beat them both against a wall. They were about to be shot. Chiussi prepared for death and thought of ski-ing. The Cossacks changed their minds. They took them down to the village again and 'Walter' was beaten once more. They were questioned separately, and the Cossacks tried to make them contradict each other. Now they were taken to the house of a Captain Burgos, *Capitano del Frigato*, (a frigate Captain/naval commander presumably a suspected Partisan), who now lived at Mione. The Cossacks were about to strike Burgos' wife when Chiussi remonstrated, 'Don't strike a woman. Strike me!' Whereupon they hit the wretched 'Walter' again. Then back to prison in Ovaro.

By this time it was New Year's Eve. Strange to say, whilst still prisoners, they were invited to the Cossack hotel, where they were all sitting on the floor singing. It was very moving. A young man of about 30 came up wearing his *Kolpaco* (fur hat). 'Would you like to hear the history of the Cossacks', the young man said. Chiussi assented.

> 'So it was like this. A nobleman drives up in a sleigh, drinking vodka and smoking a cigar. He tells the Cossacks "*Robata! Robata! Robata!*" (Work! Work! Work!). Then a little later another man drives up in a sleigh. His name is *Commissar*. He is drinking vodka and smoking a cigar. He looks at the Cossacks and gives them their orders. "*Robata! Robata! Robata!*".'

So Chiussi sang with the Cossacks.

A Great Ski-Champion But Also A Great Partisan

Now Chiussi is kept in a barber's shop, sleeping on the floor. A young Cossack who has killed a young girl is imprisoned with him. He had a big scar. He had been on guard and tried to rape the girl early one morning. When she ran, he shot her.

Chiussi and 'Walter' are next taken to Comeglians, north of Ovaro. It is now 3 or 4 January, 1945. They are forced to chop wood. The Cossacks gave them no food, only the local people supplied them. About this time there was a big 'drop' to Captain Prior (BLO). The Russians spotted the flares at Casera Razzo, came up and took everything. Now it became a bit frightening. The two Partisans were put against a wall again all night with a Cossack guard and kept there for nine hours. The Cossacks were terrified of the Partisans.

But Chiussi's ordeal had not ended. They were now taken on foot to Paluzza, a German headquarters north of Tolmezzo, a very long day's march. Here there was a frightening incident. One day, during his imprisonment, a German officer entered, accompanied by a man called Fullj, an Italian in the pay of the Gestapo. He saw Chiussi, recognised him and said 'Paolo!' But Chiussi pretended not to know him.

On 16 January, Chiussi was taken to the German commandant. Here there was an interpreter who said 'Speak Friulan to me, the Germans here understand Italian'. Chiussi said he would answer questions with unrelated replies, so that the interpreter could give the Germans the 'correct' answers. He wondered, 'Do I trust him or not?'

Then (just as it seemed that he was going to be released) Chiussi's captors noticed his ski-championship pass, allowing travel concessions on the railways. Inscribed on it was his real name. 'A great ski-champion' they scoffed, 'but also a great Partisan!' He denied it. They were just about to let him go to Ovaro with a special permit, when his old friend the Cossack major arrived, Prince – He looked at the pass and said to the German, 'This is a *grande partigiano*. You are making a big mistake.' The German officer was affronted by having his decision questioned. 'Stand to attention!' he bawled at the Cossack. 'I am in command here, not you!.

The German officer ordered the Russian to apologise to Chiussi, whereupon the very tall Cossack officer bowed, saluted, and gave Chiussi back his pass. He was then escorted by the German across a courtyard full of Cossacks. Chiussi held the German by the arm for protection. After his release, he went to a house near the prison which the interpreter had suggested to him.

What followed sounds like a dream. He finds himself in a room. In the room is a beautiful girl holding out some new clothes. Next door is a steaming hot bath. This is not the end of the story but discretion obliges us to withdraw from the room!

To cut a long story short, the interpreter asked for some rolls of cloth (Chiussi is in the clothing business) for the German officer, and said they would make sure that the unfortunate 'Walter' was released – as in fact he was.

Finally, he is free! He has thumbed a lift in a Cossack cart. Allied planes are droning overhead in large numbers 'Americani!' he cries pointing upwards. The Cossacks, dumb-founded, simply will not believe him.

APPENDICES

A. Speech on Anglo-Soviet Relations. House of Commons, 7 April 1987

B. Repatriation Statistics 21 Army Group (May–July, 1945)

C. Truman's Telegram: 12 May 1945

D. Signal by 5 Corps Defining Russian Nationals: 21 May 1945

E. Historical Note on the Cossacks

F. Anti-Tito Yugoslav Groups

G. Letter from P J Grigg (War Minister) to Anthony Eden (Foreign Secretary): 24 August 1944

Appendix A

EXTRACT OF A SPEECH BY SIR CAROL MATHER MP
ON 7 APRIL 1987 IN A DEBATE ON FOREIGN AFFAIRS
IN THE HOUSE OF COMMONS
(HANSARD VOL. 114 Colns 201–204)

(See Preface page xiii)

Sir Carol Mather (Esher): I hope that the right hon. Member for South Down (Mr. Powell) will forgive me if I do not follow his line of argument, because I am on a slightly different tack. I think that this afternoon is an opportunity to try to look at some of the origins of the problems that we face today in foreign affairs. My right hon. and learned Friend the Foreign Secretary said that, in common with the Russians, we should think long, and I believe that we should think longer than we usually do. Therefore, I make no apology for going back in time to consider some of the problems.

First, may I congratulate my right hon. Friend the Prime Minister and my right hon. and learned Friend the Foreign Secretary on their extremely successful visit to Moscow. There has been a great change of atmosphere between ourselves and the Soviet Union, indeed between the West and the Soviet Union, and that change has been greatly enhanced by this recent visit. I believe that we are witnessing the biggest change in atmosphere in the postwar period. I can think of no other period when we were involved in such dialogue with Russia other than the year of 1944 when we were allies with the Soviet Union, and the Germans and their collaborators were our enemies.

Of course, things changed in 1945 when we began to see the true nature of the Russian bear. We learnt this at the Yalta conference when we were trying to deal with the intractable problems of the reoccupation of Germany by the allied powers, free elections in

Poland and the repatriation of our prisoners, both Russian and British. I wish to dwell on the problem of repatriation for a few moments because that problem has not gone away.

The reasons why it was so important for us to come to an agreement at Yalta were, above all, that we had 50,000 allied prisoners in Russian hands. We also had a continuing war with Japan, which looked likely to continue for another two years – it was important to have the Russians on our side – and there were vast problems in Germany and the occupied territories. There were millions of emaciated people in Germany and Austria whom we were trying to feed as well as vast numbers of refugees and large numbers of displaced persons – Poles, Hungarians and so on.

Then, the urgent problem was to repatriate the people back to their homelands while we had enough food for them. I had experience of this because I was with the northern armies and was liaison officer to Montgomery. I was working on those problems, visiting the camps and trying to report on how we would repatriate all the people. It was an immense problem.

In the north there were 20 million Germans and displaced people to look after and to feed. Housing had been destroyed and the standard of health was low. There were 2.5 million German prisoners of war and 1 million displaced persons – Russians, Poles, Hungarians and so on. In West Berlin alone there were 3 million people whom we had to feed, not from the hinterland, but from the western zone of Germany. There was one policy alone – everyone must go home. It was the same in Austria.

In addition to such problems, we were faced by the frightening attitude adopted by the Soviet Union under the leadership of Stalin. At that time our future was indeed precarious. In the biography of Eden written by my hon. Friend the Member for Cambridge (Mr. Rhodes James) Churchill is reported as saying that the situation was more dangerous in 1945 than it was in 1939.

By far the most important factor in our discussions was, of course, the prisoners – the return of our prisoners to us and vice versa in the case of the Russians. My noble Friend Lord Barber wrote an interesting letter. He was a prisoner of war in Russian hands in East Germany, overrun by the Russians. He made an important point which was reported in a debate in the House of Lords in 1976. He was a member of an air crew which had been captured. His letter said:

'We realised at the time that we were being kept as hostages until the return of the Russians, who had been liberated by the British. If the Government had refused to return the Russians, I do not doubt that most of us would have accepted our unhappy lot as being a necessary consequence of the aftermath of war!'

That was a noble sentiment, but it did not wash at home. It would not have been in accordance with British public opinion at the time when the main desire was to get everyone back home. That is the background to events in Austria in 1945.

My first contact in Normandy after we landed on D plus one was, strangely enough, with a Cossack unit. They were among the first German troops that I met. I was having my breakfast. They were more surprised at seeing me than I was at seeing them. Those were the people with whom we were faced in many of the German units.

Under the Yalta agreement we repatriated about 45,000 Wehrmacht Cossacks to the Soviet Union. Inevitably, White Russians were included in those numbers. If we had not maintained the Yalta agreement we would have been in dire trouble. At the same time, major units of Russians and Ukranians were spirited away – the Ukranian division of some 10,000 men and the White Russians Schutz Corps of some 4,500 men.

That has been the subject of two books by Mr. Nicholas Tolstoi which contain some pathetic stories. But untold so far have been the successful efforts by anonymous pimpernels to thwart the Soviet intentions and free those people to the West. I have no personal axe to grind in this, but I should like to see historical justice done. Tolstoi, in his book, 'Minister and the Massacres', accuses the then Minister resident in those parts, Harold Macmillan, of conspiring to send those people to their deaths. That is the clear implication of what he said.

There is plenty of opinion by the author in that book, but very little hard fact. It casts a slur on the War Cabinet of those days and on the commanders and staff in the field as well as on our allies who were in full agreement with the policy. I utterly reject the theory that the late Lord Stockton was involved in a devious plot.

What was the outcome? Stalin insisted upon his pound of flesh and we had to send the Soviet citizens back. Many of them were shot or perished in the gulags. There were no free elections in Poland, as we had agreed, and many of the smaller old European countries were swallowed up by Stalin.

But this last outcome, in particular, could have been avoided.

Unfortunately, there was a dispute between the British and the Americans about our policy in the final stages of advance. The Americans favoured a broad front advance and we favoured a narrow one, as advocated by Montgomery. I am convinced that we could have been in Berlin by Christmas 1944 if we had adhered to the narrow front strategy. As it was, we halted and waited for the Russians to move up. We could also have occupied Czechoslovakia. I remember being sent to Czechoslovakia in 1946 by Montgomery to see the commander there. I talked to the people and I remember how fearful they were of being swallowed up by the Russians, as, indeed, they were. If we had continued with our advance, Europe would have been a different place today.

There are two more cautionary tales that I would like to tell and they concern the middle east. The Attlee Government ordered the evacuation of Palestine in October 1947. It was to be evacuated by May the following year. I and my chums who were there were told to pack up and go home. We had been keeping the peace there and we were astounded by that drastic and ill-considered decision.

As it turned out, the Arabs did not see off the Jews. The Jews were trained for war because they had been fighting us, and the Arabs, unfortunately, were seen off and lost their lands. That has set off a kind of political Chernobyl, whose noxious fumes are still poisoning the world today. We have only to look at worldwide terrorism, events in the Lebanon and the rising of the Arab Jihad to see what a pot we stirred up in those days.

My final tale concerns the events in the Persian gulf a few years ago. When the Conservative Government came to power in 1970 it was virtually a fait accompli that we had to leave the Persian gulf. That had been decided by the previous Labour Government. I want to ask some rhetorical questions to which there are no answers, but they should still be considered.

If we had retained our presence in the Persian gulf and had been in communion with the Arab rulers who were friendly towards us, would the oil crisis have taken quite the same form that it took? Would OPEC have arisen in the form that it did? Would the Shah have fallen if we had been there to hold his hand? Would the American hostages have been taken by the following Government? Would, indeed, the Iran-Iraq war have taken place?

I hope that recounting those experiences gives some clues to the problems that we are facing today. This is, in a way, my maiden speech, but, in case it is also my valedictory one, I wanted to put that on the record.

Appendix B

REPATRIATION STATISTICS 21 ARMY GROUP
(May to July 1945)

(See Chapter III page 15)
Extract from the paper:
POST SURRENDER ADMINISTRATIVE ACTIVITIES
OF 21 ARMY GROUP

Statistics

The following figures, especially for the earlier months, are, of necessity approximate, they do not take account, e.g., of an indeterminable number of Russians who passed through the Russian lines before controlled evacuation began or of an inevitable number of undiscovered DP:

	Remaining in British Zone	Repatriated from British Zone (incl. Russian exchange)	Remarks
28 May 45			
Westbound	35,000	228,000	Inc. approx 35,000 from 1 Cdn. Army area.
Eastbound	382,000		Inc. approx 85,000 in 1 Cdn. Army area.
Eastbound		65,000	
Total PWX/DP	417,000	293,000	

Grand Total 710,000

219

June 45

Westbound	11,000	309,000	
Eastbound	1,567,000	431,000	Russian only
Total DP/PXW	1,578,000	740,000	Increase due to takeover from US Army area of British zone and DP intake from Russians.

Grand Total 2,318,000

31 July 45

Westbound	5,000	529,000	
Eastbound	1,210,000	717,000	Russian and Czech.
Total DP/PWX	1,215,000	1,246,000	

Grand Total 2,461,000

By 22 July 350,000 French, Belgian and Dutch had passed through the National Reception Centres in the L of C area.

Note: This report had been compiled soon after these events as raw material for the war historians.

Source: WO 205/139 PRO.

Appendix C

TRUMAN'S TELEGRAM

(See Chapter xv page 100)

FROM FOREIGN OFFICE TO WASHINGTON
No. 4887   0.7.50 p.m. May 12th. 1945.
May 12th. 1945.
Repeated to United Kingdom Delegation San Francisco (for Secretary of State) No. 649.

IMMEDIATE
DEDIP
TOP SECRET AND PERSONAL
Following is text of personal message No. 34 dated May 12th. from President to Prime Minister.
(Begins)
Since sending you my telegram of April 30th. I have become increasingly concerned over the implication of Tito's actions in Venezia Giulia. You are no doubt receiving the same reports which indicate that he has no peaceful solution of this century-old problem as part of a general pacific post-war settlement. I have come to the conclusion that we must decide now whether we should uphold the fundamental principles of territorial settlement by orderly process against force, intimidation or blackmail. It seems that Tito has an identical claim ready for south Austria, in Carinthia and Styria and may have similar designs on parts of Hungary and Greece if his methods in Venezia Giulia succeed. Although the stability of Italy and the future orientation of that country with respect to Russia may well be at stake the present issue, as I see it, is not a question of taking sides in

221

a dispute between Italy and Yugoslavia or of becoming involved in internal Balkan politics. The problem is essentially one of deciding whether our two countries are going to permit our Allies to engage in uncontrolled land grabbing or tactics which are all too reminiscent of those of Hitler and Japan. Yugoslav occupation of Trieste, the key to that area and a vital outlet for large areas of central Europe, would, as I know you will agree, have more far-reaching consequences than the immediate territory involved. In these circumstances I believe the minimum we should insist upon is that Field Marshal Alexander should obtain complete and exclusive control of Trieste and Pola, the line of communication through Gorizia and Montfalcone, and an area sufficiently to the east of this line to permit proper administrative control. The line suggested by Alexander at Allied Force Headquarters in March extended to include Pola would, I believe, be adequate. Tito seems unsure of himself and might not put up more than a show of resistance, although we should be prepared to consider if necessary further steps to effect his withdrawal. I note that Alexander, who has lost patience with Tito's latest moves, is prepared to go ahead if we agree.

I suggest that as a first step we instruct our Ambassadors at Belgrade to address Tito along the following lines:

The question of Venezia Giulia is only one of the many territorial problems in Europe to be solved in the general peace settlement. The doctrine of solution by conquest and by unilateral proclamation of sovereignty through occupation, the method used by the enemy with such tragic consequences, has been definitely and solemnly repudiated by the Allied Governments participating in this war. This agreement to work together to seek an orderly and just solution of territorial problems is one of the cardinal principles for which the peoples of the United Nations have made their tremendous sacrifice to attain a just and lasting peace. It is one of the cornerstones on which their representatives, with the approbation of world public opinion, are now at work to build a system of world security.

The plan of Allied Military Government of Venezia Giulia was adopted precisely to achieve a peaceful and lasting solution of a problem of admitted complexities. It is designed to safeguard the interests of the peoples involved. Its implementation, while assuring to the military forces of the Allied Governments the means of carrying on their further tasks in enemy territory, would bring no prejudice to Yugoslav claims in the final settlement.

With these considerations in mind, and in view of the previous general agreement of the Yugoslav Government to the plans proposed for this region, my Government has instructed me to inform you it expects that the Yugoslav Government will immediately agree to the control by the Supreme Allied Commander in the Mediterranean of the region which must include Trieste, Gorizia, Montfalcone and Pola, and issue appropriate instructions to the Yugoslav forces in the region in question to co-operate with the Allied Commander in the establishment of military government in that area under the authority of the Allied Commander.

I have been instructed to report most urgently to my Government whether the Yugoslav Government is prepared immediately to acquiesce in the foregoing.'

I also suggest we both inform Stalin in accordance with the Yalta agreement for consultation. If we stand firm on this issue, as we are doing on Poland, we can hope to avoid a host of other similar encroachments.

(Ends).

Appendix D

SIGNAL BY 5 CORPS DEFINING RUSSIAN NATIONALS

(See Chapter xx page 130)

SECRET

Subject: *Definition of RUSSIAN NATIONALS*

MAIN 5 CORPS
405/G
21 MAY 45

6 BRIT ARMD DIV
46 DIV
78 DIV
7 ARMD BDE
GSI (a)
GSI (b)
DA & QMG
A
Q
MG LO : MGA : DEMIL
Copy to : MAIN EIGHTH ARMY
REAR EIGHTH ARMY
Ref conference am 21 May at MAIN 5 CORPS on transfer SOVIET NATIONALS.
1. Various cases have been referred to this HQ in which doubt has been raised as to whether certain fmns and groups should be treated as SOVIET NATIONALS in so far as their return to the SOVIET UNION direct from 5 CORPS is concerned. Rulings in these cases

are given below.

RUSSIAN SCHUTZKORPS (incl RUMANIANS in this fmn) will NOT be treated as SOVIET NATIONALS until further orders.

Following will be treated as SOVIET NATIONALS:-

ATAMAN Group

15 COSSACK CAV CORPS (incl COSSACKS and CALMUCKS)

Res units of Lt-Gen CHKOURO

    CAUCASIANS (incl MUSSULMEN)

2. Individual cases will NOT be considered unless particularly pressed. In these cases and in the case of appeals by further units or fmns, the following directive will apply:-

(a) Any individual now in our hands who, at the time of joining the GERMAN Forces or joining a fmn fighting with the GERMAN Forces, was living within the 1938 bdy of USSR, will be treated as a SOVIET NATIONAL for the purposes of transfer.

(b) Any individual although of RUSSIAN blood who, prior to joining the GERMAN Forces, had not been in USSR since 1930, will NOT until further orders be treated as a SOVIET NATIONAL.

(c) In all cases of doubt, the individual will be treated as a SOVIET NATIONAL.

ARM LOW
Brigadier,
General Staff.

Source WO 170/4241

Appendix E

HISTORICAL NOTE ON THE COSSACKS

Origins

The origin of the term 'Cossack' and the history of the Cossack people are lost in obscurity. Of one thing historians are fairly certain and that is that the Cossacks cannot be said to be of a separate ethnic group, or race apart, from the rest of the Russians.

They were certainly people of the steppes, as opposed to the Muscovites, who were people of the northern forests. The term Cossacks came to be used for the frontier people, outlaws and freebooters, semi-nomadic people, who gained their livelihood from their herds and from their hunting and fishing and trapping. They carried out an intermittent warfare with their neighbours on the far side of their boundaries, to which were added the rewards of war, loot, pillage and the carrying off of women. On their eastern and southern area of operations they were most likely in contact with the Tatars, the natural descendants of Gengis Khan and Tamurlaine. To the south-east were the Circassians, occupying an area north-east of the Caspian Sea, renowned for their horsemanship and dancing. And it was from them that many of these traditional Cossack arts derived. The Turkomen, also on the far side of the Caspian, were probably the nearest direct descendants of the Mongol hordes, or Golden Horde as they liked to call themselves, (from the golden tent poles of their nomadic headquarters). Peter Hopkirk in his book *The Great Game*[1] reminds us, that it was said, 'you could smell them coming even before you heard the thunder of their hooves. But by then it was too late. Within seconds, came the first murderous torrent of arrows, blotting out the sun and turning day into night. Then they were upon you – slaughtering, raping, pillaging and burning . . .'. This was in the 13th Century. No wonder fear of the Mongol hordes is still part of the 'subconscious' in many parts of Europe.

When the Mongol invasion at last began to recede, there still remained three large but isolated Khanates; at Kazan, Astrakhan and in the Crimea. By the middle of the 16th Century all these except the Crimea had fallen to the expanding Russian empire. No direct connection can be adduced between the Cossacks, the Tatars or the Circassians except by assimilation, usually by marriage, through women carried off as booty. But it is true to say that the frontiersmen who were occupied in 'cossacking' learnt many of the Tatar ways. They began to use Tatar words like *ataman* (chief), *esaal* (lieutenant), *yassak* (tribute) and *yassyr* (captives) and gang leaders began to adopt the Tatar horsetail standard as the symbol of their authority.[2] Their amazing feats of horsemanship, the *djigitovka*, were also learnt from their Tatar mentors.

On the southern borders of Russia, or Muscovy as it then was, lived the Georgians and the Caucasian tribes. The Georgians will angrily insist, if you talk to them, that the distinctive dress of the Cossacks, (*cherkeska* – the tunic with bandoliers), and their wild dance, (the *lezginka*) were borrowed from them, and that they were the originators of these traditions.

Cossack expansion

Up to the year 1700 the Cossacks occupied a vast terrain known as the 'wild country' covering almost the complete river system draining south into the Black and Caspian Seas. Large tracts of this were still occupied by the Crimean Tatars. Later, in the 17th Century, a huge migration moved east into Siberia, reaching as far as the Pacific Ocean, 4,000 miles away, and pushing Russia's frontiers to the eastern limits.

Gradually, as Russia developed into an expanding state, the Tsars used the Cossacks for imperial policy in pushing out the boundaries to the east and to the south, until they eventually threatened British India. The empty steppes of Asia had been India's buffer-zone. Now, as the 18th Century turned into the 19th Century, there appeared Cossack scouts within 20 miles of the northern frontier of India. The sight of these shaggy horsemen appearing on the 'roof of the world' in increasing numbers must have caused the gravest apprehension to British administrators in India.

By the time of the First World War, this threat had never materialised, although incursions had been made through the Caucasus and into Persia. By then the Cossack Hosts were dispersed right across the Russian empire. From west to east were the *Don Cossacks*, centred on Novocherkassk, (sometimes in alliance with the Yaik and Zaporozhiye bands); then the *Kuban Host* about Yekatorinoda; next the *Terek Cossacks*, west of the Caspian Sea; moving north, were the *Astrakhan Host* about the River Volga. Going east once more, the *Ural Host* on the river of that name; and into the Ural Mountains we come to the *Orenburg Cossacks* near the settlement of Orenburg. Their lands stretched half way to Omsk, where they met up with the *Siberian Cossacks*, (those who had made the long trek 300 years before and settled in these lands). South of them was a settlement of the *Seven Rivers Host*, between Lake Balkhash and the Altai Mountains. Then, following the border with China, on the Amur River, were the *Amur Cossacks*; and right on to the Sea of Japan where on the coastal littoral were to be found *Ussur Cossacks*.[3]

The Cossack Role

The Cossacks came to be recognised as armed frontiersmen who served a very useful purpose in controlling the unruly tribes on Russia's borderland. Gradually they were formed into regiments – *Don, Kuban, Terek*, who owed personal allegiance to the Tsars. The Tsar became the Ataman (or Head) of all the Cossack Hosts; and the Cossacks, with their ingrained loyalty, became the shock troops to be brought in at a time of civil insurrection or revolt, which was often not far beneath the surface.

As Longworth recounts: 'And they were conscientious in fulfilling their duties. In Poland they fired on a procession bearing crosses, galloped through Warsaw laying into peaceful crowds with iron-tipped whips. They beat up and killed defenceless students in St. Petersburg, trampled down demonstrators from the universities of Moscow and Kiev and attacked a meeting of women workers at Rostov ...'.[4]

Lady Williams, whose parents were White Russian *emigrés*, has told me: 'I remember a photograph of my mother and father sitting on the terrace at our estate in the Orel Province, Lebetka, surrounded by a regiment of Cossacks. These Cossacks had been sorting out defenceless villagers with their sabres – so perhaps they weren't so nice after all'![5].

On the other hand the charge of the Tsar's *Cossack Guard*, at the end of the annual review on St Petersburg's *Champs de Mars*, was a patriotic occasion which stirred those who witnessed it. No-one could remain unaffected by the romance and glamour of those intrepid horsemen. For Imperial Russia the Cossack arm was an extremely economical way of guarding or extending her borders. They were completely self-contained, having to provide their own arms and horses, they lived off the land, and on the wildest steppe they would trap, hunt or fish; in sheltered valleys they would wrest some produce out of the soil, and so were independent of any baggage train.

Cossacks in the Revolution

The history of the Cossacks is not complete without a brief description of the developments in Petrograd[6] and their part in the dramatic events that unfolded in the spring of 1917.

It is said that the March Uprising in 1917, was more about bread than Revolution. It was a spontaneous reaction against food shortages and war. The other deficiencies of the régime were a subsidiary factor. In fact the professional revolutionaries themselves were not ready for it. The Tsar, Nicholas II, was away at the Front, misinformed by his ministers of the seriousness of the riots in Petrograd. At first he under-reacted, and then over-reacted, telegraphing with a peremptory order 'that the riots must be ended tomorrow'. The Governor of Petrograd, General Khabalov, took the necessary action. The next day, on 10 March, 200 people in the streets of the city lay dead. Nicholas had been warned before he left for the Front by Rodzianko, Speaker of the Duma, of the seriousness of the conspiracy which was afoot in high places, involving even members of the royal family; that the 'German woman', Nicholas's wife, Empress Alexandra with her attachment to the evil monk, Rasputin, must be got rid of. Nicholas either dared not, or would not intervene. It was the defection of Nicholas's loyal troops that destroyed his power-base. Regiments with household names fell like nine-pins. First it was the *Volinsky* regiment, which refused to leave barracks until they marched out to join the Revolution, then the *Semonovsky*, the *Ismailovsky* and the *Litovsky* regiments. Then Peter the Great's own regiment, the *Preobrajensky Guard*, admittedly, after three years of war, all second rate material. By 14 March, the whole of the Imperial Guard deserted their Sovereign and transferred their loyalty to the Duma, by then an uneasy coalition of liberals and revolutionaries.

The French Ambassador at St Petersburg, Maurice Paléologue, saw it all from the window of his embassy and reported it thus. First of all three regiments, led by a band, marched in perfect order, a few officers wearing red cockades in their caps. 'Behind them came the Guard, including units from the garrison at Tsarskoe Selo "at the head were Cossacks of the Escort, those magnificent horsemen who are the flower ... and privileged élite of the Imperial Guard. Then came His Majesty's own Regiment, the sacred legion which is recruited from all units of the Guard and whose special function is to secure the personal safety of the Sovereign".'[7]

Finally, the *coup de grâce*, was the march of the Marine Guard, the *Garde Équipage* who served on the royal yacht *Standart*, most of whom were known personally to the royal family. To add the final insult they were led by their commanding officer, Grand Duke Cyril, 'who was the first Romanov to publicly break his oath of allegiance to the Tsar, who still sat on the throne'.[8]

It was a grand *débâcle*. The world had been turned upside down, (although the parties in the grand houses still continued). This was pageantry in reverse. Loyalty had been put in abeyance; oaths disregarded. Discipline, that indefinable ingredient, was gone. The once proud cohorts had, at the tick of the clock, become an undisciplined mob, soliciting for political favours like street-walkers. This moment conjures up more than any other the total collapse of three and a half centuries of Romanov rule. It was also the end of the Cossacks. For from this moment on, they became an anachronism. They had no role or station in a Bolshevik state (except for a brief and bitter reprieve from 1941–45).

So it was against this background that subsequent events took place. Soon the Tsar had abdicated the throne, for himself and his heirs. He and his family were sent off to Siberia, ending with the infamous Ekaterinburg murders. Kerensky was appointed by the Duma, head of the Provisional Government.

The Germans meantime, with whom Russia was still at war, had cunningly infiltrated, (in a sealed train from Switzerland), the arch-revolutionary Lenin, who promised the Germans he would take Russia out of the war; to be shortly followed by Trotsky, from exile in the United States.

By October 1917, there were two hostile camps in Petrograd, with Kerensky (himself a revolutionary of a milder form), established in the Winter Palace, and Lenin and his Bolsheviks occupying the

Smolny Institute (formerly a school for the daughters of the nobility), only a mile or two apart. Cossack leaders then came to see Kerensky in the Winter Palace and demanded a show-down with Lenin's Bolshevik supporters. Peter Krasnov, with three Don Cossack regiments, was sent for, from the Northern Front. They were intercepted by a group of Red Cossacks and Krasnov was arrested. Kerensky meantime had escaped.

The Civil War 1917–19

Amongst the scattered Cossack army and in the homelands, a state of complete confusion reigned, with some joining the Bolsheviks and others the Whites. Krasnov, now still on parole, remained an ultra-royalist and was soon elected *Ataman* of the Don Cossacks.

Krasnov alleged that the Bolsheviks 'were behaving with extreme cruelty, that they tortured priests, raped girls and tied men to windmills'. But he and his fellow generals encouraged a counter-terror which was at least as horrible '... Krasnov described "with relish" a typical occasion, when the Cossacks at Ponomarev hamlet captured the well-known [Bolshevik] Cossack Podtelkov together with seventy-three Cossacks remaining with him. A hastily convened field-court condemned Podtelkov, together with the seventy-three Cossacks of the convoy, to summary execution. Sentence was immediately carried out in the presence of all the inhabitants'.[9]

However, Krasnov's campaign carried all before it, for by late summer the Don was cleared of the Bolsheviks. But, 'While Krasnov presided over mass executions on the Don, Annenkov pursued his war of vengeance in the Seven Rivers area, General Shkuro set an example of atrocity to the Cheka men in the Kuban, and unarmed Reds were mown down wholesale in the Urals and Siberia'.[10]

This may explain why, twenty-eight years later, Stalin was so insistent on having these people returned to him for summary justice. Whatever one may think of the enforced repatriation of White Cossack leaders, here is certainly another side to the story.

The dictatorial methods of Krasnov, and his attachment to the Germans, who were supplying him with money, arms and equipment to fight the Reds; his forcible collection of grain; all this led to increasing unpopularity.

Early in 1919, Krasnov resigned and handed over his command in Russia to Afrikan Bogayevski, serving under General Denikin.

The Revolution was now reaching its final phase. In June 1919,

Dutov's front in the Urals collapsed. Admiral Kolchak went into retreat, and having resigned overall command to Denikin (succeeded by General Wrangel in 1920), was taken prisoner. The Civil War fighting dragged on in the Far East until the autumn of 1922, by then the Red Army was able to turn south against the Don Cossacks and the Ukraine. The Cossack provinces were now in ruins both materially and spiritually. Famine succeeded war. There were disputes over land, the Bolshevik grip grew ever tighter, ending in enforced collectivisation and finally the liquidisation of the '*kulaks*' which once again split the Cossacks.

Cossack refugees now scattered over Europe and the Near and the Far East. Some to Bulgaria, others to Yugoslavia, or Czechoslovakia, many to Turkey and the island of Lemnos. Some went to Brazil or found a place in the French Foreign Legion. The refugees tried to preserve their community spirit. General I G Naumenko, now in exile, was elected Ataman of the Kuban Cossacks. Eventually, many of them drifted back home and made an uneasy peace with the Soviets.

Beyond the Caucasus

Now it is necessary to see what was happening south of the Caucasus Mountains, for important events were taking place which would have an impact on the whole of the Near East.

By 1920, General Denikin, still heading the White Russian armies, had established his headquarters at Batum on the Caspian Sea. The whole area, including Baku and Enzeli, was under the Allied occupation, British military government having been established in Batum. As General Hassan Arfa tells us in his memoirs,[11] 'The British Commander ... called on my father, as well as a handsome colonel of the Russian Army [White], Prince Qajar, of Iranian origin ... The prince, who was wearing a military *cherkeska* covered with imperial Russian crosses and medals, had been in command of a regiment of the famous Wild Division of the Caucasus, entirely composed of Moslems, but officered by both Russians and Caucasians. The Caucasian Moslems, being entirely exempt from military service, this division was composed of volunteers and was organised into six cavalry regiments, according to the races and tribes of the soldiers forming them. These were the *Tatars*, the *Daghestan*, the *Chechin*, the *Ingush*, the *Osset* and *Kabarda* regiments, all of whom had served with great gallantry throughout the war in Galizia'.[12]

The Tatar regiment actually formed the nucleus of the new Azerbaijan Republic's army. (It will be remembered that the region south of the Caucasus had separated from Russia and formed a Transcaucasian Republic in 1918 – soon to split up into its component parts as Georgia, Armenia and the Moslems of Azerbaijan, all at that time daggers-drawn with one another).

When the Soviets re-occupied this area in 1920, part of the Azerbaijani army went over and joined Iran. These were the *Tatar* cavalry regiments which became part of the Iranian army, led by Prince Qajar.

By another quirk of history, there also existed at this time a Cossack division in Iran, officered by White Russians loyal to General Denikin. This division had been on, more or less, permanent loan from Russia to the Shah of Iran since before the war. It also ran a Cossack school for the training of Iranian Cossacks. Hassan Arfa had been put down for a commission in the Cossack division by his father, but, after the interview, decided he wanted to transfer to a more national Iranian force and joined instead the mounted *gendarmerie*. The Cossack division was now paid for by the British, as were most other institutions in Iran, under the Anglo-Iranian Treaty, as the country was virtually bankrupt. Sir Percy Cox was the influential British Minister at Teheran at the time, who was responsible for administering the Treaty.

Reza Khan – Cossack Soldier of Fortune

Now an extraordinary story begins. In the spring of 1917, during the first phase of the Russian Revolution, Kerensky, head of the Provisional Government, decided to replace the commander of the Persian Cossacks with a more liberal-minded fellow, one Colonel Clergé. Passing through Tiflis, Clergé met an old friend, Colonel Staroselsky, who had formerly commanded the Tatar regiment of the *Wild Division*. Staroselsky was out of a job and persuaded Clergé to take him on, as second-in-command of the Cossack division. Staroselsky, who soon decided Clergé was a communist, intrigued to get rid of him.

Meantime there was among the Iranian Cossack officers a Colonel Reza Khan, 'who had arisen from the ranks and was renowned for his strong personality, iron will and extraordinary capacity for leadership'. He came from a traditional military family of the *Bavand* clan. However, owing to a family squabble, his mother had taken him to school in Teheran. 'Being physically unusually vigorous and endowed with a strong and virile character, he enlisted at the age of fourteen in the Cossack Brigade and owing to his remarkable military qualities rose very soon from private to NCO, and then from NCO to officer rank. It was to this man that Staroselsky turned, to organise a *coup d'état* inside the Cossack division, and Reza Khan accepted.'[13]

Reza Khan was promoted to Brigadier and received command of the Cossack Guard Infantry regiment. And so he came to think how easy it would be to change the Iranian Army by transferring power from the hands of a few foreign officers to those of a strong and enterprising Iranian.[14] Soon his moment was to come. The Cossack Division rebelled, having received no pay for several months, and marched on Teheran. Following its capture, Reza Khan was made Minister of War. It was not long (1921) before Reza Shah Pahlavi, a former Cossack trooper, by a dramatic *coup d'état* over-threw the last of the Qajar Shahs, Mozaffar-ed-Din Shah, and assumed the throne of Iran. Reza's son Mohammed Reza Shah was to be the last occupant of the Peacock Throne.

Atamans in Exile

In 1937, Himmler had been approached by two senior German officers who had taken part in the Baltic campaign in 1917/19, Lieutenant General von Cochenhausen and Graf von der Goltz, who had known Krasnov when he had been with the Don Cossacks in that theatre of operations. The Germans had been aiding the anti-Bolsheviks with arms and ammunition. The generals wished to introduce Krasnov as a useful man to cultivate for the German *Drang nach osten*. Krasnov was duly vetted by the Gestapo under the auspices of Heydrich. Himmler at this time wanted ideas on anti-kidnap measures and protection for white *emigrés* working against the Bolsheviks.[15]

At that time, Krasnov was stateless, having recently moved from Paris to Berlin, where he had been writing romantic and idealised novels about Cossack life. Krasnov had incurred the bitter enmity of the Soviets, not only through breaking his parole, following release by Trotsky, but on account of his activities during the civil war, which included the massacre at Ponomarov of the pro-Bolshevik Cossack leader Podtelkov and seventy five of his supporters (see page 231). Following approval by the Gestapo, he now set up an anti-Bolshevik propaganda centre in Berlin.

'Krasnov's value to the Germans lay in his influence with the Cossacks, who could be useful to them in their drive through the Ukraine to the Kuban and the Caucasus oil-fields. Both the Cossacks and the Caucasus were the subject of studies by the *Sicherheitsdienst* [SD]'.[16]

But when in 1941, the German invasion of Russia began, most Cossacks in that country forgot their antipathy to the communists and rallied to the cause to defend the homeland against the much feared German aggressor.

Two other names became prominent at this time, but within the Soviet Union, or that part over-run by the Germans. One, Sergei Pavlov, a Don Cossack, staged a minor coup in the town of Novochek-assk and took over a government building, later seeking German support for his plans to raise a Cossack army to fight the Bolsheviks. Another, a Cossack major named Kononov, a graduate of the military academy of the Frunze, and a veteran of the Finnish war, had been allowed by the Germans to form a squadron of Cossack deserters and prisoners-of-war.

One curious consequence of the defeat of General Wrangel's White Army were the stragglers who sought refuge in Yugoslavia in 1920. Being staunchly royalist, they were given asylum by King Alexander, and there they remained, a separate caste, trying to keep alive the Cossack creed by means of schools and other activities. Out of this group, five regiments were formed in 1942 and, under German leadership, were used against Tito's Partisans. Later known as the *Schutzkorps*, they were commanded by General Rogozhin, a White Russian leader. Making their way across to the Austrian border, they surrendered to the British, and were deemed exempt from repatriation owing to their Yugoslav citizenship. They were transferred to the camp at Rimini.

Shortly after France fell and the demands for German manpower increased, SS Reichsführer Himmler began to experience serious shortages for his Waffen SS regiments. Himmler had always aspired to high military command, presumably to boost his position in the Nazi hierachy. He now obtained Hitler's approval to recruit outside the territory of the Reich, amongst *Volksdeutche*, (German expatriates) and in other countries where populations could claim nordic descent. These national contingents or *Germanic Legions*, from such countries as France, Holland and Scandinavia, augmented considerably Himmler's total command.[17]

Krasnov, using his long association with the Nazi party, now gave his support to a Cossack Nationalist Party, formed in Prague, whose members recognised the Führer as 'supreme dictator of the Cossack

Nation'.[18] Several prominent White Cossack leaders from European capitals, including Generals Andrei Shkuro and V Naumenko associated themselves with this movement.

During 1943, the long retreat of the German Army from occupied Russia, began. Those Cossacks who had collaborated with the German Army had no alternative but to fall back too. And here we have the beginnings of two distinctive Cossack divisions, one under the German leadership of Colonel Helmut von Pannwitz (a Russian-speaking Balt), and the other under Major Pavlov (later to become known as the *Domanov* Cossacks).

In March 1944, a role was found for Krasnov. A directorate of Cossack Forces was formed by Himmler in February 1994, to coordinate the Cossack 'armies'. The ageing Krasnov was put in charge, and he was joined by a contemporary of the civil war V Naumenko, the former Ataman of the Kuban. Also included was Pavlov, (shortly to be killed in anti-guerilla operations) and Colonel Kulakov from von Pannwitz's division. The Cossack directorate, the Chief Administration (*Hauptvernaltung*) of the Cossack Hosts, was closely supervised by Dr Himpel of Rosenberg's *Reichministerium Ost* (Ministry for the Conquered Eastern Territories). Pavlov had now been killed and Major Domanov took over the Don, Terek and Kuban Cossacks. During the *trek* or retreat they had a hard time, continually being promised a *stanitza* or traditional Cossack home in return for services rendered. Byleorussia was to be their first *stanitza*, but they were forced to abandon it as the Soviet offensive swept all before it. Then it was to be Poland, and the same thing happened again.

On 20 July 1944, a German staff officer, Stadler by name from the *Ostministevium*, signalled Himmler's headquarters, (the Head of the Anti-Partisan Forces Bureau) detailing plans to remove Domanov's Cossacks to the Adriatic Littoral for anti-Partisan duties. Fortunately the signal survives:

> 'After yesterday's decision by Minister Rosenberg and SS *Obergruppenführer* Berger, the move of 4,000 Caucasians and 18,000 Cossack fugitives who have hitherto been operating in Byleorussia under General Commissioner SS *Gruppen-führer* von Gottberg, to the Adriatic Littoral operations zone has been approved, specifically to the Carnic Alps and the Prealp; off-loading station, Tolmezzo'.[19]

The sender explained that all arrangements had been made with the commander of the Adriatic SS *Gruppenführer* Globocnik in Trieste. This man had a very unsavoury reputation, for whilst serving in Poland, he had established the extermination camp at Treblinka.

The contingent consisted of 9,000 armed Cossacks, 2,000 armed

Caucasians, and many dependants, wagons and horses. With this body also travelled old Whites like General Shkuro, Salamkhin from the Kuban, and Sultan Girei Klitch, a Tatar Chief from the '*Savage or Wild* Caucasian division', whose other half we have already encountered in Iran.

There was no love lost between Generals Shkuro and Krasnov, for when Himmler's headquarters decided to appoint Shkuro to command a Cossack division, Krasnov objected violently to his appointment and described him as 'a shallow-minded and often immoral individual'.[20]

In a record of a meeting held under Himmler, on 26 August, at which General von Pannwitz was present, it was envisaged that Domanov's Cossacks should come under his overall command as the xv Cossack Cavalry Corps. Pressure on the Germans from all sides meant that the amalgamation never actually took place. But at the same meeting it was envisaged that the Cossacks should be incorporated into the framework of the Waffen SS, 'but for the time being not to become evident to them. General von Pannwitz has the task, by skilful propaganda, to render the SS concept comprehensible to them and familiarise the Cossacks with it' the Minutes noted.[21]

From this has stemmed the argument as to whether the Cossacks were, or were not, designated SS. In the case of Domanov's Cossacks, they did not carry this designation, although they worked closely with the SS in the Carnia operations. In the case of von Pannwitz's division, now operating with some ferocity against the Tito Partisans in Croatia and Yugoslavia, they did have SS status, at least from December 1944 until the end of April 1945, when they were known as the *15 SS Cossack Cavalry Corps*. But their designation matters little, for they were in fact subordinate to, and under the control of, Himmler's SS headquarters. It is unlikely that SS indoctrination had much effect on the Cossacks' way of life, they had little time to absorb it, but to the Allies the term 'SS' conjured up everything that was most hateful and odious about the Nazi régime.

Pannwitz's division, consisting of 13,000 Cossacks, was staffed and officered entirely by Germans, of which there were 4,500. As can be imagined, it was a far better trained and effective fighting force than Domanov's contingent.

When Domanov's Cossacks arrived at Tolmezzo in September 1944, they were led to believe that their new homeland, named *Cossackia*, would be cleared of partisans by Globocnik's command. This was far from the case. No proper arrangements had been made for their reception or accommodation. For their part, Globocnik's people were horrified to see disembarking from the train, not the armed and disciplined Cossack squadrons that they had been expecting, but a regular 'rag, tag and bobtail' crowd, more like a gypsy caravan than anti-partisan fighters. It was months before Police, SS troops and the Cossacks themselves were able to clear and occupy their 'homeland'.

In February 1945, when Berlin was under threat from the advancing Red Armies, Krasnov moved to Tolmezzo to join Domanov's Cossacks. V Naumenko and an aide, however, fled to the United States. Krasnov and his colleagues, Shkuro, Domanov and von Pannwitz, whom the British repatriated, were tried in Moscow as war criminals and found guilty on grounds of 'armed struggle against the Soviet Union', and other crimes of espionage and terrorism, and were sentenced to death. This was carried out during January 1947. Some of the other Cossack leaders were imprisoned but, after Stalin's death, were subsequently released and made their way to the west.

One of the leading historians on the Cossacks, Philip Longworth, has pointed out that they had fought against their own people during the German occupation of Russia.

> 'Though only a third of the officers were Soviet citizens, they were most of them traitors in the eyes of any law, and some could be classified legally as war criminals. Years before Krasnov had broken his parole to the Soviet authorities. These exiles, who, for a quarter of a century, had expressed a ruthless determination to overthrow the Soviet régime, could hardly wonder that Stalin wanted them; men who had sworn loyalty to the Nazis and had accepted the protection of and fought for the SS, ought not to have been surprised at the lack of Allied sympathy'.[22]

Appendix F

ANTI-TITO YUGOSLAV GROUPS
(See Chapter XXII page 145)
*EXTRACT FROM A MEMO FROM AFHQ
(RESIDENT MINISTER) TO THE FOREIGN OFFICE
DATED 24 MAY 1945*

CONFIDENTIAL

*Notes on the various groups of non-Partisan Jugoslavs likely to be found
in VENEZIA GIULA and/or CARINTHIA and STYRIA.*

MIHAJLOVIC Cetniks
(Known also in SLOVENIA as the 'Blue Guard').

Early in 1945 it was known that, with German assistance, remnants
of MIHAJLOVIC's Cetniks were concentrating in ISTRIA and
Southern VENEZIA GIULIA, possibly under the leadership of
JEVDJEVIC, one of MIHAJLOVIC's senior commanders who had
escaped from ROME before the Allied entry. Before this, however,
there had existed here a small group of Cetniks under Major NOVAK
(since believed to have been killed) who was General MIHAJLOVIC's
representative and who had worked closely with JEVDJEVIC when
the latter was in ROME. These Cetniks of Major NOVAK were
known as the Blue Guard, and, as an anti-Partisan force, collaborated
with the Slovene White Guard, the Italians and the Germans. In
September 1945 they appear to have been loosely associated with
the White Guard in the German-sponsored formation known as the
Slovene Domobranci. The Blue Guard appear never to have been
very numerous or very active; and never formed part of the German
Armed Forces.

2. In concentrating the MIHAJLOVIC Cetniks in this area the

Germans clearly desired to add to the general confusion. The Cetniks themselves will clearly prefer to surrender to the Allies rather than to the Partisans and may still try to enlist Allied sympathy for their cause. General Draza MIHAJLOVIC himself is NOT in this area but still remains in BOSNIA.

Serb Volunteer Guard (Dobrovoltsi)

3. These are Serb forces, formed into a National Serb Guard by the Quisling NEDIC Government in BELGRADE after the German occupation of SERBIA in April 1941. They fought in SERBIA with the Germans against the Partisans, though not forming part of the German Armed Forces. Some were eventually withdrawn with the German forces from SERBIA into CROATIA and thence into VENE-ZIA GIULIA. They were originally associated with a Serb called LJOTIC, a notorious collaborator, fanatically pan-Serb and pro-German; he has since been reported killed near TRIESTE. The present commander believed to be Col. Kosta MUSICKI. These forces would probably also prefer to surrender to the Allies rather than to the Jugoslav Partisans.

Slovene White Guard (Bela Garda)

4. This force was originally known as the Vaska Straza or Village Guard; and after the Italian capitulation it was associated with the Slovene Domobranci or Home Defence. It originated in SLOVENIA and was formed after the first beginnings of Partisan resistance there, ostensibly to guard the peasantry against the Partisans. Its nucleus was the Fantovi or Youth Organisation of the Slovene Clerical Party, which has been the main instigator of anti-Partisan activity in SLOVE-NIA. This party is strongly reactionary and closely associated with the Roman Catholic Church; it opposed the Slovene Partisan policy of active resistance, as well as the latter's association with, and later domination by, the Communist Party. Collaboration with the Italians thus became inevitable and the Slovene White Guard was armed and supplied by the Italians; it also received financial support from elements in the emigré Jugoslav Government in LONDON, through contacts in ROME and the VATICAN. After the Italian collapse the White Guard was re-grouped by Colonel Leon RUPNIK, a notorious pro-German collaborator, within the Slovene Domobranci or Home Defence and came under the control of the Chief SS official (Hohere SS under Polizeifuhrer) of XVIII Military District centred at BLED. The White Guard was then used by the Germans for garri-

soning and policing and for collaboration with the German troops against the Partisans. Other Slovene officers connected with the White Guard were Colonel PETERLIN, Colonel KREN, Colonel KOKAL and Colonel RUPNIK's son, Capt. Vuk RUPNIK.

5. The White Guard were partly equipped with Italian uniforms and arms and partly with German. One of their emblems was a white stag on an azure ground worn on the right sleeve. Some of the units were commanded by German officers; and there have been reports that some members were forcibly recruited by the Germans, the only alternative offered being enlistment in the German Armed Forces. The White Guard forces will certainly try to escape from the Partisans in SLOVENIA and prefer to surrender to Allied Forces.

Slovene Domobranci (Home Defence)

6. See under Slovene White Guard.

Croat Ustase and Domobranci

7. Elements of the Croat Ustase and Domobranci (Home Defence) may manage to escape into either CARINTHIA and STYRIA or VENEZIA GIULIA. These forces come under the control of the former quisling PAVELIC Government in ZAGREB. The Ustas Militia includes the more fanatical Ustase, who have collaborated with the Germans and are enemy troops. The Croat Domobrans are conscripts, and, as many were not confirmed Ustase, numbers deserted to the Partisans; the PAVELIC Government was thus compelled to merge the two forces in order to make desertion more difficult. These Croat forces will certainly avoid surrender to the Partisans if possible, especially the Ustase, who have committed many atrocities in CROATIA. The Majority of the members of the former quisling Government in ZAGREB (excluding PAVELIC himself) have already attempted to surrender to the Allies, but their request was rejected and Marshal TITO informed. Most of these quisling Ministers appear to have escaped from ZAGREB and may turn up in VENEZIA GIULIA or CARINTHIA and STYRIA.

SOURCE PRO FO 371/48919.

Appendix G

LETTER FROM PJ GRIGG (WAR MINISTER) TO ANTHONY EDEN (FOREIGN SECRETARY)

(See Chapter xxx page 198)

24 August 1944

TOP SECRET

My dear Anthony,

I don't know how the question of Russian prisoners which you have referred to the Russian Government now stands, but the enclosed telegram from the Middle East shows that it is necessary to be quite clear as to our policy and to make that policy clear to the Military Commanders who will have to implement it.

We are in an obvious dilemma. If we do as the Russians want and hand over all these prisoners to them whether or not the prisoners are willing to go back to Russia, we are, as the telegram implies and as Selborne's minute of 25th July suggests, sending some of them to their death; and though in war we cannot, as you point out in your minute of 2nd August, afford to be sentimental, I confess that I find the prospect somewhat revolting, and I should expect public opinion to reflect the same feeling. There is also the danger that if we hand the men back there may be reprisals on our prisoners in German hands. But I think that that risk is probably growing appreciably less, and that the Germans have probably enough to think about without keeping their eye on what happens to Russians whom they forced into the German Armies.

On the other hand if we don't do what the Russians wish there may be the danger that they will not be ready to co-operate in getting back speedily to us the British and other Allied prisoners who fall into their hands as they advance into Germany. Obviously our public opinion would bitterly and rightly resent any delay in getting our men home, or any infliction of unnecessary hardship on them, and if the choice is between hardship to our men and death to Russians the choice is plain. But I confess that I am not at all convinced that, whatever we do, the Russians will go out of their way to send our prisoners westwards at once or to deal with them in any special manner.

In any case the dilemma is so difficult that for my part I should like a Cabinet ruling as to its solution. If we hand the Russian prisoners back to their death it will be the military authorities who will do so on my instructions and I am entitled to have behind me, in this very unpleasant business, the considered view of the Government.

> Yrs sincerely
> P. J. Grigg.

CHAPTER NOTES

Notes

Preface

1. Austria had been annexed the year before in March 1938. By March 1939 it had already been reported that some 40 German divisions were mobilised and massing on the Czechoslovak borders. By the time I reached Innsbruck at the end of March, it was a *fait accompli*.
2. Major John Poston MC (11th Hussars) had become Monty's ADC on the latter's arrival in the Middle East, in September 1942. He and J R Henderson (then Captain 12th Lancers) were the two longest serving ADC's. Whilst on a liaison run, Poston was ambushed and killed in Germany just a few days before the end of the war.
3. The 'northern tier', which now came under Monty's command, consisted of First US Army (General Hodges) and Ninth US Army (General Simpson), with effect from 19 December 1944. I was sent down later that night to give General Hodges special orders to block the Meuse bridges at all costs. Col. Bigland (DSO, OBE, Legion of Merit) was liaison officer between Bradley (12th US Army Group) and Montgomery (21 British Army Group).
4. As a Minister of the Crown (Government Whip), I had been unable to speak in the Commons. This was my first speech for 11 years! It proved my last one because the date of the 1987 General Election (at which I was due to retire) was announced a few days later. See Appendix 'A' for full text.

Prologue

1. '*Sir William Mather*'. Ed. by his son Loris E. Mather (Cobden-Sanderson, 1925). The firm was then known as William and Colin Mather, later to be known as 'Mather & Platt'.
2. *Ibid*. Nihilism – the rejection of all religions and moral principles – doctrine of the extreme revolutionary parties of Nineteenth and Twentieth Century Russia.
3. Grand Duchess Xenia was living in a 'grace and favour' house provided for her by her cousin, King George V. She was one of the few members of the Russian Imperial family to escape with her life from the Bolsheviks. Leaving from the Crimea on the British battleship HMS Marlborough in April 1919, she was accompanied by her mother, the Dowager Empress Marie Fedorovna, and her younger sister Grand Duchess Olga.

   Curiously enough, we were to know Xenia's grand-daughter later in Athens. 'Bebe' was married to Count Nicholai Sheremetiev. His family having been one of the wealthiest in Russia, he was now, in the 1950s, reduced to working as

a purser on a P & O cruise liner. Bebe's mother, Irina, had married Felix Yussoupov. Bebe was their only child. Prince Yussoupov was the main accomplice in the murder of the notorious *starets* Rasputin, whose evil influence assisted in the downfall of the Romanov regime.
4. The ski battalion was formed as 5th (Special Reserve) Battalion, Scots Guards.
5. I was with Lieutenant Lord Jellicoe, Coldstream Guards, (now the Rt Hon Earl Jellicoe KBE DSO MC PC FRS) on a two-man commando raid.

PART ONE – WAR-TORN EUROPE

Chapter I – Collapse and Chaos at the Heart of Europe

1. The actual surrender of the German Armed Forces to Field Marshal Montgomery had taken place on 5 May 1945.
2. The Hungarians had actually left the Axis powers during the previous year and declared themselves neutral, but their Army, like others, was fleeing to a place of safety.
3. *Notes on 'G' Activities of 21 Army Group during Post-Surrender Period.* WO 205/1025. PRO.
4. Drawn from the *History of the Second World War, Civil Affairs and Military Government in NW Europe 1944–46.* F S V Donnison. (HMSO London 1961.)
5. For further information see Nigel Hamilton. *Monty the Field Marshal* (Hamish Hamilton. London 1985).
   B H Liddell Hart. *The Other Side of the Hill* (London 1945). Revised edition 1951.
   H C Butcher. *Three Years with Eisenhower* (New York 1948).
   Alfred D Chandler. ed. *The Papers of Dwight David Eisenhower. The War Years Vol III* (Baltimore 1970).
6. Donnison. *Op. Cit.*
7. *Ibid.*
8. WO 205/1025. PRO.
9. *Ibid.*

Chapter II – Post-Surrender in Germany

1. PWX – Ex Prisoners of War.
   SEP – Surrendered Enemy Personnel.
   DP – Displaced Persons, mostly impressed workers from all over German occupied Europe recruited by the Todt (or Labour) Organization, in current parlance, 'slave-workers'.
2. W S Churchill. *The Second World War, Vol. VI. Triumph and Tragedy* (Cassell. London 1948).
3. Nigel Hamilton. *Monty. The Field Marshal 1944–1976* (Hamish Hamilton. London 1985).
4. *Ibid.*
5. Nigel Hamilton. *Op.Cit.*
6. Colonel R G Turner. *Report on the Evacuation of Stalag Luft I at Barth.* WO205/139.
7. Peter Hanbury, a former Welsh Guards (2nd Bn) platoon commander, captured at Boulogne 1940.
8. P F Hanbury. *Op.Cit.*
9. At the time of capture, Anthony Barber was a Spitfire pilot engaged on a lone

unarmed reconnaissance mission, without guns or radio. He had been photographing the North African coast and suspected the German submarine pens on the Spanish coast. He was returning from Gibraltar at 30,000 feet, but owing to adverse headwinds ran out of fuel as he was about to cross the Channel. He ditched the plane in order to destroy the evidence and came down by parachute in 3 feet of water. There was a 'reception party' waiting for him! (Conversation with Lord Barber, 11 June 1990.)

10. Quote from Rt. Hon. Lord Barber, former Chancellor of the Exchequer in a letter to Lord Allan of Kilmahew. House of Lords Debate on USSR and Exchange of Prisoners. 17 March 1976.
11. Conversation with Lord Barber. 11 June 1990.
12. Averill Harriman. *Special Envoy* (New York 1975).

Chapter III – Everyone Must Go Home

1. WO 205/139 PRO.
2. *Ibid.* The Leipzig Agreement was separate from that of Yalta, and was a working agreement between the Allies.
3. *Ibid.*
4. F S V Donnison. *History of Second World War. Civil Affairs and Military Government in North-West Europe 1944–46* (HMSO. London 1961).
5. *Ibid.*
6. *Ibid.*
7. *Ibid.*
8. In view of the Report, by Brigadier Kenchington (Chief PW and DP Division, British Control Commission for Germany at Lubbecke) (see page 21), which refers to likely 'mutinous conditions amongst the troops concerned', I have carefully checked the words I have used denying knowledge of any such conditions whilst I was there. I have also cross-checked with the then G2 (Ops) Tac HQ 21 Army Group, Major Paul Odgers, through whom all operational matters passed, who writes to me as follows: 'I have searched my memories of the immediate post-war period and I cannot recall any reports coming through our Ops Room at Tac, of the sort of problems referred to in Brigadier Kenchington's report'. (Letter to the author dated 11 April 1990.)
9. Rt. Hon. Leopold Amery, former member of the War Cabinet.
10. FO 1052/260 PRO.
11. FO 1052/13 PRO.
12. *Ibid.*
13. CAB CM 2 (46).
14. *Ibid.*
15. *Ibid.*

Chapter IV – A Roving Commission in Post-War Europe

1. Army action in imposing a curfew was deemed essential to prevent panic migration before the Soviet troops arrived.
2. The date of the General Election was 5 July 1945, although the results were not announced until later to allow time for the collection of the armed forces polling boxes.
3. Major H Wake MC. 60th Rifles. LO to Field Marshal Montgomery. Now Sir Hereward Wake, Bt. MC.
4. Montgomery was also becoming exasperated with Polish behaviour. At a confer-

ence for Corps Commanders he told them that the trouble with Polish DPs could only be stopped by completely ruthless action. 'Lublin' was the word used to describe the Soviet Puppet Government.

5. This refers to Prince Paul Sapeiha, a romantic figure, soldier and international diplomat (on refugees). He was born into the Austro-Hungarian Empire in Galicia, later served in the Polish Lancers, became a US citizen, served with Bradley and later Ridgeway in Korea. His uncle Cardinal Prince Adam Sapeiha was early sponsor to Karol Wojtyla, the present Pope. I was to meet him again in Athens in the 1950s.

6. WO 216/196 PRO.

7. *Ibid.* Dated 1 May 1946.

Chapter V – Austria

1. George Clare's *Last-Waltz in Vienna* (Macmillan 1981). See also an account of the rise to power of the Nazis.
2. Dr. Karl Renner's new Provisional Government recognised by the Soviets.
3. FO 371/44609.
4. Sir George Franckenstein was Austrian Envoy Extraordinary in London 1920–38. He received a knighthood when he became a naturalised British subject in 1938.
5. *Ibid.*
6. *Ibid.*
7. *Ibid.*
8. *Ibid.*
9. FO 1020/29.

PART TWO – THE SITUATION AT ALEXANDER'S HEADQUARTERS

Chapter VI – War on Three Fronts

1. Jackson. *History of the Second World War. The Mediterranean and Middle East.* Vol VI (HMSO London 1984).
2. *Ibid.* Brigadier G. M. O. Davy, Commander Land Forces Adriatic, in a briefing note on the Yugoslav scene for Alexander.
3. Jackson *Op.Cit.* This subject has now become more controversial, the decision to support Tito being seriously questioned. See Michael Lees (a former BLO with Mihailovic), *The Rape of Serbia* (Harcourt Brace Jovanovich. New York 1990) and David Martin, *Web of Disinformation* (Harcourt Brace Jovanovich. New York 1990).
4. My escape from an Italian POW Camp, near Parma, with one companion, Captain Archie Hubbard RB, was a 600 kilometre trek which took us 40 days to reach the Allied lines.

   Most of the combatants were unskilled in mountain warfare except for the British Indian Division and the French Goums, and at a later stage an American mountain division. The British, despite their earlier experiment with ski-troops had never taken mountain warfare seriously. But the exception was in the use of mules. My old friend and riding instructor, Colonel Paul Rodzianko had been given the task of raising the Mule Corps of some 30,000 animals and comes in for high praise from Alexander, 'a brilliant horseman ... who performed a most useful service'. *Alexander Memoirs. Op. Cit.*
5. Alexander. *Memoirs 1940–1945.*

6. It had not been Alexander's intention that General Mark Clark should capture Rome, but rather cut off the German armies fleeing from the battlefield. Fortunately the victory arrived at a good psychological moment, just as the 'Overlord' fleet was embarked for Normandy.
7. Alexander. *Op.Cit.*
8. Operation 'Anvil', later codenamed 'Dragoon'.
9. *Ibid.* Operation Dragoon took place on 15 August 1944.
10. Jackson. *History of the Second World War. Mediterranean and Middle East. Vol. VI.*
11. John Colville. *Fringes of Power* (Hodder and Stoughton 1985).
12. *Agreement Relating to Prisoners of War and Civilians liberated by Forces operating under Soviet Command and Forces operating under British Command. Signed at Yalta* FO1020/362.
13. Jackson. *Mediterranean and Middle East.* Vol. VI. Part II (p. 171 note 116). It is tempting to compare Montgomery's attitude to the arrival of a civil affairs/political adviser at an earlier stage of the Italian campaign. On hearing that Lord Rennell of Rodd had arrived in that capacity and wished to see him, Montgomery exclaimed, with his customary inability to pronounce the letter 'R', 'Wennell of Wodd? Wennell of Wodd? Never heard of him!' And he refused to see him.
14. Alexander. *Memoirs 1940–1945.*

Chapter VII – Final Phase and Surrender

1. Jackson. *History of the Second World War. The Mediterranean and the Middle East. Vol. VI.* Pt. III.
2. *Ibid.*
3. Alexander. *Memoirs 1940–1945.*
4. Jackson. *Op. Cit.* Allen Dulles was then OSS representative in Switzerland.
5. *Ibid.*
6. *Alanbrooke.* David Fraser. Collins 1982.
7. *Ibid.*
8. *Ibid.*

Chapter VIII – War and Blood in the Mountains

1. Conversation with Peter Lee. Ex SOE Italy.
2. Jackson. *History of the Second World War. The Mediterranean and the Middle East.* Vol VI Pt III. HMSO.
3. *Ibid.*
4. Peter Lee. *Op. cit.*
5. Macmillan. *Op. cit.* Diary entry 22 January 1945.
6. Macmillan *Op. cit.*
7. This is a reference to the rooting out and destruction of the 'Red Star' Partisan's base at Marzabotto by the SS with the utmost savagery, reflected in the number of Partisans killed (718), to 456 taken prisoner. Jackson. *Op. Cit.*
8. Basil Davidson. *Special Operations in Europe* (Gollancz. London 1980).
9. BBC documentary *SOE Italy 1985.*
10. Pietro Menis. *Tempo di Cossachi.* (Tip. Buttazoni – San Daniele). By kind permission of his son, Prof. Monsignor Gian Carlo Menis, Extracts translated by James Chamberlain. The book contains excerpts from the diary which his father kept in 1944/5.

11. *Ibid.*
12. Material compiled by P. Martin-Smith. SOE Italy.
13. Patrick Martin-Smith. The British in Friuli. *No 1 Special Force and Italian Resistance*. (Pub. Federazione Italiana Associazioni Partigiane (FIAP) and Special Forces Club 1990.)
14. Pat Mosdell. Report on Return from the Field. *No 1 Special Force and the Italian Resistance* Vol. II. *Op.Cit.* According to Martin-Smith, for the first *Rastrallemento*, in order to gain control of the area north of the R. Tagliamento, four columns of Germans from Austria were used and two columns from the West using Spanish and Italian fascists – 40,000 troops in all.
15. Ronald Taylor. The British 'Sermon One' Mission to Friuli. *No 1 Special Force and the Italian Resistance* Vol. II. *Op.Cit.*
16. Letter to the author from Ronald Taylor. 7 Sept 1990.
17. Troppenburg had been a trainee pilot at Gorizia at the time of the Italian armistice on 8 Sept 1943 when he joined the Action Party partisan movement.
18. The Garibaldini wore the Red Scarf of Garibaldi with the Russian Red Star and were communist dominated. The Osoppo were anti-communist and wore the green scarf. Sometimes they fought together, but more often there was keen rivalry between the two.
19. Count Gianandrea Gropplero di Troppenburg. The Bigelow Mission. *No 1 Special Force and the Italian Resistance.* Vol. I. *Op.Cit.*
20. *Ibid.*
21. Dumas Poli. The Bigelow Mission to Friuli. *No 1 Special Force and the Italian Resistance.* Vol. I. Poli Dumas writes to me (28.4.91) the following clarification:
1. The shooting of the 'peasant up the tree' was recounted to them by other people at the end of the episode.
2. The general opinion of the inhabitants of the zone that the Cossacks were harder than the Germans themselves was undoubtedly motivated by personal experience.
3. Failure to fire the fatal shot at the moment of capture led Dumas and his companion to attribute merit to their captors, whatever may have been the motive in their not doing so.
22. Tribute by Gianandrea Troppenburg. Gerald Thistlewaite, also writes how the 18 year old courier Paola Del Din (on her brother's death in a daring attack on a German Barracks), volunteered, after crossing the lines in Florence, for parachute training with No 1 Special Force. Before departing on her return mission, she expressed a wish that she should see her father, an *Alpini* Colonel then a PoW in British India. This was arranged by SOE and before she departed he appeared at Bari in full *Alpini* uniform.
23. Martin-Smith. *Op.Cit.* The women came down from the mountains and collected food south of the R. Tagliamento for the 60,000 Partisans as well as for the local inhabitants.

PART THREE – THE VENEZIA GUILIA CRISIS

Chapter IX – Tito Moves In

1. WO 214/42/
2. AIR 23/8575 386A NAF 943.
3. *Ibid.*
4. *Ibid.*
5. WO 214/42.
6. Jackson. *Op. Cit.*

7. FO 371/48814. NMF 949.
8. *Ibid.* Churchill's cable has no reference number.
9. *Ibid.* Alexander's signal ref. 1095.

Chapter X – Crossing the Alps

1. WO 170/4404. PRO.
2. Caporetto, scene of a disaster for the Italian Army in the First World War (24 Oct. 1917), is now in Jugoslavia and known as Korbarid.
3. 3rd Battalion Welsh Guards War Diary WO 170/4982. PRO.
4. 36 Inf Bde War Diary WO 170/4461. PRO.
5. Brigadier G R D Musson DSO. Commanding 36 Inf Bde.
6. 36 Inf Bde War Diary. *Ibid.*

Chapter XI – Cleaning Up

1. Brigadier Gerald Verney, Commanding 1 Guards Brigade in Austria. Formerly commanding 6 Guards Tank Brigade and 7 Armoured Division in Normandy, where I had close contact with him. Subsequently commanding British Troops, Vienna, after which he wrote the account quoted. I am indebted to his son, Major Peter Verney, for permission to use this account, and extracts from letters to his mother.
2. Letter dated 1 Guards Brigade, 18 May 1945. By kind permission of Peter Verney.
3. Macmillan, as a parliamentarian, had been on a two-man fact-finding visit to Finland in 1940 at the height of the Russian attack. He and his companion, Lord Davies, had seen many similar scenes of roads clogged with abandoned equipment.
4. Letter dated HQ 1 Guards Brigade, 18 May 1945.
5. Cowgill Report. *Op. Cit.*

Chapter XII – The Melting-Pot

1. HQ 36 Inf. Bde. war diary WO 170/4461. PRO
2. *Ibid.*
3. This Libel case opened at the Royal Courts of Justice on 2 October and continued into December 1989. The plaintiff, Lord Aldington, was awarded substantial damages.
4. Evidence J S Shuter.
5. Evidence Judge John Barrington Taylor QC.
6. *Ibid.*
7. *Ibid.*

Chapter XIII – Sorting Out the Armies of Europe

1. *The Reminiscences and Recollections of Captain Gronow 1810–1860.* (RS Surtees Society. Frome 1984).
2. Report on the 38 (Irish) Infantry Brigade (1 May to end July 1945). Written by Brigadier T P D Scott and published in The *Faugh-a-Ballach. The Regimental Gazette of the Royal Irish Fusiliers* Vol. XXXVII No. 161 (London. July 1946). By kind permission of the Regimental Museum.
3. *Ibid.*

PART FOUR – HOW WE ALMOST STUMBLED INTO WORLD WAR THREE

Chapter XIV – The Crisis Deepens

1. FO 371/48814.
2. Resident Minister to FO No. 837 9 May 1945. No dispatch time. Received FO 9.50pm.
3. FO 371/48814.
4. FO 371/48814.
5. Alexander to CIGS Ref. F.73280 at 1755 hours 10 May 45. FO 371/48814.
6. *Ibid.* FO to Belgrade No. 546 of 10 May 45. Dispatched 11.25pm.
7. FO 371/48814.
8. Alexander to CCS NAF947. Dispatched 0545 hours, 11 May 45.
9. McCreery to Alexander No. AC/173 1000 hours 11 May 45.
10. Alexander's reply to McCreery's AC/173 dispatched 18.30 hours 11 May.
11. Resident Minister to FO No. 857 of 11 May 8.35pm., and FO comments 11/12 May FO 371/48814.
12. Resident Minister to FO No. 853 of 11 May 9.00pm. FO 37/48814.
13. Resident Minister to FO No. 854 11 May 45 bears dispatch time 8.45pm, before the substantive telegram FO 371/48814.

Chapter XV – History Repeats Itself

1. Res.Min. to FO. No. 863 on 12 May 1.51 a.m. 1945. FO371/48814. PRO.
2. This telegram Res.Min. to FO. No. 867 was drafted on 11 May but not dispatched until 2.10 a.m. 12 May.
3. Alexander's message to Tito. Repeated 8 Army to 5 Corps (Keightley) No. AC/181 at 12.09 hrs. 12 May.
4. Repeated to 15 Army Group from 8 Army No. AC182 0900 hours 12 May 1945, FO. 1020/42. (Alexander's private papers). PRO.
5. Alexander's signal to Combined Chiefs of Staff, Washington, NAF980 of 11 May repeated 15 Army Group to 8 Army. Personal for McCreery from Clark. No. SGS390. 12.05 hours 12 May 1945.
6. *Ibid.*
7. *Ibid.*
8. Contained in 15 Army Group to 8 Army No. SGS390. Personal for McCreery from Clark. 12 May 12.05 hours. FO. 1020/42. PRO.
9. For full text see Appendix C.
10. FO to Washington. Truman's message to Churchill repeated to UK Delegation at San Francisco Conference. (on setting up the UN). 7.50 p.m. 12 May 1945. FO 371/48814 PRO.
11. Churchill to Truman. 12 May 1945. Churchill. *Second World War.* Vol. VI.
12. *Ibid.*
13. From Washington to FO. No. 3296 6.12 p.m. 12 May 1945. FO 371/48814. PRO.
14. Rome to FO. No. 794. 6.50 p.m. 12 May 1945. FO 371/48814. PRO.
15. Rome to FO No. 795. 7.00 p.m. 12 May 1945. FO. 371/48814. PRO.
16. Sargent to PM. No. PM/OS/45/110 13 May 1945. FO 371/48814. PRO.
17. Keightley, 5 Corps to Eighth Army. 13 May 0145 hrs. No. 394. KP 86.
18. FO 371/48814. PRO.

19. Churchill. *The Second World War*. Vol. VI. p. 485.

Chapter XVI – 'The Klagenfurt Conspiracy'

1. Nikolai Tolstoy. *The Minister and the Massacres* (Century Hutchinson. London 1986).
2. Mr. Justice Michael Davies.
3. Harold Macmillan. *War Diaries. Politics and War in the Mediterranean 1943–45*. (Macmillan. London 1984.) Entry for 12 May 1945.
4. *Ibid.*
5. *Ibid.* Entry for 13 May 1945.
6. *Ibid.* 13 May.
7. *Ibid.* 13 May.
8. Macmillan. *Op. Cit.*
9. 5 Corps to Eighth Army No. 394. 13 May 0145 hours. KP 86.
10. DISTONE was not a place in Italy but the military abbreviation for DISTRICT 1, an administrative area in Italy.
11. AFHQ No. FX75383 14 May.
12. Maj. Gen. Sir Brian Robertson, son of Field Marshal Robertson.
13. 'Russian' will have included Gen. von Pannwitz's 15 Cossacks Cavalry Corps now fleeing from Yugoslavia to the west, General Domanov's division who had been operating against the Italian Partisans in the Carnian Alps, and Georgian groups from the Caucasus nominally under Domanov. See Appendix 'F'. All of these men were under German command.

Chapter XVII – Pre-requisite for War

1. Alexander's NAF 960 is his military appreciation sent to CCS Washington.
2. PM to FM Alexander. 14 May. 1329 hours.
3. PM to Alexander. 16 May. WO 214/42 PRO. No Ref. No's. shown. except DTO 160044.
4. *Ibid.*
5. Gen. McNarney was Senior US Officer at Alexander's HQ.
6. Personal for PM, copy CIGS, from FM Alexander. 15 May. 1210. WO 214/41 PRO.
7. Eden telegram from the US is repeated in this one which goes to Alexander for info. 16 May. 0102 hours. WO 214/41 PRO.
8. Andrew Gibson-Watt. *An Undistinguished Life* (The Book Guild. Lewes 1990).

Chapter XVIII – On the Brink

1. Churchill. *The Second World War*. Vol VI.
2. McCreery from Keightley. No. 0.410 on 14 May 0015 hrs.
3. *Ibid.*
4. Clark from McCreery. AC/190 14 May 1450 hrs.
5. Key Papers (KP) from *The Repatriation from Austria in 1945. The Report of an Enquiry by Brig. Anthony Cowgill* (Sinclair Stevenson. London 1990).
6. *Ibid.* KP 88. Institute of Military History, Belgrade.
7. *Ibid.* KP 89. Institute of Military History, Belgrade.
8. *Ibid.* KP 117. Institute of Military History (III Army Files).

9. *Ibid.* KP 118. AFHQ to MACMIS No. FX75902, 15 Army Group to Eighth Army. 15 May 1611 hrs. USNA (Kirk Papers). PRO FO 371/48816.
10. From Italian Ministry of Foreign Affairs to Ambassador London (translation). 15 May 1945. FO 371/48818.
11. War Cabinet Chiefs of Staff Committee Meeting to be held on 16 May 45. WO106/4054.

Chapter XIX – 'I Must Clear the Decks'

1. To Main 8 Army from Main 5 Corps, Info. AFHQ No. 4581. 16 May 0225 hrs. WO 170/4184 PRO.
2. *Ibid.*
3. For events at Bleiburg see Chapter XXII.
4. Signal to AFHQ. copy to Main 8 Army from Main 5 Corps. 16 May 1300 hrs. WO 170/4184 PRO.
5. To Alexander from Morgan at 5 Corps. 16 May 1215 hrs. WO 170/4184 PRO.
6. Alexander to Churchill No. MA 1099 of 16 May 1115 hrs.
7. Alexander to PM. No. MA 1100 on 16 May 1430 hrs.
8. Alexander to PM. No. MA 1102 on 16 May 1750 hrs.
9. WO 241/41 PRO.
10. Special un-numbered telegram to Alexander from PM. 17 May. WO 214/41 PRO.
11. Special un-numbered telegram to Alexander from PM. 17 May. 0202 hrs (referred to as No. 170202). WO 214/41 PRO.
12. Alexander sent CIGS Brooke a signal on 18 May at 1650 hrs. say that he would be ready to eject the Yugoslavs about 1 June. He would prefer not to take action before then, which gave him just under 2 weeks to clear the decks. Cowgill Key Papers No. 155. WO 106/4059.
13. Alexander to Eisenhower (SHAEF Forward) NAF 974. 17 May 1159 hrs. FO 371/48918 PRO.
14. Kirk AFHQ to Washington. 14 May 2300. KP 107. USNA Diplomatic State Dept. 740.00119 Control (Italy) 5-1445.
15. Washington to Kirk AFHQ. 15 May. KP 125. USNA Diplomatic State Dept. 740.00119 Control (Italy) 5-1445.
16. To Main 8 Army TAC 8 Army from 13 Corps No. 4994. 17 May 1600 hrs. WO 170/4184 PRO.
17. Alexander to COS NAF 975/FX77292. 17 May 1743 hrs. KP 155. WO 106/4059 PRO.

Chapter XX – The Turning Point

1. Extract from a letter to Sir James Grigg, Minister for War from Harold Macmillan. 18 May 1945. WO170/4184 PRO.
2. *Ibid.*
3. The final Peace Conference never took place.
4. A Special Message from the Supreme Allied Commander to all the ALLIED armed forces in the MEDITERRANEAN theatre No. SGS 520. 19 May issued 11.20 hrs. WO 170/4184 PRO.
5. FO 371/48918. 17/18 May PRO.
6. *Ibid.*
7. Sir Andrew Cunningham was First Sea Lord.

8. COS (45) 132 Meeting 18 May FO 371/48918 PRO.
9. Nicholls to Mack 19 May. FO 371/46609 PRO.
10. Notes on Meeting CCL Ivanovitch-Brig ARM LOW 1900 hrs. 19 May at 5 Corps HQ.
11. Passed by AFHQ to 15 Army Group, 8 Army. No. 5860. 20 May 1351 hrs.
12. 6 Brit. Armd. Div. Adm. Instr. No. 25. 19 May. WO 170/4338 PRO.
13. Mil. Gov. to 8 Army, AFHQ. No. M1015. 17 May. KP 130. Institute of Military History, Belgrade (III Army Papers).
14. AFHQ to Mil. Gov. Info. 8 Army. 18 May 1246 hrs. KP 151. FO 371.48819.
15. These orders were amongst the 'missing documents' discovered by Anthony Cowgill and his team at the Military Field Branch of the U.S. National Archives, Washington. Cowgill Interim Report Sept. 1988.
16. Another group, the Ukrainian Division, largely made up of Poles from the pre 1939 boundaries of Poland, was also exempt under the Yalta agreement, and had already been evacuated to Italy. (See Chapter XXIX.)
17. For an historical summary of these groups see Appendix E.
18. Cowgill Interim Report.

Chapter XXI – The Climb Down

1. COS (45) 133 Meeting 22 May FO 371/48818 PRO.
2. For Alexander's plan see signal Alexander to CCS FX 76415 (NAF 972) of 16 May 1415 hrs. Cowgill Key Papers 25.10.89 KP 138. FO 371/48816.
3. *Ibid.* KP 104 FX 75436 14 May 1917 hrs. USNA (Kirk Papers) (711/4 Axis PW (0); WO 170/4183 PRO.
4. *Ibid.* KP 146. WO 106/4059.
5. *Ibid.* KP 156. USNA (Kirk Papers).
6. *Ibid.* KP 130. Institute of Military History, Belgrade (III Army).
7. *Ibid.* KP 199. (By this time agreement had been reached with the Yugoslavs to withdraw their forces the following day.) FO 371/48817.
8. *Ibid.* KP 213. USNA (Kirk Papers).
9. *Ibid.* KP 218. Controversy has since raged round this 'missing' letter of 6 Mar 1945, a corruption or typing error showed this date as 6 May. In consequence the signal could not be found in the records. It was believed by those suspecting an official 'cover-up', to prove that there was no official AFHQ sanction for the repatriation policy. The correct signal of 6 March was found by the Cowgill team in United States archives.
10. Alexander would have known that Eisenhower was heavily committed at that time with the arbitrary French occupation of the Val d'Aosta in NW Italy.
11. *Loq. Sit.* KP 23. The reader will have realised that there is an anomaly between those instructions and the ones which Alexander now issues, in that he does not now intend to use force. This may be in deference to American susceptibilities as they have not yet decided whether force should or should not be used. But clearly it is going to prove quite impossible to repatriate unwilling people without the use of force or threat of force, unless deception is to be resorted to. USNA (Kirk Papers).
12. Nicholls to Mack 21 May 1945. FO 371/46609 PRO.
13. *Ibid.*
14. Admiral Darlan, former French Vice President and Foreign Minister in the Pétain Government. Defected to the Allies in N Africa in 1942. This upset British-American relations with De Gaulle, on which Macmillan as Minister Resident at Eisenhower's Mediterranean HQ, had to mediate.

PART FIVE – WAR AVERTED – BUT A PRICE TO PAY

Chapter XXII – Balkan Backlash

1. 'An Appreciation of the Situation in Yugoslavia' by Brig. F. Maclean (Commanding British Military Mission to Yugoslavia). Feb. 1945. WO 214/41/PRO
2. *Ibid.*
3. Extract from a letter from CIGS Brooke. 11 Jan. 1945. WO 214/41 PRO.
4. Personal for CIGS from F M Alexander No. MA1073. 25 Feb. 1945. WO 214/41 PRO.
5. Jackson. Pt. IV. Vol. I. quoting Ehrman. For an authentic account of how this problem was solved see the official History, *British Intelligence in the Second World War. Its Influence on Strategy and Operations Vol. III Part 1* by Prof. Hinsley. (HMSO 1984). But also note Michael Lees's, *The Rape of Serbia – the British Role in Tito's Grab for Power* (Harcourt Brace. New York 1990). Lees was a BLO with Mihailovic's nationalists (the Yugoslav Army for Home Defence or Chetniks), and maintains that the switch of British support from Mihailovic to Tito was engendered by the skilful manipulation of left-wing sympathisers at SOE(MO4) HQ in Cairo which controlled the Yugoslav operation and through which all information on Yugoslavia was filtered; and that Churchill was mislead, by a disinformation campaign alleging Mihailovic's collaboration with the enemy. Pretty substantial evidence to support this view has also been compiled by the author David Martin (who served as Executive Secretary of the Committee for a Fair Trial of Draja Mihailovic (1959–70). His book *Patriot or Traitor: The Case of General Mihailovic* (Stanford, California, Hoover Institute Press 1978) deploys the case. A shorter version of Martin's arguments are given in *Deception Operations – Studies in the East-West Context*. Edited by David A Charters and Maurice A J Tugwell (Brassey's (UK). London 1990). (See Martin's monograph entitled 'James Klugman, SOE Cairo, and the Mihailovic Deception.) The real balance of argument may never be known, but it is not the purpose of this book to explore further these intriguing possibilities, for we are concerned solely with the effects of the decisions taken and the actions which followed. The result was that all British aid (including BLO's) was withdrawn from Mihailovic in December 1943. Later his followers were classed as 'Yugoslav dissidents' in Allied phraseology; soon to be treated as 'surrendered enemy personnel' on account of their collaboration with the Italians and Germans against Tito; they were returned to our 'ally' Tito as soon as the fighting had ceased. In considering these matters one must remember that the British officers concerned (BLOs) were fighting on opposite sides in a particularly vicious and bloody civil war in Yugoslavia, and this must colour indelibly the views of the survivors. The most recent outbreak of violence between Serb and Croat can be traced directly to the events in Croatia during 1941, where the Serbian minority was subject to the most brutal genocide at the hands of the Croatian Ustachi (ustasa), the equivalent of the German SS. According to Serbian sources, several hundred thousand members of the Serbian minority in Croatia were murdered. The policy of the Nazi puppet state of Catholic Croatia at the time was to rid themselves of the Orthodox Serbs by converting a third, by transporting a third and by liquidating a third (Michael Lees, *Rape of Yugoslavia*). During the Second World War, of a population of eleven million, one and three-quarter million went missing, of whom three-quarters of a million were taken away by Germany as slave labour. On 9 October 1934, Serbian King Alexander was assassinated in Marseilles by the Ustachi. All of this goes some way in explaining the outbreak of civil war in 1991.

6. Paper given by Fitzroy Maclean at a conference on British Policy towards war-time Resistance in Yugoslavia and Greece. Published by Macmillan, in association with the School of Slavonic and East European Studies, University of London. Edited by Phillis Auty and Richard Clogg.
7. Churchill to his Chiefs of Staff. 25 June 1944.
8. *Loq. Stat.*
9. 5 Corps signal No. 0.462 to Divs. 17 May 1250 hrs. WO 170/4241 PRO.
10. *Illustrated History of the Second World War* (Readers Digest. London 1989).
11. Fitzroy Maclean in *Eastern Approaches* (Jonathan Cape. London 1951) described the view at the time:
    'Pavelic's [Croatia's German-appointed puppet leader] accession to power had been followed by a reign of terror unprecedented even in the Balkans. He had a lot of old scores to settle. There were widespread massacres and atrocities; Serbs, first of all, especially in Bosnia where there was a large Serb population; then to please his Nazi masters, Jews; and finally where he could catch them, Communists and Communist sympathisers'.
    And he tells us, racial and political persecution was accompanied by equally ferocious religious persecution. The Ustase [Pavelic's version of the SS] were fervent Roman Catholics and they set about liquidating the Greek Orthodox Church in their domains.
12. 5 Corps to AFHQ 16 May 0200 hrs.
13. Verney Papers.
14. Cowgill. *The Repatriations from Austria 1945* (Sinclair Stevenson. London 1990). Brigadier Tony Cowgill has visited Yugoslavia and carried out fresh research on the question of the 'massacres'. He has concluded that no massacre took place at Bleiburg. He was accompanied not only by Dr. Ariprand Thurn-Valsassina, the owner of Bleiburg castle, but by Mr Robert Plan (known as 'Bob Perry'), formerly of the American OSS, both of whom were present at the meeting between Brigadier Scott and the two emissaries. Dr Archie Thurn has subsequently confirmed that this is the correct account.
15. Report on the 38 (Irish) Infantry Brigade (1 May to end July 1945). Written by Brigadier T P D Scott and published in *The Faugh-a-Ballach*. The Regimental Gazette of the Royal Irish Fusileers (London) Vol. XXXVII No. 161 July 1946. By kind permission of the Regimental Museum.
16. *Ibid.*

Chapter XXIII – The Missing Signal

1. Dr M Krek to FM Alexander. 7 June 1945. *Loq Sit* KP 291. USNA (Kirk Papers).
2. *Ibid.* KP 301. Col. Christenberry 'AG' (Adjutant General's Branch) AFHQ, to Eighth Army No. 197CEC-O. 15 June. USNA (Kirk Papers); WO 204/36898A PRO.
3. *Ibid.* KP 311. 17 July. AFHQ G-1 (Prv) to G3, and British Resmin. Internal AFHQ Memo. USNA (Kirk Papers).
4. FO Minute No. R11649/1728/92. 10 June–10 July 1945. FO 371/48919 PRO.
5. JR ('Jock') Colville had been Churchill's Private Secretary for the duration of the war, except for a short spell on flying duties with the RAF.
6. Colville. *The Fringes of Power. The Downing Street Diaries 1939–1955* (Hodder and Stoughton. London 1985).
7. 'The Prof'. Professor Frederick Lindemann, later Viscount Cherwell, Advisor to Churchill on all scientific and technical matters. For pen portrait see *Fringes of Power* p. 736.

8. *The Minister and the Massacres.* Tolstoy. *Op. Cit.*
9. *Loq Sit.* KP 154. USNA (Kirk Papers).
10. Aldington *v* Tolstoy and Watts.

Chapter XXIV – Message from Stalin

1. This message (Stalin to Truman) is contained in a report from FO to Moscow No. 2783. 23 May. 12 midnight. FO 371/48818 PRO.
2. *Ibid.*
3. COS (45) 138th. Meeting of 29 May. FO 371/48918 PRO.
4. Contained in telegram from Eden to Stevenson (Belgrade) 26 May 1945. FO 371/48818 PRO.
5. PM to FM Alexander. Special unnumbered signal. 30 May. 2127/29/10128/0315/ 30. WO 214/41 PRO. Churchill had already told Alexander in a telegram sent on 26 May (KP 222), that he expected him to move forward in full strength on 1 June 'to the limits that have been decided'.
6. *Ibid.*
7. *Ibid.*

Chapter XXV – Operation of War

1. 36 Inf. Bde. Order 'Caucasians & Cossack Personnel'. No 129/9. WO 170/4461 PRO.
2. 36 Inf. Bde. Order No 129/9. 26 May. WO 170/4461 PRO.
3. Report. 'Evacuation of Cossacks and Caucasian Forces from 36 Inf. Bde area May–June 1945' dated 3 July 1945 in response to 5 Corps call for a detailed report. WO 170/4461 PRO.
4. *Ibid.*
5. *Ibid.*
6. WO 170/4404.
7. Conversation with Anthony Cowgill, 13 March 1991. For some reason, General von Pannwitz's execution was not mentioned in the *Pravda* report.
8. 36 Inf. Bde. War Diary. WO 170/4461 PRO. (The Appendices are not included).
9. 3rd Battalion Welsh Guards War Diary WO 170/4982 PRO.
10. 5 Corps War Diary WO 170/4241 PRO.
11. The story is not complete without recording an unexpected aspect of the repatriations. Not all Cossacks were unwilling to go home. The author of this story is Lady Williams (née Masha Poustchine). Her family had fled to England following the Revolution. In 1945 she was working as Russian Interpreter to the four-power Allied Commission for Austria in Vienna. She told me, 'I had an appendix out in Rome in a hospital – some wives of Cossacks were recovering from an American bombing of their train. They [their menfolk] had fought with the Germans in Vlassov's army. A Uniate priest from the Vatican said he would take care of them and their husbands.' He tried to persuade them to stay and not go home, saying, 'Why you yourselves say that you've been fighting for the Germans, and will be punished. Why do you want go home? At the risk of being killed?' They replied that they wanted to go home, 'We don't know the language. We don't know the people. We can't get on with them. We've had enough. We want to go home.' Then their husbands, two officers and some men, arrived. The Cossack officers said to their men, 'If you go back, of course you'll be shot'. And do you know, said Masha Williams, 'these men chose to go back. It was incredible. I couldn't believe it. They just said they wanted

to go back to their own people. They all went back. But you cannot fight against your own people and survive.'

Chapter XXVI – Alexander Visits 5 Corps

1. LO Report on visit to 5 Corps 7–8 June. FO 1020/39 PRO.
2. 36 Inf Bde Sitreps 1–7 June. WO 170/4461 PRO.
3. Lt. Col. Colin Mitchell's letter to the author. 7 Feb 1989. 8 Argyll's Intelligence Officer at the time. Member of Parliament 1970–74.
4. W S Churchill. *The Second World War* Vol. VI. Appendix C (Cassell. London 1954).
5. F S V Donnison. *History of the Second World War. Op. Cit.* p. 289.
6. Extract from an account written by Brigadier Scott of 38 (Irish) Brigade.
7. *Ibid.*

PART SIX – THE AFTERMATH

Chapter XXVII – Summer Solstice

1. John Colville. *The Fringes of Power* (Hodder and Stoughton. London 1985).
2. *Ibid.*
3. Army Bureau of Current Affairs. ABCA.
4. FO 371/4409 PRO.
5. Statement by Eighth Army 22 July 1945. FO 1020/39 PRO.
6. SHAEF G-5 Division Meeting held on DP's 2 July 1945. WO 204/3464 PRO.
7. Notes on a visit to Carinthia July 6–8 by W H B Mack. FO 371/46609 PRO. '*Herrenvolk*' German term for 'gentlemen'.
8. Eighth Army to 5 Corps. Evacuation of Yugoslav EX PW from SHAEF. 26 May 1945. FO 1020/2838 PRO.
9. Eighth Army to 5 Corps. 13 June. No. 90. FO 1020/2838 PRO.
10. *Ibid.*
11. Lt.Col. Colin Mitchell was a very young officer at the time and has a clear memory of these happenings.
12. *Ibid.* Letter to the author 21 March 1989.
13. The meeting was between Lady Falmouth and Lt.Gen. Sir Charles Keightley, but the report comes from Lady Limerick, representing the International Red Cross in Geneva, who was probably also present.
14. DP status was granted following a detailed screening, to weed out war criminals and other undesirables. Once DP status was obtained they were eligible to apply for emigration to other countries willing to accept them. Although these people were generally referred to as Displaced Persons, very few at this stage would have been through the screening process, which was a lengthy one. This did not apply to those governed by the Yalta Agreement.

Chapter XXVIII – Winter of Discontent

1. The Foreign Office (T Brimelow) to the War Office (Lt. Col. V M Hammer of Displaced Persons Dept). N 16720/409/38. 6 December 1945. FO 371/47910 PRO.
2. From Vienna to FO No. 234 dated 13 December 1945 referring to telegram 409. FO 1020/2843 PRO.

3. BERCOMB (Berlin Comd) to TROOPERS (War Office). Date not readable. FO 371/47910 PRO.
4. FO (Signed T Brimelow) to WO (Lt. Col. Hammer) N 16842/409/38 dated 11 December 1945. FO 371/47910 PRO.
5. Vienna (Mr Mack) to FO. No. 246. 16 December 1945. FO 371/47910 PRO.
6. ACABRIT (McCreery to WO). No. 10146. 16 December 1945. FO 371/47910 PRO.
7. FO (T Brimelow) to WO (Lt. Col. Hammer). No. N 17094/409/38 FO 371.47910 PRO.
8. *Ibid.*
9. J S M Washington to Cabinet Offices. DON 101. 23 December 1945. FO 371/47910 PRO.

Chapter XXIX – Repatriation in Reverse

1. 'Undesirables' whom it is claimed the Russians and their collaborators liquidated, comprised the community/political leaders of the country and the educated classes generally, including such personalities as the Chief Scout of Latvia. The Germans, during their re-occupation, unearthed mass graves and exhumed the bodies many of whom were still recognisable. This was their excuse for the extermination programme for the Latvian Jews, who had become commissars or other officials under the Russians. They were of course marked men.
2. It has been alleged in some quarters that those figures are unreliable as they stem from a 'collaborationist' organisation, the Latvian Red Cross.
3. These figures are given in the Hetherington Report HMSO (CM744). 16 June 1989.
4. War Crimes. A report by Thomas Hetherington KCB, CBE, TD, QC, and William Chalmers CB MC. HMSO (CM 744). 1989. This report originated from an approach by the Simon Wiesenthal Centre in Los Angeles to the Prime Minister on 22 October 1986 concerning 17 alleged war criminals said to be living in Britain. It was presented to Parliament in July 1989.
5. Conversation between the author and Sir Fitzroy Maclean. 26 October 1990.
6. Minute on Cabinet Conclusions paper dated 22 January 1947. FO 371/66709 PRO.
7. Rome to FO No. 373. 12 February 1947. FO 371/66604 PRO.
8. Rome to Foreign Office 22 February 1947. FO 371/66604 PRO.
9. FO 371/66605 PRO.
10. Rendel 27 February 1947. FO 371/66605 PRO.
11. Rome to FO 7 March 1947. FO 371/66605 PRO.
12. A W K Wilkinson minute WR 612.
13. Wilkinson minute 11 March. FO 371/66605.
14. Carew Robinson. 14 April 1947, FO 371/66711 PRO.
15. Hector McNeil to PM. 19 March 1947. FO 371/66709 PRO.
16. Minute from C J Edmonds, Head of Refugee Department. 2 April 1947. FO 571/66710 PRO.
17. Chairman. The Rt. Hon. Merlyn Rees, PC MP. November 1988.
18. It was indeed 'a time-bomb' with a very long fuse. For, 44 years later, the House of Commons took unprecedented powers to legislate retrospectively for 'war-crimes'. It had become evident that certain war criminals were still at large in Britain.

The War Crimes Bill was much criticised in that it legislated for acts committed outside the jurisdiction of the United Kingdom and retrospectively at that. This led to a clash between the two houses of Parliament, the Lords rejecting the bill on two occasions, and the Commons giving it overwhelming support. It was only resolved by the Government bringing in the little used Parliament Act, which over-ruled the Upper Chamber. The War Crimes Act received the Royal Assent in May 1991. The verdict of Parliament was quite clear in condemning the admittance of suspected war criminals into this country.

Chapter XXX – How it all Began

1. War Cabinet Meeting 91/44. 17 July 1944. CAB 65/43 PRO.
2. Caserta to FO No. 39. 27 July 1944. WO 32/11137 PRO.
3. FO 371/40441. 26 July 1944 PRO.
4. Sir Frederick Bovenschen to Sir Orme Sargent. 1 Aug 1944. WO 32/11137 PRO.
5. *Ibid.* Sargent, then a Deputy Under-Secretary at the Foreign Office, was to become Permanent Under-Secretary in 1946.
6. Prime Minister from Anthony Eden. No. PM 44/566. 2 Aug 1944. WO 32/11137 PRO.
7. *Ibid.*
8. Appendix G. Grigg to Eden. 24 August 1944.
9. War Cabinet 115/44/ 4 September 1944. FO 371/40448 PRO.
10. Res. Min. Caserta to FO. No. 345. 19 September 1944. WO 32/11137 PRO.
11. FO to Res. Min. Caserta. 0/7482/93G. 27 September 1944 as drafted for approval by the WO WO32.11137 PRO.

Epilogue

1. Brigadier M C Thursby-Pelham, former Captain 3 Welsh Guards.
2. T J Chamberlain of Udine University.
3. Claudio Magris. *Illazione su una Sciabola. Rivisita Milanes di economia. Cass De Risparmio Dolle Province Lombardo 1986.* (English translation. Polygen Edinburgh 1990).
4. This account comes to me from Osoppo records, through the good offices of ex-Partisan leader, Dotoressa Paula del Din Carnielli. Her brother, Renato Del Din, was awarded a posthumous *Medaglia d'Oro* for bravery in an attack on the German Barracks at Tolmezzo.

Appendix E – Historical Note on the Cossacks

1. Peter Hopkirk. *The Great Game. On Secret Service in High Asia* (John Murray. London 1990).
2. Philip Longworth. *The Cossacks* (Constable. London 1969).
3. Source. Longworth. *Op. Cit.*
4. Longworth. *Op. Cit.*
5. Lady Williams, née Masha Poustchine. Her father was a member of the Duma at the time of the Revolution. He was also a gentleman-in-waiting to Nicholas II. On hearing that there were no volunteers to accompany the Emperor and family into exile in Siberia, he himself immediately volunteered. The Emperor replied 'I am sorry, but no. You have a wife and five children. I only take bachelors'. Another famous ancestor was Jeannot Poustchine, one of the Decembrist plotters. A great friend but no relation to Pushkin.
6. St. Petersburg's name was changed to Petrograd in 1914 for patriotic reasons as it sounded more Russian.

7. Robert Massie. *Nicholas and Alexandra* (Victor Gollancz. London 1968). As told by Robert Massie quoting Paléologue.
8. *Ibid.*
9. Longworth. *Op. Cit.* Quoting Chamberlain Vol. II. Podtelhov's two deputies along with himself were actually hanged, making a total of 76.
10. Longworth. *Ibid.* Quoting Krasnov, '*Vsev. Voi. Don*' p. 226.
11. Hassan Arfa. *Under Five Shahs* (John Murray. London 1964). Hassan Arfa was half Russian, his mother being from the Demidoff family, from the Urals. His father, Prince Mirza Reza Khan Arfa, was one time Iranian Minister at St. Petersburg. General Hassan Arfa (the son) married an English ballet dancer, Hilda Bewicke (a cousin of my wife's). It was a romantic story, how Hassan, as a young officer, conceived an attachment for this English ballerina touring with the Diaghilef Russian Ballet, and followed her half round Europe.
12. Hassan Arfa. *Ibid.*
13. Hassan Arfa. *Ibid.*
14. *Ibid.* The other foreign-officered part of the army was the South Persia Rifles, all of whose officers were British.
15. Research by Patrick Martin-Smith.
16. *Ibid.*
17. Source for the above paragraph – P H Buss *Hitler's Germanic Legions* (Macdonald and James. London 1978).
18. Longworth. *Ibid.* Quoting Alexander Dallin, *German Rule in Russia 1941–45* (Macmillan 1957).
19. *Bundersarchiv Freibourg*, and Berlin Document Centre (US).
20. Patrick Martin-Smith.
21. *Ibid.*
22. Philip Longworth. *The Cossacks.* (1969). *Op.Cit.*

Index

ADC xi
Addis, Mr S M 127
Africa 199
Agents provocateurs xxvi
Air Force
 Desert 99
 RAF 55, 150
 US 150
 US Twelfth 46
 Yugoslav 117
Air Ministry 137
Alamein, Battle of xi
Alanbrooke, Field Marshal Lord (*see
 also* Brooke) 51
Aldington, Lord (*see also* Low,
 Brigadier Toby) 80, 104
Alesso 204
Alesso, Enrico 59
Alexander II, Emperor (1855–81) xxv,
 xxvi
Alexandra, Empress (wife of Nicholas
 II, 1894–1917) 229
Alexander, Field Marshal Viscount
 as Supreme Allied Commander
 Mediterranean 43
 his responsibilities 43
 his strategic goal 45
 restrictions on 45
 withdrawal of divisions from 46
 his role at the Crimea Conference 47
 Brooke scorns his methods 48
 starts talk with Tito 50
 visits Marshal Tolbukhin 50
 Brooke's views on 51, 52
 and Italian Partisans 53
 his lifeline 66
 and Tito crossing into Italy 66
 his telegrams on Tito crisis 91–6

plans to eject Tito 91
 American backing 92
 rebuff from Tito 93
 Churchill's warning 93
 failure of Morgan's mission to
 Tito 94
Alexander assesses the prospects 94
 and Tito's incursions into Austria 95
 sends Macmillan to brief the
 generals 98
 his military requirements, his
 ultimatum to Tito 99
 questions morale of troops 99
 considers his resources 99–101
 his doubts brushed aside by
 Churchill 101
 and Macmillan's visit to the
 Generals 104, 105
 and the Robertson telegram 108
 his doubts about morale, Churchill's
 scathing riposte 109–11
 the role of Russia 115
 agrees repatriation of Croats to
 Tito 115, 116
 compares forces available 116, 117
 prepares to 'clear the decks' 118
 strives to free L of C 121, 122
 dispute with Washington 122
 disposal of enemy personnel 123,
 124, 127
 relations with Macmillan 126
 his 'order of the day' 126
 seeks Eisenhower's aid 133, 134
 his reactions to Yugoslav
 'massacres' 152
 final approval for repatriations 154
 and Churchill on Pola 160
 and repatriation of Cossacks 166

Alexander, Field Marshal Viscount
—(*contd.*)
  his visit to 5 Corps   167, 168, 171
  his knowledge of events   170
Alexander, King of Yugoslavia   235
Algiers   51
Allied Commission in Vienna   177
Allied Forces Headquarters
  (AFHQ)   36, 115, 129, 130, 133,
  134, 152, 154, 166, 168, 177
Allied Military Government/(AMG)
  61, 68, 79, 94, 179
Alps
  Carinthian   78
  Carnic   204
  Dolomite   202
  Gross Glöckner   78
  Hohe Tauern   78
  Karawanken Range   49, 146
Altai Mountains   228
America/USA   x, xi, 238
Amery, The Rt. Hon. Leo   19
Ampezzo   202
Amsterdam   6
Amur, River   228
Anders, General   131, 136
Annenkov   231
Anschluss   33
Anti-Titoists   239–43
Antwerp   xii
Anzio   45
Appenines   45, 46
Arbuthnott, Major General   164, 167,
  171
Archbishop of Gorizia   67
Ardennes   xi, xii, 46, 47
Arfa, General Hassan   232, 233
Argentine brides   31
Argonaut Conference   47
Argyll and Sutherland Highlanders (A &
  SH) (*see* Regiments)
Armenia   xxvi, 233
Army
  American   xii
  American Fifth   43, 44
  Azerbaijani Republic   233
  British Eighth   43, 44, 50, 118, 121,
  129, 130, 134, 145, 146, 152, 155,
  156, 167, 178, 179, 180, 201
  Bulgarian   84, 85, 86, 87, 88, 106
  Croatian   149
  German Twenty-Fifth   7
  Hungarian   75, 84

  Imperial Tsarist   51, 131
  Iranian   234
  Red (Soviet)   10, 162, 232, 238
  Russian Liberation   70
  First US   xii
  Third US   133
  Ninth US   15
  White (Russian)   203, 232, 235
  Yugoslav   123, 149
  Yugoslav First   145
  Yugoslav Third   128
  Yugoslav Fourth   50, 51, 67, 118
Arnhem   5
Arnoldstein   75
Arta   71
Artegna   58
Arvenis, Mount   210
Asia   227
Astrakhan   227
Ataman   234
Athens   43
Atlantic   10
Attimis Resistance Group   208
Attlee, Clement   154, 175, 189
Aurich   31
Auschwitz   31
Australia   199
Austria(ns)   ix, x, xi, 21, 33, 34, 37, 43,
  49, 72, 78–82, 106, 116, 121, 122,
  124, 125, 128, 129, 130, 132, 144,
  157, 162, 166, 167, 171, 176, 182,
  195, 202
  Lower   3
  Southern   116, 127, 133, 158
  Upper   177
Austrian military personnel   122
Austro-Hungary   141
Austro–Yugoslav border   114, 134, 146
Axis   144
Azerbaijan(is)   3, 71, 131, 233

Bailey, Brigadier   81
Baku   232
Balkans   43, 44, 49, 141, 145, 159
Balkhash, Lake   228
Balsan, Louis   74
Baltic campaign   53, 203
Baltic States   16, 22, 189, 190
Balts   189, 191
Barber, Flight Lieutenant (later The Rt.
  Hon. Lord Barber of
  Wentbridge)   13

Bari xi
Barker, Lieutenant General Sir
  Evelyn 24, 26, 27
Barrier zones 15
Barth, *Stalag Luft-I* 12
Batum 232
Bavaria 12
Bayeaux xii
Beckett, Manfred (Czernin) 209
Belgium 4, 17, 30, 191
Belgrade 91–5, 142, 175, 240
Belgrade Agreement 66
Belsen 7, 19, 25, 27
Benson, 'Con' 105
Berlin 5, 10, 25, 70, 162, 183, 234
Berne 30
Bevin, Ernest 182, 183, 190
Bigland, Colonel Tom xii
Bixio 62
Blackmarket 123
Blackpool 26
Blaskewitz, Colonel General 8
Bled 240
Bleiburg 118, 141, 146, 147, 148, 149,
  151, 168
Bohemia 29
Bolla 209
Bolsena, Lake 50
Bolshevism(ists) 149, 168, 230, 231,
  232, 234
Bosnia 141, 240
Boulogne 12
Bovenschen, Sir Frederick 196
Bowen-Colthurst, Paddy 171
Bracken, Brendan 120
Bradley, General, (US Army) xii
Brandenburger Regiment (*see* War
  Crimes – Special Category) 131
Brasichia, General 178
Braulins 204
Brazil 232
Brigade
  1 Guards 73, 146, 164, 167, 168
  36 Infantry 69, 78–82, 161, 162, 164,
    165, 169
  38 (Irish) Infantry 83–6, 146, 147,
    167, 171
  6 Osoppo 209
Brimelow, Thomas (Sir Thomas, later
  Lord) 186
British Control Commission for
  Germany 20
British Empire 32

Brooke, CIGS, General Sir Alan (*see
  also* Alanbrooke) 44, 48, 51, 52,
  93, 120, 142, 159
Bruck 38
Brussels xii
Buja (Buia) 55, 58, 59, 61
Bulgaria(ns) 38, 43, 75, 85–7, 98, 125,
  131, 148, 232
Burgos, Captain 211
Byelorussia 189, 190, 236

Cabinet (British) 52, 137, 158
  considers repatriation for first
    time; 195–200
Cabinet committees (British) 127, 154
  (18 May 1945), 158
Cadet School, Hungarian 87
Cairo 142, 143
Caledon Camp 105
Cambridge x
Canada 199
Cantacuzine xxvii
Caporetto 69
Carinthia ix, x, 35, 49, 50, 69, 78–82,
  91–6, 118, 119, 125, 133, 144, 153,
  158, 160, 175, 177, 241
Carnia 201, 202, 203, 205, 208, 237
Carnielli, Paola del Din 201
Casera Razzo 211
Caserta 43, 108, 136, 137, 168, 196,
  199
Cassacco 209
Cassino 45
Castiglione xii
Caucasians 3, 59, 71, 78, 131, 161–4,
  176, 227
Caucasus Mountains 71, 131, 201, 228,
  232, 233, 235
Celje 147, 175
Cergneu 209
Chamberlain, James 201
Champs de Mars 229
Charles, Sir N 101
Chequers 136, 137
Chetniks (Cetniks) (*see also*
  Partisans) 239–41
  Michailovic (Mihajlovic) 239
  FO view on disposal of 158
Chevaliers Gardes xxvii
Chialminis 209

Chiefs of Staff
 British   94, 121, 123, 127
 Combined (CCS)   44, 45, 67, 94, 99,
  100, 119, 121, 123, 133, 154, 159
 US   101
China   228
Chiussi, Giancarlo   210–12
Christian Orthodox   141
Churchill, Winston S   10, 44, 45, 47, 48,
  66, 68, 91–5, 99–103, 105, 109, 110,
  112, 119, 120, 136, 142, 143, 154,
  157, 160, 170, 171, 175, 197, 198
Circassians   226, 227
Cividale   60, 67, 69
Civil War (*see* Russian Revolution)
Clan, Bavand   233
Clark, General Mark   98, 145
Clerge, Colonel   233
Cold War   11, 37, 182, 189
Collaborators   ix
Colley, Madame   xxvi
Colosomano   59
Colville, John (later Sir John)   47, 153,
  154, 175
Combined Administration Committee
  (CADC)   127
Comeglians   211
Comintern   141
Commands
 Central Mediterranean Forces
  GHQ   184
 German Adriatic Littoral   60
 German High   12
 South East Asia, (Allied)   25
 Sudost, Ob   67
 Supreme Allied Commander,
  Mediterranean (SACMED)   43,
  46, 48, 52, 152
Commonwealth, British   44
Communism/Communist Party   107
Copenhagen   29
Corfu   10
Cormons   94
Corps   46
 1 Canadian   46
 2 Canadian   7
 2 Hungarian   87
 5 British   37, 80–2, 104, 119, 123,
  131, 133–35, 146, 152, 155, 170, 171,
  177–80
 HQ   34, 118, 128, 130, 144, 166,
  167–69
 8 British   15, 19
 District   24, 30

13 British   67, 133
13 US   178
15 Cossack Cavalry   85–7, 131, 144,
  164, 237
18 US Airborne   15, 16
97, of Army Group E (German)   67
 Croat, commander   146
 French Expeditionary   46
 German Staff   147
 Polish   131
 Russian Staff   147
 Schütz Korps   130, 131, 189
Cosacchi, I (by Petro Menis)   201, 205
Cossacks   x, xxviii, 70, 73, 75, 104, 119,
  121, 122, 124, 125, 127, 128, 158,
  161–6, 176, 180, 185, 201–12
 in Carnia   55–62
 FO view on disposal of   158
Cossack Hosts (traditional
  groups)   226–38
Cossackia   202, 237
Cossack Nationalist Party   235
Court Case (Aldington v Tolstoy)   80–
  2, 130
Coventry   11
Cowgill, Brigadier Anthony   76, 130,
  147
Cox, Sir Percy   233
Crerar, Lieutenant General (Sir)
  Henry   6
Crimea   xxv, 227
Crimea Conference (see Yalta)
Croatia/Croats   49, 75, 84, 106, 118,
  119, 121, 124, 127, 128, 141, 144–51,
  153, 158, 176, 208, 237, 240, 258,
  259
 Domobranci   129, 147, 153, 241
 FO view on disposal of   158
 Ustachi (Ustase)   106, 125, 129, 145–
  7, 169, 241
Cunningham, Admiral Sir Andrew   127
Cunningham, Lieutenant Colonel
  Bill   119
Czechoslovakia   x, 29, 232
 army commander   29

Dalmatia(ns)   50, 51, 141
Dalton, Dr H   175
Darlan, Admiral   137
d'Astiev, M   196
D-Day   xii, 45
Definition letter (Nationals)   130

Deputy Director Medical Services
(DDMS) 81
Deganutti, Prof. Lorenzina 208
De Gasperi (Italian Prime
Minister) 116
De Gaulle, General 120
Denikin, General 231, 232
Denmark 17, 29
Din, Paola del (Renata) (see
Carnielli) 61
Distone 107, 155
Distone Signal 155
Divisions
British
6 Armoured 73, 76, 80, 129, 131,
144, 164, 165
46 Infantry 37, 144, 164
56 Infantry 67
78 Infantry 144, 164, 167, 168, 177
Indian 99
South African 99
Allied
91 US 67
82 and 101 Airborne, US 5
14 Yugoslav 97, 128
Brazilian 99
Polish 99
Axis
16 SS Panzer Grenadier 55, 189
42 Jaegar 87
1 Ukranian (Waffen SS) Panzer
Grenadier Galizien, 189, 193
369 Croat 87
Laszlo Hungarian 87
Other
Iranian Cossack Division 233
Wild Divison, The 232, 233
Dodecanese 43
Doenitz (Dönitz), Admiral 67, 69
Dolfuss, Chancellor Otto 33
Dolsach 169
Domanov, Major (later General) 71–3,
162, 236
Domobranci (Croat Home
Defence) 239–241
Don, River 231
Donnison, FSV 16, 17, 171
DPs 15, 16, 25
Polish 22, 24
Drau, River (*see also* Drava) 75, 78,
114, 149, 177
Drava (*see* Drau)
Dravograd 118, 129, 146

Drummond, Sir Jack 7
Dublin 86
Dulles, Allen 51
Duma, The Russian 229, 230
Dunkirk 12
Dutov 232

EAM/ELAS 54
Eastern Front 33, 37, 44
Eboli 191
Eden, The Rt. Hon. Anthony (later
Lord Avon) 93, 111, 195, 197, 198
Edinburgh 26
Eindhoven 5
Einsatz-Gruppe 193
Eisenach 10
Eisenhower, General Dwight D xii, 5,
14, 46, 52, 119, 121–3, 127, 128, 133,
134, 171, 176, 181
Ekaterinburg 230
Elbe, River 10, 15
Emancipation of the Serfs xxv, xxvi
Ems, River 15
Enzeli 232
Erfurt 112
Estonia(ns) 189, 190
Europe x, xi, 10, 189
Central 23
Eastern 14
North West 4, 14, 46
Western 7
Ewart, Colonel Joe 11

Falmouth, Viscountess 180, 181
Fantovi (Slovene) 240
Far East 10, 14, 25, 172, 232
Fascists 107, 123, 176
Felmy, Lieutenant General 69
Ferro 59
Ferro, Livio (Barba Livio) 208–9
Finland xxvii
Fiume 49, 67
Flensburg 24
Florence 54
Floyd, General 177
Forces
Allied Expeditionary 19
Central Mediterranean 184
German 134, 239, 240
Soviet 187, 196
Tito's 133, 209

Forces—(*contd.*)
Yugoslav 153, 157
Foreign Legion, French 196, 232
Foreign Office 19, 34, 35, 91–5, 126, 127, 136, 152–4, 158, 159, 180, 182–6, 193
Departments
Northern 186
Refugee 191
Southern 127, 153
Forni 202
Forni Avoitra 70
France/French xxvii, 4, 17, 46, 79, 80, 126, 135, 145, 197, 235,
Franckenstein, Sir George 34
Franz Josef Barracks 79
Fraser, General Sir David 51
Fraternisation 28, 81
Freccia 61
Friedeburg, Admiral von 11
Friulian Plain 201, 205
Friuli 55, 60, 201
Fullj 211

Gaevernitz, Gero von 51
Gail, River 78, 177
Galitzine xxvii, 191
Galizia 232
Gemona 55, 58
Gendarmerie, Iranian Mounted 233
Geneva Convention 199
Georgia(ns) 70, 201, 227, 233
Germanic Legions 189
German(y) ix, x, xi, 17, 119, 121, 122, 125, 131, 143, 144, 161, 163, 171, 176, 182, 190, 195, 196, 198, 202, 211, 230, 234, 235, 237, 238
East 10
Economy 31
People 28
West 10, 11, 18
Gestapo 26, 36, 132, 211, 234
Giovanni, Mount (Ioanis) 60
Globocnik, *Gruppenführer* 60, 208, 236–8
Gogol 183
Golden Horde 226
Golden Star, The 203
Goltz, Graf von der 234
Gorizia 49, 67, 116, 159
Gothic Line 46

Gottburg, General Commissioner SS *Gruppenführer* 236
Government
British/HMG 136, 158, 183, 184, 191
Imperial (Russian) 47
Lublin (Pro Soviet Polish) *see* Lublin
Pavelic (Croatian) 241
Provisional (Russian) 233
Renner (Austrian) 34
Royal Dutch 5
Royal Yugoslav 129, 152
Soviet 197, 198
US 158
Graf Spee 31
Gray, Charles, QC 80
Graz 37, 115
Greece 43, 44, 46, 55
Grew, Mr 111
Grigg, Sir James 125, 198
Grönow, Captain 83
Group
British
21 Army 5–7. 15–22
Royal Artillery (AGRA); 144
Allied
15 Army 43, 52, 121, 133, 134, 145, 146, 155, 158
German
Army C 67
Army E 67, 87, 114
Army SE 83
Axis
Ataman 131
US
12 Army 133, 134
Guards
Blue 239
Garde Équipage 230
Imperial 229
Preobrajenzky 229
Serb Volunteer (*Dobrovoltsi*) 240
Slovene Home 153, 240
Slovene White (*Bela Garda*) 240, 241
Tsar's Cossack 229
Welsh, 3 Bn. 69, 76, 165
White 129, 239, 240, 241
Gulags 19
Gurk 165

Hague, The 6
Halifax, Earl 92, 101, 159

Hamburg 19, 23, 28, 30, 31
Hammer, Lieutenant Colonel V M
 186
Hampton Court xxvii
Hanbury, Lieutenant P F 12
Harding, Lieutenant General Sir John
 105, 107, 160, 164
Harriman, Mr Averell 14
Heimwehr 33
Herrenvolk 17
Herzegovina 141
Hetherington, Thomas 190
Hetherington-Chalmers Report 190
Heydrich, Reinhardt 234
Himmler, Heinrich 27, 60, 203, 234–7
Himpel, Dr 236
Hitler, Adolf 3, 4, 33, 60, 69, 75, 108,
 126, 208, 235
Hitler Youth School 171
Hocevar, Lieutenant Colonel 118
Holland (The Netherlands) 4–7, 17,
 235
Home Office 192
Hopkirk, Peter 226
Hostages, Western 11
House of Commons xiii, 190
Howard, D F 158
Hubbard, Captain Archie 53
Hungary/Hungarians 3, 75, 119, 121,
 141

Ijjssel Meer 7, 8, 15
Imponzo 202, 204
India 199, 227, 228
Innsbruck x
Interneppo 204
Iran 233, 234
 Shah of 233
Iron curtain 112
Ismay, General (Lord) 170
Isonzo, River 67, 93, 116, 119, 155
Istria 157, 239
 Peninsula 43
Italy/Italians 43, 44, 53, 78, 121–4, 130,
 131, 152, 154, 158, 160, 162, 185,
 189, 190, 192, 202, 210, 211
 North East 133
 Northern 54, 105
 North West 99
Itzerhoe 29
Ivanovitch, Colonel 128, 135

Jackson, General Sir William 46, 50
Japan 11, 47, 112, 126, 169
Jesenice 146
Jevdjevic 239
Jews 39, 189, 190
Joint Staff Mission, Washington
 (JSM) 127, 158, 187
Judenburg 133, 134, 164, 168
Judendorf 169
Jugoslavia *see* Yugoslavia

Kazan 227
Keightley, General Sir Charles (5 Corps
 Commander)
 advances into Austria 67
 halts Russians 81
 hard pressed 98
 dispute over surrendered
  Yugoslavs 102
 accusations against 104–8
 receives visit from Macmillan 106
 faces open warfare with
  Yugoslavs 113
 and refugee problem 113
 his equanimity 125
 the Distone signal 155
 and General Murray's
  objections 165
 and the conspiracy theory 170
 his skill in handling the Tito
  crisis 177
 meeting with Lady Falmouth 180,
  181
 his evacuation of Ukranian division
  and *Schütz Korps* 189
Kelitsch-Ghirei, Sultan 71, 72, 163,
 165, 237
Kenchington, Brigadier 20
Kerensky 230, 231, 233
Kesselring, Von 55, 60
Khabalov, General 229
Khan, Colonel Reza 233, 234
Khan, Gengis 226
Khanates 227
Kiel Canal 24
Kiev 228
Kirk, Alexander (Resident UK Minister
 AFHQ) 122, 123
Klagenfurt 34, 49, 74, 80, 81, 92, 97,
 98, 104–8, 116, 118, 119, 125, 126,
 128, 136, 146, 147, 167, 168
Klein St. Viet 131
Klitch, Sultan Girei (see Kelitsch-Ghirei)

Kokal, Colonel 241
Kolchak, Admiral 232
Konjice-Sotanj 115
Kononov 235
Krasnov, General Peter N 162, 165, 203, 231, 234–8
Krasnov, S N 165
Krek, Dr. Mika 152, 153
Kren, Colonel 241
Krushchev 165
Kuban 231, 235
Kulakov, Colonel 236

Labour, Government/Party 25, 187
Lancashire Fusiliers *see* Regiments
Lancers, 27 *see* Regiments
Latvia(ns) 79, 189, 190
Lavamund 84, 86, 148
Lavant-Leinz 169
Lavenberg 29
League of Nations 102
Lebetka 228
Lecky, Rupert 149
Lee, Peter 201
Lees, Michael 250, 258
Leibnitz 115
Leinz 36, 79, 80, 133, 134, 163, 177
Leipzig 112
  Agreement 16
Lemnos 232
Lenin 230
Leningrad 37
Levantines 25
Liaison Officers xi, xii, 5, 19, 23, 168, 169
  American (ALO's Special Forces) 54
  British (BLO's Special Forces) 54, 60, 210, 211
Liege xii
Lindemann, Professor Frederick ('The Prof') 154
Lithuania 189, 190
Livadia 48
Livio, Barba (Livio Ferro) 208, 209
Ljotic 240
Ljubljana Gap 44, 49
Lloyd, Major Guy 153
Löhr, General (Loehr) 67, 69, 114
Löibl Pass 49, 74
London 4, 26, 34, 136, 159, 180, 240
Long, Colonel Walton 131

Longworth, Philip 228, 238
Low, Brigadier Toby *see also*
  Aldington 118, 128, 130, 135, 136, 144, 155
Lübbecke 20
Lübeck 10, 24, 26, 29
Lublin 26, 29, 47
Lückenwalde 13
Luneberg Heath 11, 67
Lunn-Rockcliffe, Paul 149
Luxembourg 17

Maas, River 5
Macedonia 141
Macek 115
Mack, W H 36, 128, 135, 136, 177, 185
Maclean, Brigadier (Sir) Fitzroy 116, 141–3, 190–2
Macmillan, The Rt. Hon. Harold (later Earl of Stockton)
  his joint communique, Brooke's disapproval 48
  caution over Italian patriots 54
  his skill as statesman 55
  comparisons with Winter War in Finland 76
  telegrams on Tito crisis 91–5
  his four alternative courses of action 95
  proposes to brief Generals McCreery and Harding 98
  envoys in favour of Macmillan's 'ultimatum' to Tito 101, 102
  and the 'Klagenfurt conspiracy' theory 104–8
  advises return of Cossacks 107
  endorses Alexander's repatriation policy 124
  he confides in War Minister Grigg 125, 126
  his close relationship with Alexander 126
  denigration of 136
  a distressing evening with General Anders 136
  summoned from Italy by PM for crisis talks 154
  leaves Italy to take up Cabinet post 136
  his earlier forecast of events 196
  and the Geneva Convention 199
Macmillan, Ernest 180

MACMIS (Maclean's Mission to
    Tito) 115, 155
MacPherson Mission 209
McDermott, G L 158
McNarney, General 110
McNeil, Hector 192
Madonna 59
Magris, Claudio 203
Malcolm, Alex 180
Mallnitz 178
Malta 48, 51
Maquis
    Belgian 26, 27
    French 196
Marchetti, Dr Romano 202, 203
March Uprising 229
Maria Elend 146, 147, 168, 169
Martin-Smith, Patrick 60, 62
Mather, William xxv, xxvi
Mauthen 49, 71, 78, 79
McCreery, General (Sir Richard) 50,
    94, 95, 105, 107, 130, 145, 160, 167,
    171, 179, 185, 186
Mecklenburg 16, 23, 24
Mediterranean Theatre 55
Melikoff, Loris xxvi
Mels 61
Menis, Pietro 55
Mennell, Major 76, 77
Michailovic, General Draza 44, 142,
    143, 239, 258
Middle East 195–7, 199
Military
    Academy, The Frunze 235
    Administration, British 176
    Government 15, 23
Mille, Cecil B de 15
Ministry of Finance, French 74
Mione 210
Mitchell, Lieutenant Colonel
    Colin 170, 180
Mohammed Reza Shah 234
Molotov-Ribbentrop Pact 189
Monfalcone 123
Mongols 55, 226, 227
Monmouthshire 16
Montenegro 141
Montgomery, Field Marshal Sir Bernard
    (later Viscount)
    his practice of command in war xi
    his use of liaison officers xi
    battle headquarters Normandy xi,
    xxviii

in the Ardennes xii
a commander and 'time to think' xii
operation 'Market Garden' 5
stage-management of the German
    surrender; 11, 12
and 'the party is over' 16
briefs the War Cabinet 21, 22
at Schloss Östenwalde 23
closes Neuengamme camp 27
and fraternisation 28
and Czechoslovakia 29
convalescent in Switzerland 30
valedictory dispatch from
    Germany 31
Brooke's opinion of
    Montgomery 51, 52
his methods compared with
    Alexander 126, 164, 168, 170
and the 'use of force' 183
Moore, Peter 143
Morale, Army 25
Morgan, General (Chief of Staff,
    Alexander) 92–4, 98, 119, 124,
    152
Morgenthau Plan 18
Morrison, The Rt. Hon. Herbert 175
Morteglinao 206, 208
Mosanghini, Sig. A 206–8
Moscow xxvi, 14, 44, 66, 95, 176, 185,
    228, 238
    Conference 183, 184, 186, 187
    Declaration 93, 118
Mosdell, Lionel (Pat) 60, 210
Moslems, Caucasian 232
Mozaffar-ed-din Shah 234
Muravieff, Count M N xxv
Murmansk 103
Murray, General Horatio 73, 164–6
Muscovites/Muscovy 122, 226
Musicki, Colonel Kosta 240
Muslim 141
Mussolini, Benito 126
Musson, Brigadier (later General Sir
    Geoffrey) 71, 77, 161, 162, 179

Nationals, Russian/Soviet 130, 131
Naumenko, General V & I G 232, 236,
    238
Nazi 4, 38, 144, 162, 171, 190, 203, 237
    Germany, disgust at 37
    Putsch 33
    Sympathisers 37

Nazification/de- 4, 37
Near East 232
Nedics 240
Netherlands *see* Holland
  East Indies 4
  Military Administration 5, 6
  Queen of the 4
Neuengamme Camp 26
New Zealand(ers) 67, 199
Nicholas II, Tsar (1894–1917) xxvi,
  xxvii, 229
Nicholls, Mr Jack 37, 38, 128, 135, 146
Nihilism xxvi
Nijmegen 5
Nimis 61
Nives Sant 59
NKVD 12
Noel-Baker, Philip 153
Normandy xi, xxviii, 195
Normandy landings 195
North Africa 192
Norway 17
Novak, Major 239
Novocherkassk 235
Nuremburg Tribunal 193

Oberdrauberg 169
Occupation, The 4, 5, 7
Odessa 106
Omsk 228
Oncedis 204, 205
Operations
  Barbarossa xxvii
  Barleycorn 26
  Beehive 113
  Dragoon (Anvil) 46
  Gelignite 44
  Market Garden 5
  Overlord 46
Oppicina 123
Orel Province 228
Osoppo *see* Partisans
Osovani Patriots *see* Partisans
OSS 44
Ost Ministry (*Ostmin*) *see also*
  Reichministerium Ost
Ottoman Empire 141
Ovaro 208, 210–12

Pacific Ocean 227
Pahlavi, Reza Shah 234

Paléologue, Maurice 230
Palestine 31
Palmer, Murphy 85, 86
Paluzza 211
Pannwitz, Colonel Helmut von (later
  General) 85, 131, 236, 237, 238
Panzers xii, 5
Parilli, Baron 51
Paris 70, 234
Paris Summit 11
Partisans
  Chetniks xi, 44, 75, 79, 106, 122,
    124, 125, 127, 129, 142, 143, 146,
    147, 152, 155, 158, 167, 169
  Garibaldi 61, 206, 209, 210
  Greek 53, 143
  Italian 53–62, 70, 162
  Osoppo 61, 62, 201, 202, 206–8, 210
  Osovani patriots 209
  Tito's 71, 79, 147, 153, 167, 235, 237
  Yugoslav 53, 116, 143, 171, 208, 240
Patton, General 13
Pavelic(h), Ante 241
Pavlov, Major Sergei 235, 236
Peace Conference 15, 154
Peacock Throne 234
Peggetz 169
Peninsula War 83
Peonis 204
Peressini, Antonia 205
Persia 228
Persian Gulf xiii
Peterlin, Colonel 241
Peter the Great 229
Petrograd 229
Pistoia 55
Plöcken Pass 72, 78
Plön 24
Po, River 49, 51, 65
Podtelkov, Red Cossack 231, 234
Pola 49, 120, 154, 159, 160
Poland/Poles 10, 14, 16, 29, 60, 120,
  131, 136, 193, 198, 208, 228, 236
Poli, Dumas 61, 62
Polish DPs 26, 29
  Pro-London 26, 29, 47
  Pro-Lublin 26, 29, 47
Poljana 148
Ponomarov 231
Porter, Lieutenant Colonel Andrew 83
Poston, Major John xi
Potsdam 31
Potsdam Conference 10

Poustchine (*see* Williams) xxvii
PoW ix, xi, 26, 121, 192
  Allied 12, 74
  Allied PoW overrun by Russians 14
  Commonwealth 14
  Release of 12–14
  Russian; 12, 15–22
PoW camps xxviii
  Barth, *Stalag Luft 1* 12
  Eichstat, *Offlag VII C* 12
  Lückenwalde, *Stalag Luft* 13
Prague 29, 235
Pravda 176
Prealp/i 201, 209
Predil Pass 49
Price, Lieutenant Colonel C R 158
Prior, Captain 211
Prof, The (see Lindemann)
PWX 15, 16, 73–7, 78–91

Qajar, Prince 232, 233
Qajar Shahs 234
Queen's Own (see Regiments)
Quislings ix, 145–7, 158

Railways, Trieste–Monfalcone 123
Rasputin 229
Rastrellamento 53–65
Ration scales 18
Red Cross
  British 18, 131, 180, 208
  Latvian 190
Regiments/Units
  British
    8 Argyll and Sutherland
      Highlanders (A & SH) 70, 169,
      170, 180
    17 Field Artillery 87, 148
    Fusiliers, Royal Irish (RIF) 83–
      86, 148
    2 Inniskillings 169
    2 Lancashire Fusiliers (LF) 169
    27 Lancers 83, 149
    London Irish 87
    Queen's Own 70
    6 Royal West Kent (RWK) 169
    3 Welsh Guards 111, 147, 165
  German
    Brandenburger 131
    Waffen SS 189, 235, 237
  Cossack Regiments 169, 234

Domanov's group 59, 71, 73, 131,
  162, 236, 237
  Including
  Circassians 227
  Caucasians 3, 59, 71, 72, 161–7,
    169, 170, 176, 227, 232, 233
  Don 71, 203, 207, 231, 232, 234,
    236
  Kuban 71, 232, 236
  Iranian Cavalry and Cossack
    (WWI) 232–4
  Red Army Stalin Bn. 71
  Terek 71, 236
  Tsarist Russia Imperial Regiments
    (WWI) 229, 230
  Chevalier Gardes xxvii
Reichministerium Ost 236
Renato/Renata 61
Rendel, Sir George 153, 191
Renner Government (Austria) 34
Repatriations 38
Resistance, Dutch 4, 5
Revolution (Russian) xxvi, xxvii, 131,
  231
Reyels, Major 129
Rheims 67
Rhine, River 5, 15
Rimini 189, 190, 191
Risiera, The 208
Robert of Austria, Archduke 35
Roberts (British Ambassador
  Moscow) 102
Robertson, Lieutenant General Sir
  Brian 108, 122
Robertson telegram 107, 144, 155
Robinson, Carew 192
Rodzianko, Paul xxvii, 250
  Speaker 229
Rogozhin, Colonel (later
  General) 131, 189
Roman Catholics 106, 240
Romanov 230
Romano, Zoffo 208
Rome 45, 54, 152, 239, 240
Roosevelt, Franklin D 48, 100
Rosenbach/Station 76, 141, 146, 147
Rosenberg 60, 236
Rose-Price, Lieutenant Colonel R
  165
Rosselli 61
Rostock 12
Rostov 228
Rotterdam 6

Roumania(ns) 43, 131
Royal Military Academy Sandhurst
   (RMAS) xxvii
Ruhr, The 5, 25, 32
Rundstedt, General Gerd von xii
Rupink (SS 'Butcher') 176
Rupnik, Colonel Leon 240
Rupnik, Captain Vuk 241
Russia(ns) x, xxv, xxvi, 3, 33, 37, 45,
   120, 127, 128, 134, 135, 159, 161,
   166, 170, 176, 179, 181, 184, 189,
   192, 193, 195, 196–9, 211, 227, 230,
   235, 237
   DP/PWX 20
   Wartime losses 48
   White xi, xxvi, xxvii, 71, 75, 96, 106,
   125, 135, 136, 166, 168, 232, 233

Saar, The 32
St. Andre (St. Andra) 75
St. Petersburg *see also* Petrograd xxv,
   228, 230
S. Floriano 58
Salamkhin 237
Salerno 45
Salisbury-Jones, Brigadier Guy (later Sir
   Guy) 176
Salzburg 177
Sandown Park xxvii
Sangro, River 45
Sant Andrat 206
Sapieha, Lieutenant Paul (Prince) 29
Sargent, Sir Orme 101, 196
SAS xi
Satrio 202
SBO 13
Scandinavia 235
Schleswig-Holstein 9, 12, 24, 25, 29
Schloss Östenwalde 23
Schuschnigg, Chancellor Otto von 33
Scott, Brigadier T P D 83–6, 91, 147–
   51, 167, 171
Screening 135, 180, 189–95
Sea
   Adriatic 43, 44, 49, 189, 201
   littoral 60, 209, 236
   Black 189
   Caspian 226–8, 232
   Mediterranean 44, 137
   North 10, 43
   of Japan 228
Secondo/dino 61, 62

Secondo Risorgimento 53
Secret Intelligence, German 132
Seeler, Oberst von 145
Selborne, Lord (later Earl) 143, 195–8
Selva Carriza 209
Serbia/Serbs 106, 141, 176, 240
   Royalist Officers 178
Seven Rivers 231
Seyss-Inqhart, Dr. Arthur, *Reich
   Kommissar* 4, 7, 33
Shakovskoi, Princess xxv
Sheremetiev, Count Nikolai xxvii
Shkouro (Shkuro), Lieutenant General
   Andrei 131, 162, 165, 231, 236,
   237
Shuter, John Stanley 80
Siberia 230, 231
Sicherheitsdienst (SD) 235
Slessor, Air Marshal 54
Slovene(ia) 50, 75, 106, 119, 121, 128,
   141, 152, 153, 167, 176, 240, 241
   Clerical Party 240
   Domobranci 240, 241
   Minority 49
Smolny Institute 231
Soca, River 159
SOE
   British Liaison Teams (BLOs) 59–62
   Cairo 142, 258
Sotanj-Slovenjgradec 115
South Africa, Union of 80, 199
Soviet
   Allies xxviii, 9
   Embassy 197
   Nationals/Citizens 19, 21, 135
   Repatriation Representatives 19, 20
   Union ix, 19, 71, 163, 165, 187, 190,
   193, 238
Spa xii
Spittal 80, 164
Sprong Commandos *see also* War
   Crimes 131
SS *see also* War Crimes 108, 193, 202,
   204, 237
   Camp 27
   Cossack Campaign 53–65, 201
Stadler 236
Stalin, J ix, 10, 44, 48, 97, 128, 157,
   158, 161, 238
Stalingrad 37
Standart, royal yacht 230
Stanitsas 60
Starhemburg, Prince 33

Staroselsky, Colonel 233, 234
State Department 19
Stella D'Oro (Golden Star) 203
Stevenson, Mr (British Ambassador
  Belgrade) 96
Street, Lieutenant Colonel Vivian 143
Styria 34, 37, 38, 98, 239, 241
Sudakov Commission 196
Supreme Headquarters Allied
  Expeditionary Force (SHAEF) 3–
  9, 15–23, 118, 119, 133, 134, 175–88
Surrender, The 68
Sweden 25
Switzerland 30
Syria 120

TAC HQ (21 AG) 5, 23
Tagliamento, River 58, 60, 61, 201,
  209
Talmassons (-massone) 206
Tamurlaine 226
Tarcento 55, 209
Tarvisio (Tavisio) 49, 50, 69, 94
Tatar (Tartar) 226, 227, 233
Taylor, Judge John Barrington,
  QC 80–2
Taylor, Major Ronald 60
Teheran 233
Tempo di Cosacchi (Petro Menis) 55
Third Reich x, 3, 4, 12, 45, 60
Thorl 69
Thursby-Pelham, Brigadier
  Christopher 201, 203
Tiflis 233
Times, The 7
Tito 43, 44, 66, 75, 91–6, 97–103, 119,
  121, 126, 128, 129, 136, 137, 141–5,
  147, 157–60, 175, 241
Titoists ix, 36, 145
Tito's signals 115
Tobruk xxvii
Todt Organisation 131, 206, 207
Togliatti, Signor 91
Tolbukhin, Marshal 51, 69, 98, 106,
  107, 114, 115, 125, 127, 158, 168
Tolmezzo 49, 60, 69, 71, 202, 211, 237,
  238
Tolstoy, Nikolai 104, 155
Torre, River 55
Trade Unions 22
Transcaucasian Republic 233
Trasaghis 204

Travemunde 26
Treblinka 208, 236
Treaty
  Anglo-Iranian 233
  of Versailles 141
Treppo, Joseph 204
Treviso 105
Trieste 10, 49, 116, 123, 133, 154, 157,
  159, 208, 236, 240
Tripoli 135
Trischamps 210
Troops
  Allied 6
  British ix, 3, 12, 131, 184
  German 4, 6
  Russian 9
  US 3, 12
Troppenburg, Gianandrea Gropplero di
  (Count) 61
Trotsky 230, 234
Truman, President 10, 102, 103, 109,
  128, 136, 154, 157, 160
  message 100
Tsar xxvi, 228, 230
Tsarskoe Selo xxvi, 230
Turkomen 3
Turkey 43, 141, 232
Turner, Colonel R G 12
Tyrol 209

Uccea 209
Uden 5
Udine 67, 71, 94, 116, 201, 206, 208
Ukraine/ians 38, 80, 131, 184, 189–92,
  232, 234
  Internees 193
Ultimatums 95, 98
United Kingdom 6, 14, 180, 191, 192,
  199
United Nations 47, 126, 157
Ural Mountains/Urals 228, 231, 232
US War Department 187
Use of force 19, 161–6, 182–8

Val Torre 209
Vatican 240
VE Day 180
Veghel 5
Venezia Giulia ix, 49–51, 55, 65, 67,
  91–6, 109, 112, 116, 120, 125, 127,
  128, 154, 157, 239–41
  Anglo-American difference 65

Vergendo 202
Verney, Brigadier Gerald 73–7, 146, 167
his views on English soldier 76
Vienna 33, 34, 44, 184, 185
destruction in 34, 35
entry of Russians into 35
and food supplies 36
Viktring 119, 131, 145–7, 152, 156, 167, 168
Villach 49, 69, 73, 74, 119, 146
Villa
Orter 209
Santina 202
Scoccimarro 209
di Verzegnis 203
Vlassov, General 70
Volga, River 228
Volkermarkt 98
Volksdeutche 235
Voralberg 177

Waal, River 5
Wake, Major H (later Sir Hereward) 25, 29
Wales, 16
'Walter' (Albino Venier) 210–12
War Cabinet 103, 159, 186, 195, 199
War Crimes, Group, All-Party Parliamentary 193
German Special Category Troops 131, 206
Warner, Miss 180
War Office 120, 127, 154, 183, 186
Warsaw 228
Pact 11
Radio 24
Washington 44, 91–5, 101, 122, 156, 159, 185
Wehrmacht 51, 189, 206
Weir, Major General 164
Weitensfield 165, 166
Welsh Guards see Regiments
Weser, River 15
Western Allies 10, 11, 17

Western-Front 44, 195
White Guard, Slovene (*Bela Garda*) 239–241
Whitehall 156, 192, 193
Wilderness, The xxvii
Wilkinson, A W H 191, 192
Williams, Lady see Poustchine xxvii, 228, 260
Winter Palace 230, 231
Winter War (Finland) 76
Wismar 24
Wismar Cushion 16, 23, 24
Wolff, Karl 51, 55
Wolfsberg 83
World War
First xxv, xxvii, 51, 126
Second xi, 4, 182
Third 112
Wörthersee 118
Wörzen Pass 49
Wrangel, General 232, 235

Xenia, Grand Duchess xxvii, 247

Yalta 9, 24, 47, 112, 114, 135, 187, 197
Agreement 20–22, 50, 123, 127, 163, 171, 182, 184–6, 198, 199
on exchange of prisoners 47, 48
Yugoslavia (slavs) x, 14, 43, 44, 49, 50, 91–6, 118, 123, 125, 128, 131, 134, 141, 143–5, 148, 151, 152, 154, 155, 157, 161, 167, 168, 176, 178, 179, 189–92, 202, 232, 235, 237
Anti- x,
Government of see Government
Chargé d'Affaire 159

Zagreb 241
Zones
American x, 187
British 10, 14–16, 18, 20, 23, 28, 123, 128, 142, 178, 184, 199
Soviet 16, 28

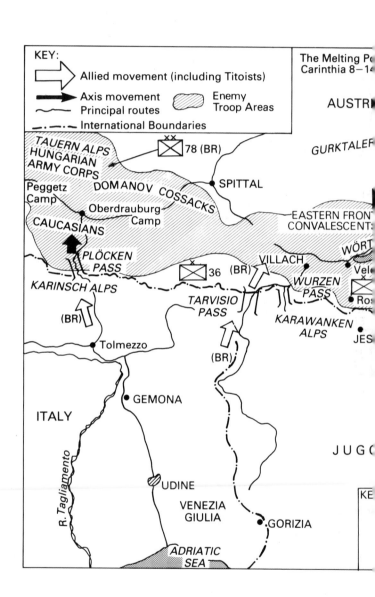

KEY:

Allied movement (including Titoists)

Axis movement

Principal routes

International Boundaries

Enemy Troop Areas

The Melting Po
Carinthia 8–14

AUSTR

GURKTALER

TAUERN ALPS
HUNGARIAN
ARMY CORPS

78 (BR)

SPITTAL

Peggetz
Camp

DOMANOV COSSACKS

Oberdrauburg
Camp

CAUCASIANS

EASTERN FRONT
CONVALESCENTS

WÖRT

PLÖCKEN
PASS

VILLACH

Vel

KARINSCH ALPS

36 (BR)

WURZEN
PASS

Ro

(BR)

TARVISIO
PASS

KARAWANKEN
ALPS

JES

Tolmezzo

(BR)

GEMONA

ITALY

R. Tagliamento

JUGO

UDINE

VENEZIA
GIULIA

GORIZIA

KE

ADRIATIC
SEA